Lessons and Activities for Building Powerful Numeracy

Pamela Weber Harris

HEINEMANN
Portsmouth, NH

Heinemann
361 Hanover Street
Portsmouth, NH 03801–3912
www.heinemann.com

Offices and agents throughout the world

Cataloging-in-Publication Data is on file with the Library of Congress.
ISBN: 978-0-325-04804-8

Editor: Katherine Bryant
Production editor: Sonja S. Chapman
Cover design: Suzanne Heiser
Compositor: Eric Rosenbloom, Kirby Mountain Composition
Manufacturing: Steve Bernier

Printed in the United States of America on acid-free paper

7 8 9 10   MP   24 23 22 21
February 2021 Printing

contents

WORKOUTS

TEACHER-DIRECTED ACTIVITIES

**An ANSWER KEY
is available online at
www.heinemann.com/lessonsandactivities.
Click on Companion Resources.**

---

acknowledgments

Many, many thanks to all the wonderful people who helped, cajoled, poked, and encouraged me, including:

My Father in heaven, by whose grace all of this is possible;

My kids, for being the ultimate guinea pigs, for your advice, for mocking up illustrations, for brainstorming, for your powerful numeracy, for your patience while I clicked away on my laptop, and for your humor and love. And especially Matthew, who created most of the graphics. Your attention to detail is unbeaten.

My husband, Daniel, for unwavering support.

My parents, Clyde and Ursula Weber, who taught me I can do anything and who are proud of me no matter what I do.

My eight siblings, with whom there is always a party, a loud and fun one.

Mylisa Jones Larsen, my college roommate extraordinaire, who taught me more about writing than anyone and who helped me write my first sample chapter. It worked!

My personal professional learning community including Kim Montague, Brittany Goerig, Sarah Hempel, Monica Hettenhausen, Abby and Rick Sanchez, Sue Simmons, Ann Roman, Leslie Martin, Kathy Hale, and anyone else who has joined the team lately.

The good folks in the Education Service Centers in Texas, especially Regions 12, 14, 15, and 17 and their wonderful teachers.

Brittany Goerig, for advising me about middle school and for piloting ideas in your classroom.

Kim Montague, a true friend and wise colleague. When I grow up I want my math and teaching brain to be like yours.

Tim Pope, who helped me get my numeracy project off the ground. You are a great professional colleague and friend.

Scott Hendrickson, a wonderful mentor who has demonstrated integrity throughout your teaching and your life. How grateful I am to have had those two years of teaching with you.

Pam Giles, my cooperating teacher, from whom I learned so much and who didn't tell me how bad I was when I first started.

My math method students at the University of Texas at Austin, for your helpful suggestions.

Teachers in the many, many workshops I have held who have given great feedback, shared your strategies with me, and listened to way too many of my stories.

My wonderful editor, Katherine Bryant, and the good folks at Heinemann.

introduction

As secondary teachers, we are often frustrated by the lack of number sense in our students. Students seem to either reach for a calculator or just shrug and say, "I don't know," when asked simple arithmetic questions. They seem ill-prepared to learn higher math because they have not memorized basic facts. Many students make careless errors with nonsensical results, yet do not recognize how far off their answers are. We are in the age of *algebra for all*, yet we have students who were obviously never in the *arithmetic for all* movement.

FROM BUILDING POWERFUL NUMERACY FOR MIDDLE AND HIGH SCHOOL STUDENTS, P. 10.

I wrote *Building Powerful Numeracy for Middle and High School Students* to bring the wonderful world of research in numeracy at the elementary level to the secondary world. *Lessons and Activities for Building Powerful Numeracy* continues that work, providing classroom resources for you to help your students build numeracy.

By using models and problem strings in a systematic way, with an eye toward the major, efficient strategies, we can help secondary students construct mental numerical relationships. For those students who come to us with some elementary work in numeracy, we can build on their understanding and support their continued development, while at the same time helping those who lack that understanding gain the foundation they need. When we give secondary students this numerical power, we also help them engage in learning higher mathematics with more confidence and more success.

FROM BUILDING POWERFUL NUMERACY FOR MIDDLE AND HIGH SCHOOL STUDENTS, P. 10.

When we help students construct and use numerical relationships, they begin to believe that they can learn higher math. Mathematics becomes less a counterintuitive world where they must memorize abstract, isolated facts, and more an area in which they can reason and use their intuitive sense. We can build numeracy in our students and use this understanding to construct higher math.

There are two main types of activities in this workbook: Student Workouts and teacher-directed activities (strings, as close as it gets, and relational thinking). The Workouts (new in this book) are to be distributed to students to work on independently or in pairs. The teacher then leads a class discussion of the problems and the relationships and strategies they reveal. These are often used as warmups. The teacher-directed activities, on the other hand, involve you, the teacher, actively throughout the activity. Both types help build a solid numeracy base.

Student Workouts

These reproducible sheets evolved in response to teachers' requests for conversation starters for students. Many teachers new to numeracy find these Student Workouts to be good entry points for students to begin to *think* about numbers, to reflect on alternative strategies, and to consider the efficiency and sophistication of different strategies. The discussions that follow students' work is critical; these Workouts are not intended as worksheets that students complete and hand in, but as starting points for discussions that help students build important relationships and choose effective strategies.

Some Workouts (such as those in Figure I.1) present several different strategies for solving the same problem. Students fill in the blanks to complete the strategies and then compare the strategies to discuss which they think works well for the numbers in the problem.

FIGURE I.1   EXAMPLES OF ADDITION AND MULTIPLICATION WORKOUTS

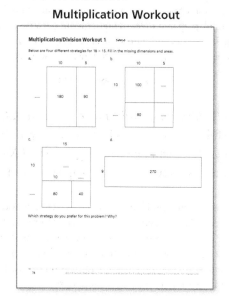

After students have worked on a Workout such as the one in Figure I.1 for a few minutes, the teacher leads a conversation to help them compare the strategies and discuss when it might be most efficient to use each one. (You will find sample classroom discussions in each Workout chapter.)

Other Workouts present students with common errors and ask them to analyze the errors (Figure I.2), or provide students with a model and scaffolding to help them begin to use the model as a tool (Figure I.3).

FIGURE I.2   EXAMPLE OF ERROR ANALYSIS: ADDITION OF FRACTIONS WORKOUT

Addition of Fractions Workout—Error Analysis

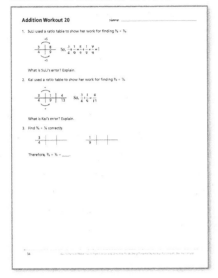

FIGURE I.3   EXAMPLES OF ADDITION OF FRACTIONS AND MULTIPLICATION WORKOUTS

Addition of Fractions Workout	**Multiplication Workout**

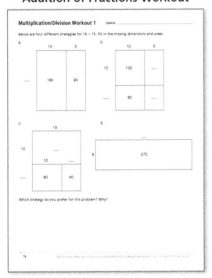
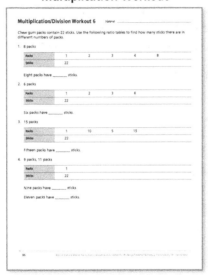

Teacher-Directed Activities: Problem Strings, As Close As It Gets, and Relational Thinking

Problem strings, as close as it gets, and relational thinking are teacher directed whole-class activities. (I introduced these activities in *Building Powerful Numeracy for Middle and High School Students*, where you can find more about the background for them.) They are five- to fifteen-minute activities meant to help students construct numerical relationships as they work together with the teacher. They often involve asking students to solve problems on their own, then to discuss, compare, model, verbalize, find and describe patterns, and make generalizations. Unlike the Workouts, these activities do not have pages to be distributed to students.

Problem Strings (Chapter 5)

A problem string is a series of problems presented in a certain order and intended to construct numerical relationships in the learner's mind (see Figure I.4). As students develop these relationships, they become inclined toward a particular strategy for computation. While strings are not all delivered in exactly the same way, the following guidelines generally apply: The problems are done one at a time, in order. Start by giving students the first problem, which is often easy and sets up the rest of the string. After students have solved it, ask them what answer they found and invite them to share their strategies as you purposefully model these strategies using a particular model (such as a number line, open array, or ratio table). Then give students the next problem. After they solve it, call on students who have used certain strategies to share, modeling the shared strategies. This continues with each problem. As the string progresses, you may want to limit the sharing to students who have begun to use the target strategy. By the end of the string, many students will likely be trying the target strategy. You may find that for some strategies you need to repeat the same kind of string (using different numbers) several times to encourage more students to use the target strategy. You will find sample classroom discussions on problem strings throughout Chapter 5.

FIGURE I.4 SAMPLE PERCENT PROBLEM STRING

100% of 15
50% of 15
25% of 15
10% of 15
5% of 15
1% of 15
11% of 15
0.5% of 15
13.5% of 15

This book contains examples of problem strings for key strategies using addition, subtraction, multiplication, and division (including fractions and decimals), ratios, proportions, and percents.

As Close As It Gets (Chapter 6)

As close as it gets activities contain multiple-choice questions where the answer choices do not list the correct answer. Instead, students must estimate and use number sense to choose an answer choice that is as close to the correct answer as possible (Figure I.5). These activities get students to consider the numbers in the problem before choosing a strategy and to use the magnitudes involved to determine the reasonableness of the answer choices. Because the correct answer is not listed, students cannot just use a memorized procedure; they must reason using the numbers and the operations. The power of these seemingly easy exercises is in the conversations students have as they think about the problems.

FIGURE I.5   AS CLOSE AS IT GETS

$\frac{4}{9} \times \frac{29}{30}$

a. 0	b. 0.5
c. 1	d. 2

In the problem shown in Figure I.5, a student might suggest that b is correct because "⁴⁄₉ is about ½ and 29/30 is about 1. So about ½ times about 1 is about ½." You will find more sample discussions in Chapter 6.

Once students demonstrate numerical fluency with these operations, it is time for relational thinking activities.

Relational Thinking (Chapter 7)

Relational thinking activities are equation-solving problems where students use numerical relationships to either complete an equation or determine if the equation is true or false. These exercises help students solidify which strategies work for which operation. Often the true/false section presents an equation that suggests using a strategy that only works for a different operation, thus giving a false result. For example, students learn a doubling and halving strategy for multiplication where they would fill in the blank in the equation $16 \times 35 = \_\_\_ \times 70$ with 8. In the true/false section, students would explain that $360 \div 90 = 180 \div 180$ is false, because you cannot double and halve with division because if you do, the ratios are not equivalent: $360/90 \neq 180/180$ (Figure I.6). As students are faced with false equations, they must reconcile why they are false. As students discuss their reasoning, they solidify numerical relationships using appropriate strategies.

FIGURE I.6   RELATIONAL THINKING

Fill in the blank:
$16 \times 35 = \_\_\_ \times 70$

True or False? Why?
$360 \div 90 = 180 \div 180$

The Importance of Models

To build numeracy, we take advantage of the power of representation. Representing student strategies on models such as the open number line, the open array, and the ratio table promotes discussion of relationships rather than procedures, which helps students build and solidify numerical relationships in their minds.

All the activities in this book allow students to visualize strategies and use and develop models *of thinking*. As students *see their thinking*, they can begin to use the model as a tool to solve problems, a tool *for thinking* (Gravemeijer 1999). Students begin to compute using the model. Then students continue to develop more sophisticated strategies using the model as a tool to solve problems. The major models, as mentioned, are the open number line, the open array, and the ratio table.

The models work because they beg for action. Suppose you're trying to find $99 + 27$. Once you put 99 on an open number line, the proximity to 100 prompts a short jump of 1. Then, since you've already added 1, just add the remaining 26, $100 + 26 = 126$ (Figure I.7).

FIGURE I.7

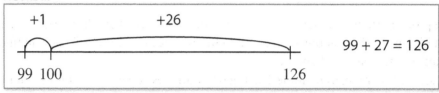

To multiply 99×87, you can use a ratio table to find $(100 \times 87) - (1 \times 87) = 8{,}700 - 87 = 8{,}613$ (Figure I.8).

FIGURE I.8

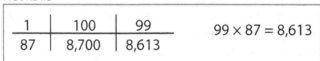

To find 18×35, consider the area of the 18 by 35 array. Cut the array strategically in half, rearrange the pieces, and find the area of the resulting array, $9 \times 70 = 630$ (Figure I.9).

FIGURE I.9

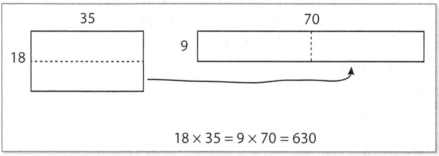

Strategies

The strategies in this book are not tricks or procedures to memorize. The goal is to teach as much mathematics as possible with as little memorization as possible, building on prior understanding, not repeating rote steps. The hallmarks of these strategies are that they are transparent actions, they maintain the magnitudes in the problem, and they develop mathematical habits of mind that students need for higher math.

For examples of key strategies and models for each operation, see the beginning of the Workout chapters and the descriptions of problem strings in Chapter 5. You can read much more about these models and strategies and how to help students develop them in *Building Powerful Numeracy for Middle and High School Students*, Chapters 2, 5, and 8.

How to Use This Book

The following are some suggestions for materials you might use for particular topics or sequences of topics. Consider these as menus of possible options, not as required sequences — you know your own students, and can judge best what they need.

Middle School

Measures of Central Tendency: Division strings (p. 250), division ratio table Workouts (p. 114), and activities in Chapter 7, "Relational Thinking," help students develop multiplicative thinking and transparent strategies for dividing the sums of data points.

Geometry: Array multiplication Workouts (p. 78) and doubling/halving array multiplication strings (p. 239) help students develop multiplication strategies useful for finding the surface area of prisms.

Integer Subtraction: Whole number and decimal subtraction strings (p. 223) and subtraction Workouts (Chapter 2) help reinforce the difference meaning of subtraction before beginning work on integer operations. The integer subtraction strings (p. 229) are then helpful.

Multiplication and Division of Decimals: Over the course of several lessons, the multiplication of decimals strings (p. 236) and the division of decimals strings (p. 250) help students build efficient strategies based on place value. The Workouts can be interspersed throughout several lessons, and the exercises in Chapter 7, "Relational Thinking," used as warmups, help students cement the difference between strategies.

Fraction Addition: Starting a unit with the activities in Chapter 6, "As Close As It Gets," helps students estimate fractions. Subtraction Workouts (Chapter 2) emphasize the two meanings of subtraction, providing a foundation for students' work with fractions. The money and time fraction addition and subtraction strings (p. 264) help students work with equivalent fractions and find common denominators. Double number line Workouts (pp. 27, 57) are useful interventions for students who struggle with these ideas. Multiplication ratio table Workouts (p. 86) can refresh students' memories for finding equivalent ratios, and ratio tables for adding and subtracting Workouts (pp. 30, 64) (especially the error analysis problems) further build students' understanding.

Solving Proportions: The multiplication and division Workouts and strings help students construct multiplicative strategies that can be used to solve proportions. The Workouts in Chapter 4, "Student Workouts for Proportions and Percents," help students use proportional reasoning and ratio tables to solve proportions involving similar figures and equivalent ratios.

Algebra I

Rate of Change: Subtraction Workouts (Chapter 2) reinforce the difference meaning of subtraction, critical to understanding the formula for slope.

Transformations, $y = f(x - h)$: Constant difference strings (p. 227) and subtraction Workouts (Chapter 2) give students a framework from which to understand why the transformation $f(x - h)$ shifts the graph of $f(x)$ to the right when $h > 0$ and to the left when $h < 0$.

Collecting Like Terms: The using factoring to add strings (p. 219) help students understand the arithmetic of terms as they add $6x + 2x$.

Linearity: The multiplication Workouts (p. 86) that use ratios in ratio tables to find products and quotients and the fraction Workouts (pp. 30, 64) that use ratio tables to find equivalent ratios help students gain the sense of ratio and rates that students need to have facility finding and understanding the slope of lines as a constant rate of change.

Geometry

Distance Formula: The distance versus removal subtraction strings (p. 225) help students think about the difference meaning of subtraction, which can be applied to the meaning of subtraction in the distance formulas used to find the perimeters of polygons and the area of triangles. Subtraction Workouts (Chapter 2) help students develop more sophisticated strategies for these calculations.

Surface Area: The multiplication Workouts (Chapter 3) and the multiplication strings (p. 236) use arrays to help students learn to chunk areas and connect factors and products with dimensions and areas.

Algebra II

Addition and Subtraction of Rational Expressions: The ratio table adding and subtracting fractions Workouts (pp. 30, 64) are great warmups; you can use them to connect real-number work to addition and subtraction of rational expressions.

Transformations: To start a weeklong unit on graphing functions using transformations, you could use a multiplication with the ratio table string (p. 248) to promote proportional reasoning. Throughout the week, you can reinforce these skills with ratio table Workouts (p. 86) and connect this multiplicative thinking and ratio work with the transformation $y = af(x)$, where a is the vertical scale factor that multiplicatively stretches or compresses the function vertically. The fractions as operator strings (p. 269) help students understand the effect of a when $0 < a < 1$.

Precalculus

Radian Measure: Get to a friendly number strings and give and take strings (p. 217) help build students' ideas of friendly numbers, which can be extended to the friendly numbers useful in radian measure (such as π or $\pi/2$). Using factoring to add strings (p. 219) helps students as they add values such as $6\pi + 2\pi$.

Calculus

Derivative: Using an addition Workout (Chapter 1), a subtraction Workout (Chapter 2), and a constant difference string (p. 227) can help students cement the difference meaning for subtraction, which provides a foundation for understanding the formula for the slope of the secant line.

Mean Value Theorem: The subtraction Workouts (Chapter 2) help students compare the removal and difference strategies shown for subtraction. You can then relate the difference meaning of subtraction to the subtractions in the Mean Value Theorem.

Solids of Revolution: A constant difference string (p. 227) ending with the functions $f(x) + b$ and $f(x - c)$ provides a basis for students to interpret graphs based on the graph of $f(x)$. Then you can relate the constant difference strategy to the formulas for finding the volume of solids formed as a curve is rotated about either the line $y = b$ or $x = c$. Students can shift the function back to the axis to make an equivalent, easier to solve problem.

Answer Key

The answer key is available online at www.heinemann.com/lessonsandactivities, under the Companion Resources tab. The answer key for the Workouts lists answers written on each page. For the problems that call for one correct answer, the correct answer is listed. In places where the Workouts call for strategies, a possible strategy is shown for your consideration. If you find a more sophisticated or clever strategy, I would love to hear from you! Send queries, suggestions, and slick strategies to my Facebook page, facebook.com/numeracy.

References

Harris, P. 2012. *Building Powerful Numeracy for Middle and High School Students.* Portsmouth, NH: Heinemann.

Gravemeijer, K. P. E. 1999. "How Emergent Models May Foster the Constitution of Formal Mathematics." *Mathematical Thinking and Learning.* 1(2):155–77.

Student Workouts for Addition

There are twenty Student Workouts for addition: five with whole numbers, five with decimals, five with fractions on double number lines, and five with fractions in ratio tables. Each is a five- to ten-minute activity to be completed by individual students or student pairs and then discussed as a class.

How to Use Addition Workouts

The first few whole number and decimal Workouts ask students to describe strategies to solve an addition problem. It is an opportunity for students to analyze strategies they are seeing for perhaps the first time on paper.

After students have completed a Workout, discuss their work as a class. Encourage students to explain their thinking and justify why they prefer a particular strategy for a particular problem. As the teacher leads discussion about their descriptions, students learn a shared vocabulary to explain how to use relationships among numbers to solve the problems. This chapter contains details and sample questions to help you plan and implement the Workouts.

What to Do

- ▶ Hand out the Student Workout.
- ▶ Clarify the directions. Starting with addition Workout 2, students are to fill in the blanks for a strategy.
- ▶ Circulate and ask clarifying or scaffolding questions.

▶ Discuss the Student Workout together as a class, encouraging students to explain their thinking. Discuss which strategy they prefer and why. Note that when describing a strategy, perhaps the most important thing to consider is the first move. It's about how the student decided to use the relationships among the numbers. What the students decides to do first dominates the strategy.

Clarifying Questions

▶ What is the question asking?

▶ What kind of answer is the question expecting (describing a strategy, filling in a blank with a number, recording a strategy on a blank number line)?

Scaffolding Questions

▶ How would you verbalize the strategy shown on this number line?

▶ How does that differ from this one?

▶ What is a friendly number?

▶ What are some friendly numbers in our number system?

Focusing on "How Much More to Add?"

▶ So, this strategy says to jump 3 to get to 70. Ah, 70 is a nice number. Now, how much more do they need to jump, to add?

▶ This strategy shows a nice jump of 20 to get to 40. If you have already jumped 20, how much is left?

Class Discussion Questions

▶ Why start with this number?

▶ Why start with the bigger number?

▶ What made this a friendly jump?

▶ Looking at this strategy, how many steps or jumps does it show?

▶ What about these numbers make these strategies work?

Comparing Strategies

▶ Which strategy seems more efficient? Why?

▶ Which strategy seems easier to do mentally?

▶ Which strategy seems more sophisticated?

▶ What about the numbers makes that strategy your favorite for this problem?

▶ How might you change the numbers so that a different strategy would fit better?

The Strategies and Models Used in the Addition Workouts

The primary model for addition of whole numbers and decimals is the open number line. A splitting model and equations, both horizontal and vertical, are also used.

The whole number and decimal addition Workouts and strings use two main strategies: place-value splitting and keeping one number whole. Place-value splitting is a fine place to start, but the eventual goal is to get students to be able to give and take, strategically taking a bit from one addend to give to the other addend, resulting in an easier problem.

Place-value splitting — splitting both of the numbers into place-value parts and then adding the parts together (Figure 1.1).

FIGURE 1.1

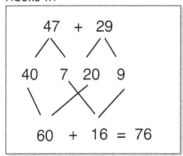

Keeping one addend whole and

► Jumping by a friendly number that is too small and adjusting up.

FIGURE 1.2

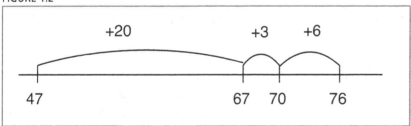

► Jumping by a friendly number that is too big and adjusting back.

FIGURE 1.3

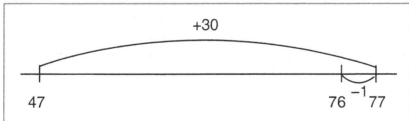

► Jumping to a friendly number and then jumping the rest.

FIGURE 1.4

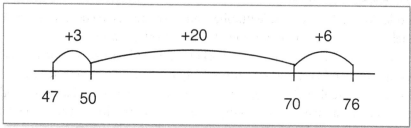

► Giving and taking.

FIGURE 1.5

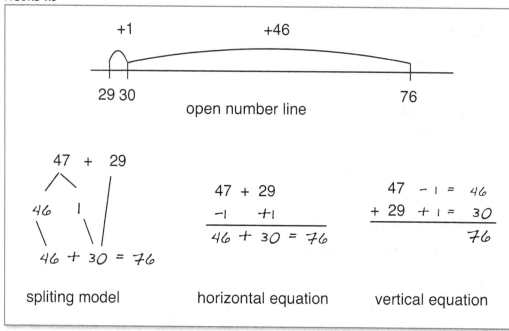

The primary models used for adding fractions are the double open number line and the ratio table. These models help students find equivalent fractions in order to then add.

The fraction addition Workouts and strings with the double open number line use the strategy of finding a unit fraction of a friendly number and then scaling up to find equivalent fractions. For example, for ⅘ + ⅑, use a double number line that represents a race course and choose a friendly course length that works for both fifths and ninths, like 45. Then find an equivalent fraction for ⅘ by first finding ⅕ of 45. The double open number line helps because as students have to decide where to mark the ⅕ on the top, they visualize dividing the line into 5 equal sections. This prompts the student to also divide the 45 into 5 equal groups, $45 \div 5 = 9$, so ⅕ of 45 is 9. This goes on the bottom (Figure 1.6).

FIGURE 1.6

Similarly, as the student then considers where four of those ⅕s are, the student is prompted to scale up the ⅘ by finding a length 4 times as long, 4 × 9 is 36. Since the whole is 45, ⅘ is equivalent to 36 out of that 45, which is ³⁶⁄₄₅ of the course (Figure 1.7).

FIGURE 1.7

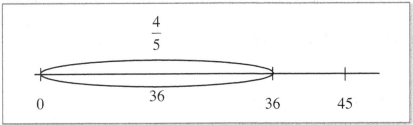

To add ⅘ + ⅑, the student similarly finds ⅑ of 45 to be 5, landing on 36 + 5 = 41, or ⁴¹⁄₄₅ of the course. So the answer to ⅘ + ⅑ = ³⁶⁄₄₅ + ⁵⁄₄₅ = ⁴¹⁄₄₅ (Figure 1.8).

FIGURE 1.8

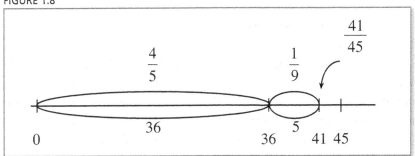

The fraction addition Workouts and strings that feature the ratio table use the strategy of finding equivalent ratios by scaling up or down. For example, to add ⅔ and ¾, students use a ratio table for each fraction to find an equivalent fraction (Figure 1.9).

FIGURE 1.9

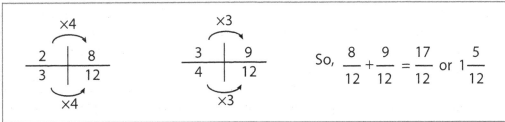

The Progression

Whole Numbers: Workouts 1 Through 5

Addition Workout 1 asks students to describe addition strategies modeled on the open number line. Then students solve the problems themselves on the open number line, starting with the second addend. This is an opportunity for students to try a problem on their own. A Sample Dialog gives you a feel for how you might lead a discussion of this Workout.

Addition Workouts 2 and 3 continue to ask students to describe strategies, but now students also fill in the blanks of missing numbers for each strategy. Again, students try a problem on their own.

Addition Workouts 4 and 5 ask students to fill in the blanks in strategies but now students have to decide what problem all four students solved. Relational thinking problems are introduced to further work on giving and taking. The Sample Dialog for Workout 4 shows a teacher discussing all the key addition strategies with students as they discuss their work.

Decimals: Workouts 6 Through 10

Addition Workouts 6 through 10 follow a similar progression but use decimal numbers. The Sample Dialog after Workout 7 shows a discussion of addition strategies with decimals, exemplifying how to use money to help students understand the magnitudes in the decimals.

Fractions: Workouts 11 Through 20

Addition Workouts 11 through 15 use the open double number line to add fractions.

Addition Workout 11 starts with unit fractions and then 12 builds to non-unit fractions.

Addition Workout 13 finds a sum greater than 1 and asks students to find non-unit fractions of a number, given the unit fraction of that number. This reasoning helps students find common denominators as a natural extension. The Sample Dialog for Workout 13 shows a discussion of using a double open number line to find unit fractions and scale up to find common denominators when adding fractions. Since the answer is greater than 1, the discussion includes the teacher's asking about the unit involved.

Addition Workouts 14 and 15 ask students to fill in the blanks in strategies but now students have to decide what problem the students solved.

Addition Workouts 16 through 20 use a ratio table to find equivalent fractions.

Addition Workout 16 gives students an example of using ratio tables to find equivalent fractions and then asks students to apply that example for a similar problem.

Addition Workout 17 adds the step of simplifying using a ratio table.

Addition Workouts 18 and 19 show parts of a strategy to find equivalent fractions, where students fill in the missing parts.

Addition Workout 20 uses ratio tables to show common errors. Students are asked to explain the errors. The Sample Dialog for Workout 20 shows an example of analyzing common errors with students.

Addition Workout 1

Carol bought concert tickets for $47.00. She also paid $29.00 for concessions at the concert. How much did the whole evening cost?

1. Five students solved this problem using the different strategies shown below. Analyze and describe each strategy.

Description

a.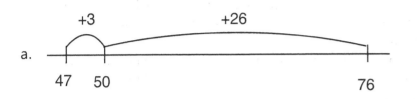

b.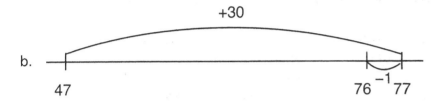

c.

d.
```
        47  +  29
        /\     /\
      40  7  20  9
        \  \ /  /
         \  X  /
      60  +  16  =  76
```

e.   40, 60, 67, 76

2. Which strategy do you prefer for this problem? Why?

3. Use the number line below to add 47 + 29, but start with the 29.

```
   +
   |
   29
```

Sample Dialog for Addition Workout 1

Teacher: Now that you've had a chance to look this Workout over, what is Carol's question? *The teacher introduces the workout.*

Peter: How much did it all cost?

Teacher: Yes, and five students solved the problem and this Workout is showing the five students' strategies, *a* through *e*. What are you asked to do in item 1?

Catherine: Analyze them and describe them.

Teacher: Then in no. 2, to choose the strategy that you prefer and tell why. And in no. 3, to solve the same problem, but start with the 29. Any questions? *Students work and teacher circulates.*

Teacher: Now that you are all about finished, let's discuss your thinking. How did you describe student *a*'s strategy? *By having students describe the strategies to each other, the class can build a common vocabulary.*

Gale: They started with 47 and added 3 to get to 50. Then they added the rest, 26, to get 76.

Teacher: Why do you think this person would add 3 first? *This question is important because the first move in a strategy is often the descriptor of the whole strategy—the first move is the indicator of how the student is planning to use the relationships among the numbers to solve the problem.*

Gale: They wanted to get to a friendly number like 50. It's easy to add on to 50.

Peter: Yeah, if you can get to 50, then you can just add what's left over, the 26.

Catherine: Student *b* added too much so they had to adjust back 1.

Rose: Instead of adding 29 like the problem says, student *b* added 30 to land on 77 and then went back 1 to 76.

Teacher: Why do you think student *b* would add 30 instead of 29? *Again, this question helps students focus on the overall strategy—how the student is using the relationships to solve the problem.*

Rose: It's a nice number, easy to add, and it gets you close to the answer.

Annie: Student *c* added a friendly number too, but it wasn't as big, so student *c* still had to add more, the rest, to add all of the 29.

Teacher: So far we have some students who are adding to get to a friendly number and some who are adding a friendly number. *The teacher helps students focus on the main ideas of the strategies.* What about student *d*?

Rose: Student *d* split up both numbers, added the similar pieces together, and then added those together.

Teacher: How did student *d* split up the numbers? *How a student splits the numbers is key—place-value splitting is a fine place to start but too cumbersome as the numbers get bigger. Another splitting strategy, give and take (like student a used), will be more efficient for many problems. It's less important that the students split up the numbers and more important how the numbers were split. In future Workouts, the strategy will be shown as more of a simultaneous give and take where you split the numbers strategically to give just the right amount to make a very friendly number. This uses the associative property.*

Annie: By place value, the tens and ones.

Teacher: And what is going on with *e*?

Peter: I don't know. I mean, the answer is 76 and that's the last number, so . . .

Gale:	I think that maybe he started with the 40 from the 46 and then added the 20 from the 29 to get 60.
Peter:	Oh, yeah, then added the 7 from the 47 to get 67 and then 9 from the 29.
Rose:	It's kind of like *d* but it's more of a running total.
Teacher:	What do you mean by running total? *The teacher knows what Rose means, but wants to make sure that all students do too.*
Rose:	Start with the big numbers and add them but then keep adding the smaller numbers one by one, first the 40 + 20 to get 60, then the 7 to get 67, then the 9 to get 76.
Teacher:	Which of these strategies do you prefer and why? *A very important question—getting students to consider the merits of different strategies for these numbers. We want students to seek more efficient and sophisticated—even clever—strategies.*
Catherine:	If I didn't have a pencil to keep track, I'd like *a* or *e* because with *e* you keep track as you go. With *a*, once you get to 50, you just add 26.
Peter:	I think you can do the same thing with *b*, just add 30, that's easy, and then back up 1.
Teacher:	Do you think you might always like the same strategy for every addition problem? I wonder if it might depend on the numbers in the problem.... *This leads toward the big idea that the numbers should suggest the strategy. We want students to use the relationships to solve the problem, not be stuck in the same strategy for every problem.*

Addition Workout 2

Keith bought a used game for $39.00 and a new game for $58.00. How much total did he pay?

1. Four students solved the problem using the different strategies shown below.

   Fill in the blanks. Analyze and describe each strategy.

Description

a.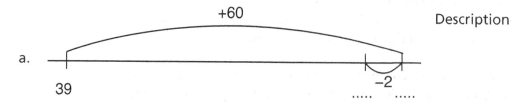

b.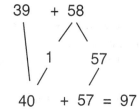

c.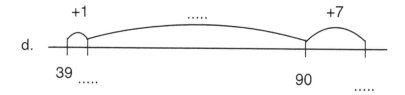

d.

2. Which strategy do you prefer for this problem? Why?

3. Use the number line below to add 39 + 58, but start with the 58.

58

Addition Workout 3

Alexia has 387 songs on her MP3 player and 514 different songs on her computer. How many songs does she have in total?

1. Four students solved the problem using the different strategies shown below.

   Fill in the blanks. Analyze and describe each strategy.

   Description

   a.

   b.
   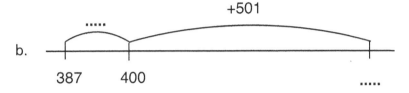

   c.
   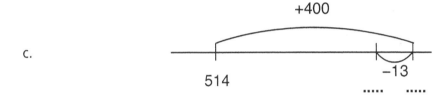

   d.
   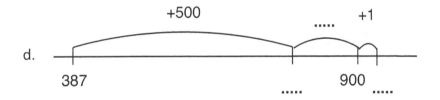

2. Study the strategy below. Which number line above models the same strategy?

   387 + 514

   13   501

   400 + 501 = 901

3. Fill in the blanks in two different models of the same strategy.

   387 + 514
   +.....   −13
   400 + ... = ...

   387 + 13 = ...
   + 514 − ..... = +501
                    901

---

1. Four students solved the SAME problem using the different strategies shown below. Fill in the blanks
    What question were they all solving? _____

a.

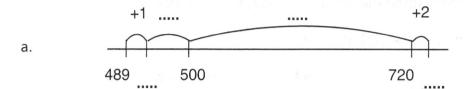

b.

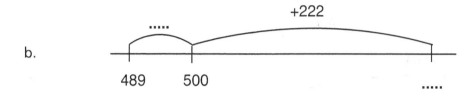

c.

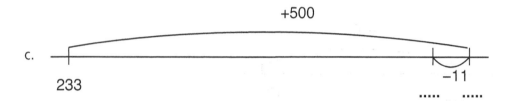

d.

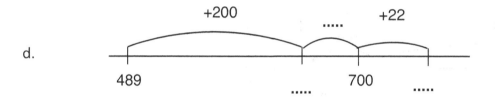

2. Fill in the blanks using relational thinking (do not compute).

   a. $67 + 28 = $ _____ $+ 25$

   b. $42 + 139 = 41 + $ _____

   c. $387 + $ _____ $= 400 + 502$

Sample Dialog for Addition Workout 4

Teacher: Let's talk about your thinking on this Workout. John, what problem did you think all four students were solving? *The teacher starts the conversation by having students agree on the equation that represents the problem and the answer.*

John: 489 + 233.

Teacher: And the answer too?

John: 489 + 233 = 722.

Teacher: Did anyone get anything different? No? OK, so if you had to point to one number line that shows that problem the most clearly, which would it be? *Asking this question gets students to describe the strategies at an analysis level.*

Sue: I think that starting with the 233 and adding 500 to get 733 and then backing up 11, that's easy to see that the problem is 233 + 489 is 722.

Marco: To me, I can see it easiest in the one that starts with 489 and adds 11 to get to 500. Then it's just 11 + 222 and that's 233.

Teacher: Great! Any other things you noticed about these strategies?

Renn: I noticed that the first and second ones are sort of the same but the second one just took bigger jumps.

Teacher: Did anyone else notice that? Can you say more about that? *The teacher knows this is a potentially confusing situation, so she keeps the conversation going so more students can work out the relationships.*

Renn: They both keep the 489 whole and then get to 500 by adding 11, it's just that the first one did it by adding 1 and 10 and the second one just added 11 all at once. Then the first one added 200 and then 22. But I can see that the second one just thought about 500 + 222 all at once.

Tiana: I'm not sure that I could do 489 + 11 all at once, but I do think I could do 500 and 222 in one jump. That would save some time.

Teacher: Thanks for those thoughts. Which of these would you say is more of an "add a friendly number" strategy? *The term* add a friendly number *is not important. It's more important that students know to which relationships the teacher is referring.* Friendly, landmark, *and* nice numbers *are some words that you can use. The big idea with this strategy is that you are keeping one number whole and adding that friendly, landmark, nice number.*

Bob: The last two—one of them adds a "too big" friendly number and has to back up. The last one adds 200 and then messes with the rest.

Teacher: And which of these is more of a get to a friendly number strategy? *And here the teacher begins to juxtapose two big strategies—adding a friendly number versus getting to a friendly number.*

Craig: The top two are, but the top one does it in smaller pieces. Once the second one gets to 500, they just added what was left over.

Nat: It's like the one we looked at yesterday—you give and take. Give 11 to get to 500. Then you just have 222 left.

Teacher: Fabulous! Let's talk about the three problems at the bottom. How did you think about 2a, Marci?

Marci: It looks like you took 3 to get from 28 to 25, so you would give that 3 to 67 to get 70.

Teacher:	*Fills in the blank with 70.* And which of these problems is easier? 67 + 28 or 70 + 25? *This focuses students on the reason for giving and taking — turning the problem into a nice, easy to solve problem.*
Renn:	70 + 25 is much easier to solve.
Teacher:	That might be a nice reason to give and take 3 to turn the problem into such an easy one. How about 2b?
Rob:	Well, the 42 went down to 41 so the 139 goes up to 140.
Teacher:	What does that do for you? *It's not just about answers, but also strategy.*
Rob:	Well, now you can just add 41 + 140 — that's easier than 42 + 139.
Roberta:	And on the last problem, you can just give and take 13 to fill in the blank with 515.
Teacher:	And which of those problems would you rather do? *With this question, the teacher helps students clarify that the strategy makes a simpler problem to solve.*

Addition Workout 5

Name _____

1. Four students solved the SAME problem using the different strategies shown below. Fill in the blanks. What question were they all solving? _____

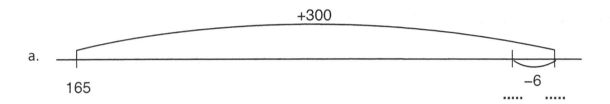

a. +300

165 −6

b. +159

294 300

c. +100 +59

294 400

d.
$$165 \quad -6 = \ldots$$
$$+ \; 294 \; + \ldots = + \; 300$$

$$\ldots$$

2. Fill in the blanks using relational thinking (do not compute).

_____ + 2,343 = 98 + 2,345

415 + 289 = _____ + 300

754 + 1,995 = 749 + _____

Addition Workout 6

Terrance owes his friend $4.80 for lunch yesterday and $3.90 for lunch today. How much total does he owe?

1. Five students solved the problem using the different strategies shown below.

    Fill in the blanks. Analyze and describe each strategy.

    Description

a.   4, 7, 7.8, ...

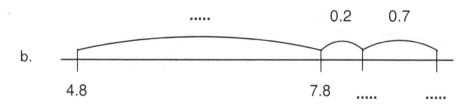

b.

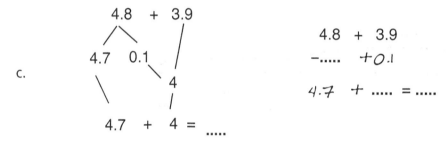

c.

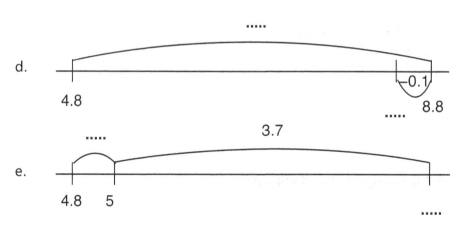

d.

e.

2. Use the number line below to add 4.8 + 3.9, but start with the 3.9.

    3.9

Addition Workout 7

Name _____

Ally has $1.90 in her pocket and $9.80 in her wallet. How much money does she have?

1. Four students solved the problem using the different strategies shown below.

    Fill in the blanks. Analyze and describe each strategy.

    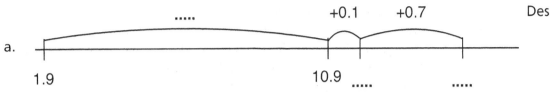

    a.

    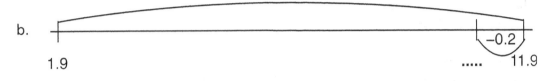

    b.

    c.

    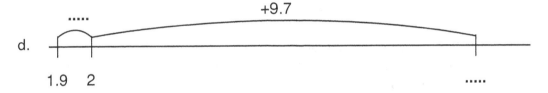

    d.

2. Which strategy do you like the best for these numbers? Why?

3. Study the strategy below.

    Which of the above number lines show the same give and take strategy?

    Fill in the blanks for an alternative give and take strategy.

    1.9 + 9.8   1.9 + 9.8
         / \   / \
       0.1 9.7   ..... 0.2
      /   /   \   \
    2   + 9.7 = 11.7   ..... + ... = ...

Sample Dialog for Addition Workout 7

Teacher: Let's talk about your thinking. Who will start us off with *a*?

Harry: That is add a friendly number because you kept one number whole and added 9.

Teacher: Anyone disagree? OK, how about the next one, *b*?

Lily: I think it is also adding a friendly number. It's just that for this one, they added a friendly number that was a bit too big, 10, so then they had to back up.

James: I think about it as over and adjust back.

Teacher: So, you added a friendly number that was too big, so you went over. Now you have to adjust. Why do you think you might add 10 when the problem asks you to add 9.80? *This question helps students focus on the relationships between 9.80 and 10 and why you might use the strategy.*

Tom: Because 9.80 is really close to 10 and it's easy to add 10 to anything.

Teacher: How close is it?

Virginia: 2 dimes.

Harry: 2 tenths.

Katie: Point 2.

Teacher: So, use your choice of naming 0.2 and tell us what 11.9 − 0.2 is.

Virginia: It's 11 dollars and 90 cents minus 20 cents, that's $11.70.

Harry: I would say that it's 11 and 9 tenths minus 2 tenths, so it's 11 and 7 tenths.

Katie: Yeah, so 11 point 9 minus point 2 is 11 point 7.

Teacher: Great! We can think about decimals in all those ways. How about the third one, *c*?

Katie: I think it's to get to a friendly number, $1.90 plus a dime is $2.00.

Teacher: Then what?

Katie: Well, you added a dime but you were supposed to add $9.80, so you still have $9.70 left to add. So they added 9 to get from 2 to 11, and then you just add 70 cents, so $11.70.

Teacher: Nicely explained. Those are nice, easy jumps to see. The one underneath it looks a lot like it. What do you think? *The teacher wants to direct the conversation to compare the get to a friendly number and the give and take strategies.*

Virginia: That is also get to a friendly number. It's just that after they added the dime, they added the $9.70 all at once.

Teacher: Can you add 2 bucks and $9.70 all at once? Sure enough! *This invites students to consider bigger jumps.*

Virginia: But I think that the last one is give and take — take a dime to get to 2 bucks and then just add what's left over, $9.70 to get $11.70.

Teacher: What do the rest of you think?

Lily: I think they are related.

Teacher: How?

Lily: One has more little jumps and one is just give and take and you're done.

Teacher: So, when you get to a friendly number and then take stock of where you are and continue to add in chunks, that is the get to a friendly number strategy. When you give and take in concert, all at once, then you are adding a big chunk all at once. What we call the strategies is less important and having you recognize what your brain is doing is more important. I want to encourage you all to make bigger, fewer jumps. Then you can be really efficient. I encourage you to try to look for clever solutions, ones where a seemingly difficult problem just falls out, sort of solves itself because of how you manipulated the numbers. So, looking at item 3, do you see that give and take strategy?

Ron: On the left. Both it and *d* added a dime to get 2 and then just added what was left.

Teacher: So, what about the last problem, no. 3, on the right? How did you think about a different give and take? *The numbers in 1.9 + 9.8 lend themselves to 2 different, nice give and take compensation strategies where you can use the associative property (1.7 + 0.2) + 9.8 = 1.7 + (0.2 + 9.8) or 1.9 + (0.1 + 9.7) = (1.9 + 0.1) + 9.7. The Workout asks students to look at both of them. On this Workout, the models are an open number line and a splitting model. In the next few Workouts, the same strategies are modeled with equations.*

Ralph: You can just give 20 cents to $9.80 and it becomes 10 bucks. Ten dollars plus $1.70 is the easiest problem up there.

Teacher: So, of all of these strategies to find 1.90 + 9.80, which do you like best and why?

Addition Workout 8

Name _____

Heather had $2.78. During the day, she earned $6.83. How much money does she have now?

1. Four students solved the problem using the different strategies shown below.
   Fill in the blanks. Analyze and describe each strategy.

Description

a.

2.78 3   9   9.61

b.

2.78 3   9.61

c.

2.78   8.78 ....

0.22 ....

d.

2.78   .... 9.78
                                        −0.17

2. Which strategy do you like the best for these numbers? Why?

3. Study the strategies below.

   Fill in the blanks for an alternative give and take strategy.

   Which of the above number lines shows one of the give and take strategies below? _____

   $$2.78 + 6.83$$
   $$\underline{+..... \ {}^-0.22}$$
   $$3.00 + ... = ...$$

   $$2.78 - ...... = ...$$
   $$\underline{+ 6.83 + 0.17 = 7.00}$$
   $$......$$

Addition Workout 9

1. Five students solved the SAME problem using different strategies shown below. Fill in the blanks. What question were they all solving? _____

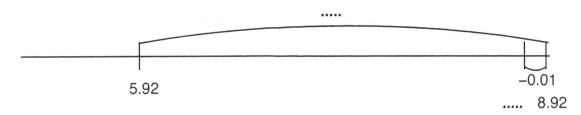

5.92   −0.01
                   ..... 8.92

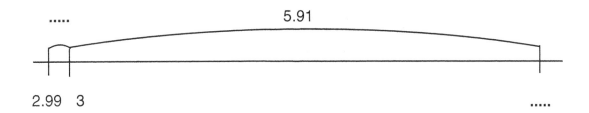

2.99   3   5.91   .....

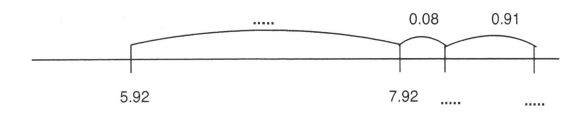

5.92   7.92 .... 0.08 0.91

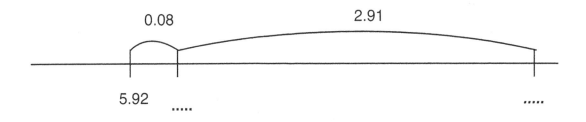

5.92 .....   2.91   .....

2.99 − ...... = ...   2.99 + ...
+ .... + 0.08 = 6.00   +0.01   −0.01
          ....   3.00 + ... = ...

2. Fill in the blanks using relational thinking (do not compute).

2.54 + 5.97 = _____ + 6.00

_____ + 2.09 = 79.91 + 2.18

3.8 + _____ = 4 + 2.7

1. Five students solved the SAME problem using different strategies shown. Fill in the blanks.
   What question were they all solving? _____

$$15.7 + \dots\dots$$
$$\underline{+0.3 \quad -0.3}$$
$$16.00 + \dots\dots \ = \dots\dots$$

$$0.49 \ + \dots\dots \ = 1.00$$
$$\underline{+ \dots\dots \ - 0.51 = 15.19}$$
$$\dots\dots$$

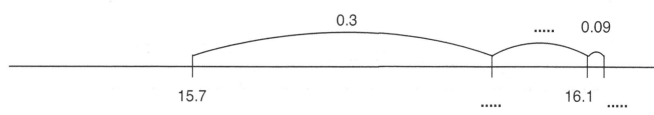

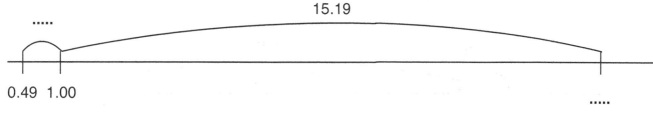

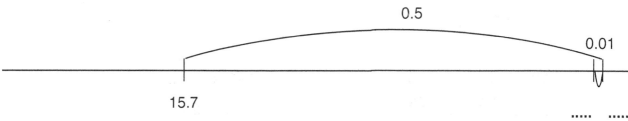

2. Fill in the blanks using relational thinking (do not compute).

   $9.99 + \_\_\_\_ = 10.00 + 3.44$

   $0.53 + 8.89 = \_\_\_\_ + 9.00$

   $\_\_\_\_ + 3.2 = 9.89 + 3.31$

Addition Workout 11

1. Jade was solving ⅕ + ¼. The double number lines show her thinking.

    Fill in the blanks.

    What answer did she find? _____

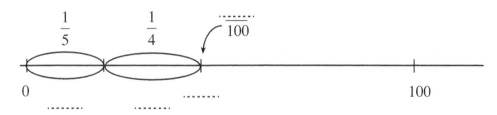

2. Tianna was also solving ⅕ + ¼. The double number line shows her thinking. Fill in the blanks.
    What answer did she find? _____

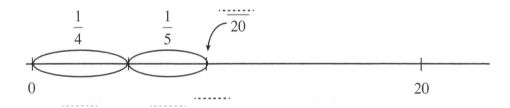

3. Amara was also solving ⅕ + ¼. The double number line shows her thinking. Fill in the blanks.
    What answer did she find? _____

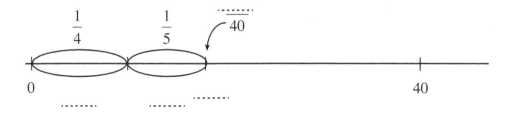

Name _____

1. Trevor was solving ⅕ + ⅔. The double number lines show his thinking. Fill in the blanks. What answer did he find? _____

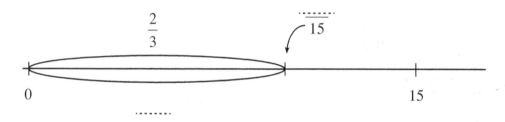

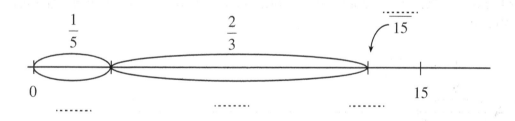

2. Joel was also solving ⅕ + ⅔. The double number line shows his thinking. Fill in the blanks. What answer did he find? _____

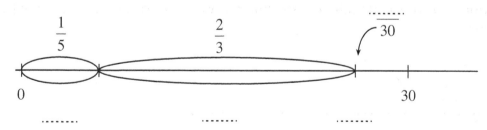

Addition Workout 13

1. Lillie was solving ³⁄₇ + ⁴⁄₅. The double number lines show her thinking. Fill in the blanks.
    What answer did she find? _____

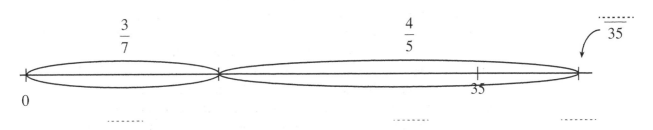

2. Keegan was also solving ³⁄₇ + ⁴⁄₅. The double number line shows his thinking. Fill in the blanks.
    How do Lillie's and Keegan's strategies compare? _____

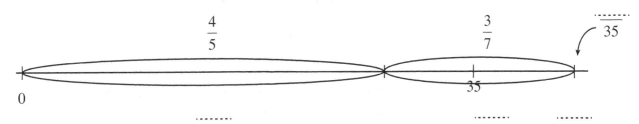

3. If ⅛ of a number is 5, what is

    ¼ of that same number? _____

    ½ of that same number? _____

    ⅜ of that same number? _____

    ⅞ of that same number? _____

    ¾ of that same number? _____

Sample Dialog for Addition Workout 13

Teacher: Let's talk about this double number line Workout. Can someone tell me why Lillie might have chosen 35? *The teacher invites the students to consider the choice of 35 for denominators 5 and 7. Students might be able to fill in numbers in the Workout, but the teacher wants the students to also consider the reasons behind the moves.*

Scott: Both 5 and 7 are factors of 35, so it's easy to find $\frac{1}{5}$ and $\frac{1}{7}$ of 35.

Angie: And that's what she did first. She found $\frac{1}{7}$ of 35, that's 5, and $\frac{1}{5}$ of 35, that's 7.

Teacher: And what did she do next? *Since the Workout is static, the teacher calls attention to the probable sequence of moves to invite students to consider how they might approach similar problems.*

Courtney: She found $\frac{3}{7}$ of 35. That is 3 times $\frac{1}{7}$, so 3 times 5 is 15.

Taylor: And then she added $\frac{4}{5}$ of 35. Since $\frac{1}{5}$ is 7, then $\frac{4}{5}$ is 4 times 7, 28.

Natalie: Then 15 and 28 are 43. So the answer is $\frac{43}{35}$.

Teacher: Who can explain why she drew the jump of $\frac{4}{5}$ over the 35? Isn't the 35 the total that she's basing everything on? Is that a typo? *The teacher knows from experience that this is confusing for some students and she wants to bring it to the forefront so students can work through it.*

Melanie: Well, the answer is $\frac{43}{35}$, right? So, that's more than 1.

Haley: It's like, she ran $\frac{3}{7}$ of a track that is 35 meters long and then she ran $\frac{4}{5}$ of the track, so she ran 15 meters and 28 meters. She ran longer than the track.

Tanner: Yeah, maybe she ran on two different days and she wanted to know how much of the track she had run. She ran more than the whole track, $\frac{8}{35}$ more.

Teacher: OK, so we are comfortable that the jumps on the double number line go over the total that Lillie was using? *Continuing the conversation to help cement the idea.*

Garrett: Yes, because $\frac{43}{35}$ is more than 1.

Teacher: Let's talk about item 3. If $\frac{1}{8}$ of a number is 5, how did you find $\frac{1}{4}$ of that same number?

Angie: I know that $\frac{1}{4}$ is the same as $\frac{2}{8}$, so since we know that $\frac{1}{8}$ is 5, then two of those $\frac{1}{8}$s is 10.

Teacher: Any questions on that? No? Then, can someone repeat that in their own words? *If there are no questions, then students should be able to restate. If students cannot restate, that might encourage them to ask a question.*

Marc: If $\frac{1}{8}$ is 5, then double that is 10. Double $\frac{1}{8}$ is $\frac{2}{8}$ so $\frac{1}{4}$ of the number is 10.

Teacher: So $\frac{3}{8}$? *This helps students think about scaling up from the unit fraction. If you know $\frac{1}{8}$, then $\frac{3}{8}$ is three of those $\frac{1}{8}$s.*

Courtney: Since $\frac{1}{8}$ is 5, then three of those $\frac{1}{8}$s is 15.

Teacher: How about $\frac{1}{2}$?

Alia: One-half of 5 is 2.5.

Andy: But the problem doesn't ask for $\frac{1}{2}$ of 5. It wants $\frac{1}{2}$ of the same number that 5 is $\frac{1}{8}$ of.

Deb: Yeah, so you're not looking for $\frac{1}{2}$ of 5. Since $\frac{1}{8}$ is 5, then $\frac{4}{8}$ is 20.

Alia: Oh, and $\frac{4}{8}$ is $\frac{1}{2}$, so that works. Got it.

Teacher: Great. How about $\frac{5}{8}$?

Ryan: If $\frac{4}{8}$ is 20 and $\frac{1}{8}$ is 5, then $\frac{5}{8}$ is 25.

LESSONS AND ACTIVITIES FOR BUILDING POWERFUL NUMERACY

Brandon: I went back to ⅛ is 5, so 5 times ⅛ is ⅝ and that is 25.

MacKenzie: I did all of these differently. I started thinking about the number. Since ⅛ of the number is 5, then number is 40.

Jackson: How did you get that?

MacKenzie: Because ⅛ is 5 and you need eight ⅛s, so 8 times 5 is 40.

Teacher: Let's take a minute and check what we just got and see if the ¼, ⅜, etc., all work if we know the number is 40. *The teacher waits to the end to acknowledge that the number is 40 because she wanted to keep the conversation focused on using the relationships between the fractions.*

Addition Workout 14

1. Four students solved the SAME problem using the different strategies shown below. Fill in the blank
   What question were they all solving? _____

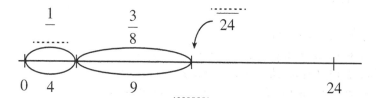

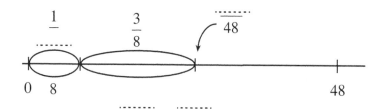

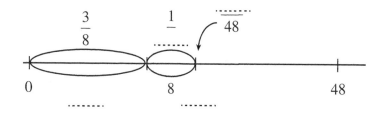

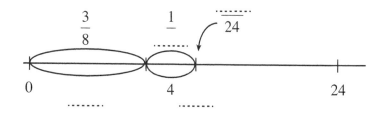

2. If ³⁄₁₀ of a number is 12, what is

   ¹⁄₁₀ of that same number? _____

   ¹⁄₅ of that same number? _____

   ²⁄₅ of that same number? _____

   ½ of that same number? _____

   ⁹⁄₁₀ of that same number? _____

Addition Workout 15

Name _____

1. A student used the double number lines below to solve a problem. Fill in the blanks. What question was the student solving? Write the question and the answer. _____

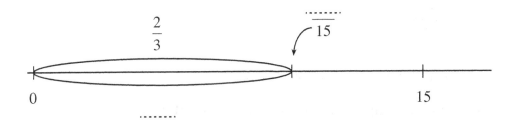

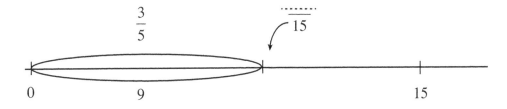

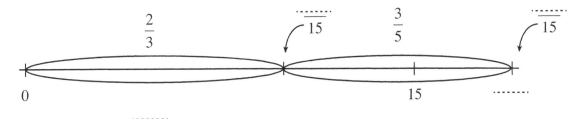

2. If ⅓ of a number is 12, what is

⅙ of that same number? _____

½ of that same number? _____

⅔ of that same number? _____

³⁄₂ of that same number? _____

¹⁄₁₂ of that same number? _____

The cookie recipe called for ⅔ C milk chocolate chips and ¾ C semi-sweet chocolate chips. Kayla doesn't like milk chocolate, so she decides to put in all semi-sweet chips. How many cups of semi-sweet chips should she put in the batter?

1. Kayla used ratio tables to model her thinking.

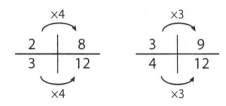

⁸/₁₂ + ⁹/₁₂ = ¹⁷/₁₂ or 1⁵/₁₂ so she put in a little less than 1½ cups.

2. How could Kayla similarly use ratio tables to find a different sum: ⅗ + ¼? Fill in the blanks.

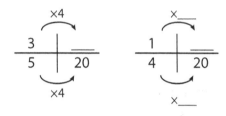

Therefore, ⅗ + ¼ = ——/₂₀ + ——/₂₀ = _____.

Addition Workout 17

Name _____

1. Kurt ran ³⁄₁₀ of the race and took a water break. Then he ran ¼ more of the race. How much of the race has he run so far?

2. Tanner used ratio tables to show his thinking. Fill in the blanks.

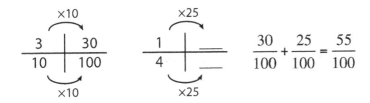

$$\frac{30}{100} + \frac{25}{100} = \frac{55}{100}$$

He also used a ratio table to simplify ⁵⁵⁄₁₀₀.

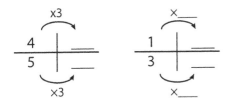

So, ⁵⁵⁄₁₀₀ = ¹¹⁄₂₀

3. How could Tanner similarly use ratio tables to find a different sum: ⅘ + ⅓? Fill in the blanks.

Therefore, ⅘ + ⅓ = _____.

©2014 Pamela Weber Harris from *Lessons and Activities for Building Powerful Numeracy*. Portsmouth, NH: Heinemann.

Addition Workout 18

1. Brent is working on ⅛ + ¹⁄₁₄. He showed his work in ratio tables. Fill in the blanks.

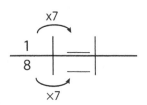   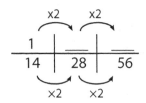

Therefore, ⅛ + ¼ = _____.

2. How could you similarly use ratio tables to find ¾ + ⅑? Fill in the blanks.

   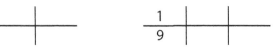

Therefore, ¾ + ⅑ = _____.

Addition Workout 19

1. Ann is working on ⅟₇ + ⅗. She showed her work in ratio tables. Fill in the blanks.

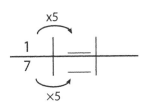 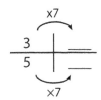

   Therefore, ⅟₇ + ⅗ = _____.

2. How could you similarly use ratio tables to find ⅗ + ⅙? Fill in the ratio tables.

   Therefore, ⅗ + ⅙ = _____.

Addition Workout 20

1. SuLi used a ratio table to show her work for finding ¾ + ⅑.

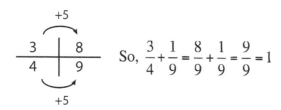

   So, $\dfrac{3}{4} + \dfrac{1}{9} = \dfrac{8}{9} + \dfrac{1}{9} = \dfrac{9}{9} = 1$

   What is SuLi's error? Explain.

2. Kai used a ratio table to show her work for finding ¾ + ⅑.

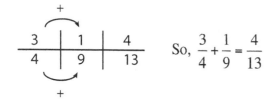

   So, $\dfrac{3}{4} + \dfrac{1}{9} = \dfrac{4}{13}$

   What is Kai's error? Explain.

3. Find ¾ + ⅑ correctly.

   Therefore, ¾ + ⅑ = ____.

Sample Dialog for Addition Workout 20

Teacher: Let's talk about the Workout with the errors. Who will explain what you think SuLi was doing and why it's an error? *This workout poses a common student error and asks students to make sense of it.*

Jack: These are called ratio tables, right? That means that the ratios have to stay the same.

Teacher: Yep, we call that equivalent — the ratios need to be equivalent. *Jack has the right idea. By reflecting the idea back using more precise vocabulary, Jack has the opportunity to connect the idea with correct language.*

Jack: So, if you have a ratio of 3 to 4, like 3 boxes each have 4 toys in them, you can't just add 5 boxes and add 5 toys. If you add 5 boxes, you now have 20 more toys, not 5 more. Each box has 4 toys.

Lainey: Yeah, when you're finding equivalent ratios, you can multiply the number of boxes and the number of toys by the same thing, because if you have 5 times as many boxes, you have 5 times as many toys. But you can't just add 5 like that.

Reese: I think of it as parts of a candy bar. If you have $\frac{3}{4}$ of a candy bar — to get an equivalent amount, you could cut the pieces in half — then you'd have eighths. So you'd need 6 of those $\frac{1}{8}$ pieces. So $\frac{3}{4}$ is equivalent to $\frac{6}{8}$. To get equivalent fractions, if you cut the pieces in half, you have to take twice as many.

Teacher: But I have seen you guys adding in ratio tables before . . . *The students' conversation about ratios is spot on, but the teacher focuses on the adding in ratio tables.*

Luke: Yes, but it's like Jack said, if you add 5 boxes, then you have to add 20 toys, not 5 toys.

Teacher: Great! Let's talk about Kai's error. What's going on there? *Focusing on the error shown.*

Josh: He just added the numerator and the denominator. You can't do that.

Teacher: Why not? Say more about that. *The conversation is going well, but the teacher wants to invite other students to comment.*

Josh: It's like Jack said, if you're going to add in a ratio table, you have to add an equivalent ratio, adding 1 box would mean adding 4 toys, not 9. You're not adding equivalent ratios here — the question is $\frac{3}{4} + \frac{1}{9}$. Those are not equivalent. They are not even close.

Delaney: Yeah, you're adding totally different fractions. So, to add them, you need to find equivalent fractions so that you have the same kind of pieces to add.

Teacher: What do you mean, the same kind of pieces?

Delaney: Like you could turn them both into thirty-sixths. Then you can add those thirty-sixths.

Jessica: So, $\frac{3}{4}$ is $\frac{27}{36}$ and $\frac{1}{9}$ is $\frac{4}{36}$. Now you can add them.

Ryan: Because you have the same denominators, thirty-sixths.

Teacher: So, you're telling me that there are times you can add in a ratio table and times you cannot? *This invites students to make a generalization.*

Ryan: Yes, you can add when you are adding equivalent ratios. You can't add the numerator and the denominators when you are adding fractions.

Student Workouts for Subtraction

There are twenty Student Workouts for subtraction: five with whole numbers, five with decimals, five with fractions on double number lines, and five with fractions in ratio tables. Each is a five- to ten-minute activity to be completed by individual students or student pairs and then discussed as a class.

Here are some general questions to have handy:

Clarifying Questions

► What is the question asking?

► How can you fill in the blanks?

Scaffolding Questions

► How would you verbalize the strategy shown on this number line/ratio table?

► How does that strategy differ from this one?

► What is a friendly number?

► What are some friendly numbers near the number you are working with?

Focusing on "Difference Versus Removal"

► Subtraction can mean removing a number from another number. It can also mean finding the difference (distance) between them. Which do you see here? How do you know?

- If both numbers in the subtraction problem are on the number line, is the strategy finding the difference or removing?
- If the answer is on the top of the number line, is the strategy finding the difference or removing?
- If the answer is where you land on the number line, is the strategy finding the difference or removing?

Focusing on "What Equivalent Problem to Create?"

- You are trying to create an equivalent problem that is easier to solve? Would it help to put the numbers on the number line and look near them?
- So, this is the distance (difference) you are looking for? Where could you shift it so that the resulting problem is easier to find?
- Do you want to make the first number (minuend) or the second (subtrahend) nice?

Class Discussion Questions

- Can you give and take with subtraction? Give and give? Take and take? Why or why not? How might you prove that on a number line?
- If the numbers are close together, which strategy might you use? If the numbers are far apart?
- When using the constant difference strategy, which number in the subtraction problem do you prefer to shift to a nice number?

Comparing Strategies

- Which strategy seems more efficient? Why?
- Which strategy seems easier to do mentally?
- Which strategy seems more sophisticated or clever?
- What about the numbers makes that strategy your favorite for this problem?
- How might you change the numbers so that a different strategy would fit better?

The Strategies and Models Used in the Subtraction Workouts

The primary model for subtraction of whole numbers and decimals is the open number line.

Vertical equations are also used at times.

The whole number and decimal subtraction Workouts and strings use three main strategies: removal, finding the difference, and the constant difference strategy.

Removal

When the numbers in a subtraction problem are far apart, it can be helpful to remove the second number (subtrahend) from the first number (minuend). Since the numbers are far apart, the second number is relatively small compared to the first number and there is not much to remove. For example, $13.72 - 0.89$ (Figure 2.1) can be found by removing 0.72 from 13.72 to get to 13 and then removing the remaining 0.17 to land on 12.83. The answer is where you land on the number line.

FIGURE 2.1

$13.72 - 0.89$

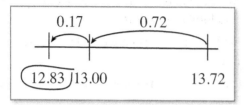

Difference

When the numbers in a subtraction problem are close together, it can be helpful to find the distance between them. Because the numbers are relatively close together, the distance between them is small. For example $13.72 - 12.98$ (Figure 2.2) can be found by placing both numbers on the number line and finding the distance between them: $0.02 + 0.72 = 0.74$. The answer is the distance between the numbers, on the top of the number line.

FIGURE 2.2

$13.72 - 12.98$

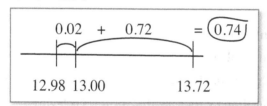

When operating with integers, both removal and difference must be considered. After finding the difference between the numbers in the subtraction problem, you determine the sign of the answer by considering removal. If you are removing a smaller number from a greater number, then answer is positive. If you are removing a greater number from a smaller number, the answer is negative. For example, to find $13 - (-2)$ (Figure 2.3), first find the difference, which is 15. Then, are you removing a larger number or a smaller number from 13? Since -2 is smaller, the answer is $+15$. For $-2 - 13$, the difference is still 15, but 13 is greater than -2, so the answer is -15.

FIGURE 2.3

$13 - (-2) = 15$ and $(-2) - 13 = -15$

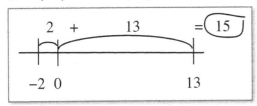

Constant Difference

Often it is helpful to shift a problem up or down the number line such that the resulting problem is easier to solve. For example, $23.15 - 16.89$ (Figure 2.4) is equivalent to $23.26 - 17.00$ because you can shift both numbers in the problem to the right 0.11 on the number line.

FIGURE 2.4

$23.15 - 16.89$

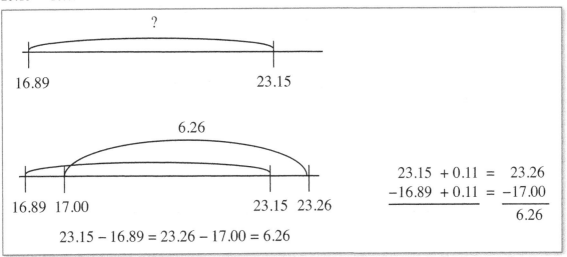

Subtracting Fractions

The primary models used for subtracting fractions are the double open number line and the ratio table. These models help students find equivalent fractions in order to subtract.

The fraction subtraction Workouts and strings with the double open number line use the strategy of finding a unit fraction of a friendly number and then scaling up to find equivalent fractions. For example, to find $\frac{3}{7}$ of 35, first find $\frac{1}{7}$ of 35 (Figure 2.5). The double open number line helps because as students have to decide where to mark the $\frac{1}{7}$ on the top, they visualize dividing the line into 7 equal sections. This prompts the student to also divide the 35 into 7 equal groups. $35 \div 7 = 5$ so $\frac{1}{7}$ of 35 is 5. The portion of the number line that is marked is $\frac{5}{35}$.

FIGURE 2.5

Similarly, considering where 3 of those ⅐s are (³⁄₇) prompts the student to scale up to ³⁄₇ by finding a length 3 times as long: 3 × 5 is 15. Since the whole is 35, ³⁄₇ is equivalent to 15 out of that 35, or ¹⁵⁄₃₅ (Figure 2.6).

FIGURE 2.6

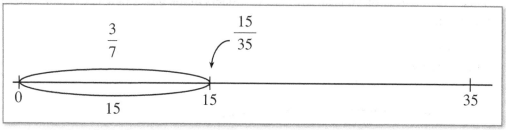

To find a fraction equivalent to ⅘, a student would reason similarly to find ²⁸⁄₃₅ (Figure 2.7).

FIGURE 2.7

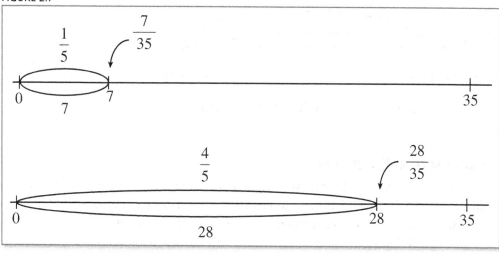

To subtract ⁴/₅ − ³/₇, the student uses these equivalencies, ²⁸/₃₅ − ¹⁵/₃₅ = ¹³/₃₅ (Figure 2.8).

FIGURE 2.8

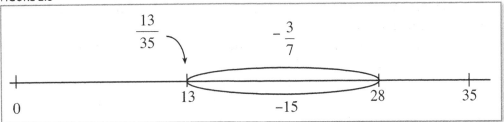

The fraction subtraction Workouts and strings that feature the ratio table use the strategy of finding equivalent ratios by scaling up or down. For example, to find ³/₄ − ²/₃, students use a ratio table for each fraction to find equivalent fractions (Figure 2.9).

FIGURE 2.9

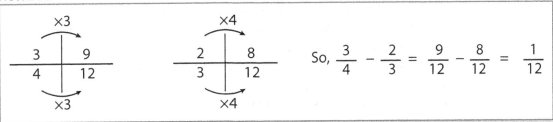

The Progression

Whole Numbers: Workouts 1 Through 5

Subtraction Workouts 1 and 2 ask students to describe subtraction strategies modeled on the open number line and fill in the blanks of missing numbers for each strategy. Then students solve a different subtraction problem themselves on the open number line. This is an opportunity for students to try a problem on their own.

Subtraction Workouts 3 through 5 ask students to fill in the blanks in strategies, but now students have to decide what problem all four students solved. Relational thinking problems are introduced to further work on the constant difference strategy.

The Sample Dialog after Workout 4 shows a teacher discussing all the key subtraction strategies with students. It includes a conversation about how students solve the same problem with both a removal and a difference strategy.

Decimals: Workouts 6 Through 10

Subtraction Workouts 6 through 10 follow a similar progression but use decimal numbers.

The Sample Dialog after Workout 7 shows a discussion of subtraction strategies with decimals, where the teacher asks students to compare strategies.

Fractions: Workouts 11 Through 20

Subtraction Workouts 11 through 15 use the open double number line to subtract fractions.

Subtraction Workout 11 starts with unit fractions and then Workouts 12 through 15 build to non-unit fractions.

Subtraction Workouts 14 and 15 ask students to fill in the blanks in strategies but now students have to decide what problem the students solved.

The Sample Dialog for Workout 15 shows a discussion of using a double open number line to find unit fractions and scale up to find non-unit fractions with common denominators when subtracting fractions. Students also discuss the problems at the bottom where they are given a fractional value of an unknown number and asked to find other fractional values.

Subtraction Workouts 16 through 20 use a ratio table to find equivalent fractions.

Subtraction Workout 16 gives students an example of using ratio tables to find equivalent fractions and then asks students to apply that example for similar problems.

Subtraction Workout 17 adds the idea of simplifying using a ratio table.

The Sample Dialog for Workout 17 showcases students discussing which common denominator to use as they subtract fractions.

Subtraction Workouts 18 and 19 show parts of a strategy to find equivalent fractions, where students fill in the missing parts.

Subtraction Workout 20 uses ratio tables to show common errors. Students are asked to explain the errors.

Subtraction Workout 1

Emmett started with $41 and spent $18. How much money does he have now?

1. Four students solved the problem using the different strategies shown below.

   Fill in the blanks.

   Analyze and describe each strategy.

Description

a.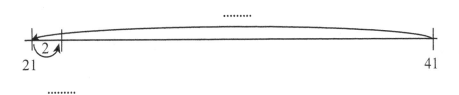

b.

c.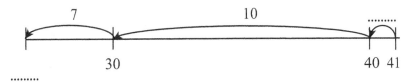

d.

2. Use the number line below to subtract 63 − 16, using any of the strategies above.

Subtraction Workout 2

Name _____

Brittany has $52 and is planning to spend $17. How much money will she have left?

1. Four students solved the problem using the different strategies shown below.

   Fill in the blanks.

   Analyze and describe each strategy.

Description

a.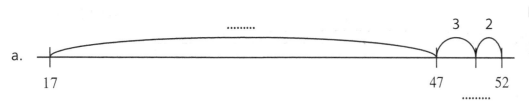

b.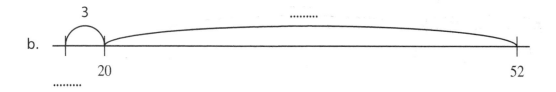

c.

5 ········ 10

35   40   52

········

d.

5   10   ·········

35   50 52

·········

2. Use the number line below to subtract 71 − 19, using any of the strategies above.

Subtraction Workout 3

Name _____

1. Four students solved the SAME subtraction problem using different strategies shown.

   Fill in the blanks.

   What were they all solving? _____

   a.
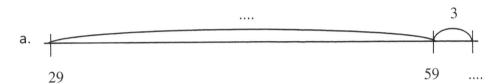

   b.
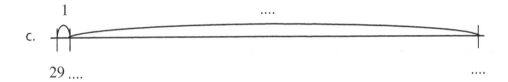

   c.

   d.

2. Solve 31 − 18 using the number line below.

   Subtract 18 from 31:

   Find the difference between 18 and 31:

(number line with 18 and 31 marked)

Subtraction Workout 4

1. Four students solved the SAME subtraction problem using the different strategies shown.

    Fill in the blanks.

    What were they all solving? _____

    a.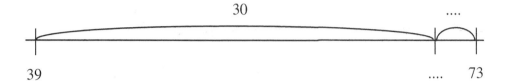

    b.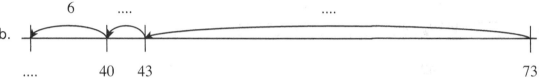

    c.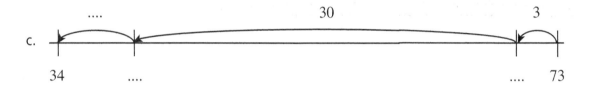

    d.

2. Solve 42 − 19 using the number lines below.

    Subtract 19 from 42:

    Find the difference between 19 and 42:

Sample Dialog for Subtraction Workout 4

Teacher: This Workout is a little different because they don't tell you the problem! There are four strategies to solve the same problem, but you have to figure out what the problem is. Remember, the same problem for the whole page. We'll talk after you work.

Students work.

Josue: I think there are two different problems, not just one.

Teacher: Say more about that.

This is a typical confusion. The teacher wants the students to work out how all the strategies can represent the same problem.

Josue: The first and last ones are both the same problem and the middle ones are the same, but they are not all the same.

Emily: Yes, I agree with Josue. Letters *a* and *d* are 73 − 34. Letters *b* and *c* are 73 − 39.

Fernando: I thought so, too, except since they have to be the same problem, I looked again. Look at the arrows.

Emily: What about the arrows? I wasn't sure what to think about them. I think I just ignored the arrows.

Shannon: In the middle two problems, the arrows show you taking away, removing 39 from 73, so, yes, they are 73 − 39.

Fernando: Now look at *a* and *d*. What if you were solving the same problem, 73 − 39 but instead of minus-ing the 39, you counted up instead?

Daniel: It's like *a* and *d* are finding the difference between 39 and 73 by counting up. So, that's still 73 − 39.

Josue: Are you saying that *a* and *d* can't be 73 − 34?

Shannon: They could be either 73 − 34 or 73 − 39, except on this page we know they are all solving the same problem, so it has to be 73 − 39.

Hayley: So it's not enough to figure out what they could be, we have to compare them to figure out what they all are? OK, I get it.

Teacher: So, of all of these strategies to find 73 − 39, which do you like best and why?

Josue: I like *b* because you just subtract the 30 in one big jump and then you can just subtract the 9.

Lucero: I like to subtract, too, but I prefer *c* because once you subtract 3 to get to 70, then you can just think of getting rid of 36 more.

Teacher: It looks like you both like to subtract, or remove, Josue by the friendly 30 and Lucero to the friendly 70.

The teacher summarizes and describes the two strategies.

Teacher: Who likes to find the difference?

Melissa: I like *d*. Once you get to 40, it's easy to see that you just have 33 more.

Teacher: You like to get to that friendly 40 and then it's easy to see the rest. Nice work. It's interesting that subtraction can be found be removing or by finding the difference. Would someone please tell us your strategy for subtracting 19 from 42?

Alexander: I started on 42 and took away 20, landing on 22, and then added back 1 to end on 23.

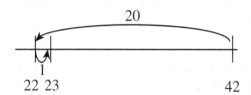

Teacher: A little "over" subtraction! Subtract a bit too much. Nice. Did anyone remove by subtracting too little and then adjusting?

Angelica: I subtracted 10 to 32 and then 9 more to 23.

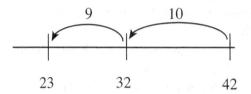

Teacher: And who will share their difference strategy? Jonathan, tell me what you did very first, please.

Jonathan: I put both the numbers, 19 and 42, on the number line. Then I could see that there was 1, 20, 2 — equals 23 — between them.

Lily: I did the same thing but once I got from the 19 to 20, I could just see the 22 left to make a total of 23.

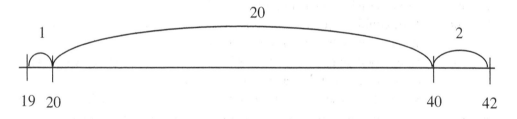

Teacher: Nice work.

Subtraction Workout 5

1. Four students solved the SAME problem using the different strategies shown below.

   Fill in the blanks.

   What were they all solving? _____

   a.
   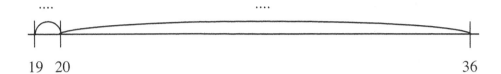

   ....

   19 20   36

   b.

     6   ....

   17   26   36

   c.

   ....

   19   29   36

   d.
   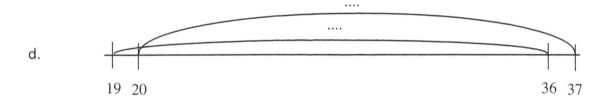

   ....

   ....

   19 20   36 37

2. Fill in the blanks using relational thinking (do not compute).

   a. 36 − 19 = _____ − 20

   b. _____ − 28 = 79 − 30

   c. 238 − _____ = 241 − 20

©2014 Pamela Weber Harris from *Lessons and Activities for Building Powerful Numeracy*. Portsmouth, NH: Heinemann.   49

Subtraction Workout 6

Name _____

Daphne had $4.10 and then lost $1.70. How much does she have now?

1. Five students solved the problem using the different strategies shown below.
   Analyze and describe each strategy.

$$4.10 - 1.70$$ Description

a.

$$\overset{+0.30 \qquad +0.30}{\underline{}}$$

$$4.40 - \text{.......} = \text{.......}$$

b.

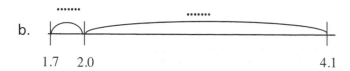

c.

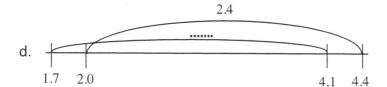

d.

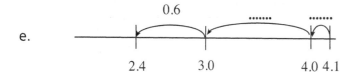

e.

2. Solve 5.3 − 1.8 using the number lines below.

   Subtract 1.8 from 5.3:

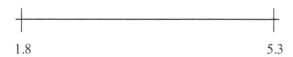

   Find the difference between 1.8 and 5.3:

©2014 Pamela Weber Harris from *Lessons and Activities for Building Powerful Numeracy*. Portsmouth, NH: Heinemann.

Subtraction Workout 7

Name _____

Toby had $6.30 and then spent $4.90 for lunch. How much does he have now?

1. Five students solved the problem using the different strategies shown below.

   Analyze and describe each strategy.

a.    Description

b.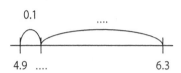

c.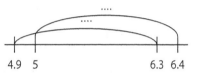

e.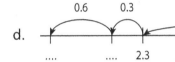

2. Fill in the blanks using relational thinking (do not compute).

   a. $3.6 - 1.9 = $ _____ $- 2$

   b. _____ $- 2.7 = 7.9 - 3.0$

   c. $35.2 - 3.8 = 35.4 - $ _____

Sample Dialog for Subtraction Workout 7

Teacher: You've worked on this problem, starting with $6.30 and spending $4.90 and finding how much you have left. How would you describe the first strategy, *a*?

Maddie: They started with the $6.30 and took away the 30 cents. That's 6 bucks. They backed up 4 bucks to 2 and then had 60 cents left so they landed on $1.40.

Teacher: Anyone disagree? No? That's how you filled in the blanks and what they did to solve the problem. How would you describe the strategy?

Maddie: Subtract to a nice number and then keep going.

Jonathan: It's a removal strategy.

Teacher: How do you know?

Sami: One way to tell is that the two numbers in the problem, 6.3 and 3.9, are not on the number line.

Mark: The 3.9 is what they are removing. It's on top of the number line being subtracted.

Teacher: Please describe strategy *b*.

Trent: Both numbers are on the number line, so it's a difference strategy.

Phil: They found the difference by getting to a friendly number, 4.9 to 5 is a dime, and then it's easy to add the dime to the rest, $1.30, to get $1.40 as the total.

Teacher: Does everyone agree this is a difference strategy? Yes? OK, how would you describe strategy *c*?

Jose: That's the equivalent problem one, where they find the difference by making an equivalent problem that's easier.

Robin: Instead of finding the distance between 4.9 and 6.3, they did 5 and 6.4. That's just 1.4 or $1.40.

Rory: It's the constant difference strategy.

Clark: And *e* is the same strategy as *c*, just not on a number line.

Preston: Both *c* and *e* show making a nicer problem to solve, 6.4 minus 5.

Teacher: Anyone else? No? OK, how about the next strategy, *d*?

Jerome: That's like *a* because it's subtracting. It's different from *a* because they subtracted a nice number first, the 4 bucks. Then they adjusted back the rest of the 90 cents.

Sue: It's removal like *a*, I agree.

Teacher: Which of these strategies do you like the most, or do you wish it came naturally for you when you run into a subtraction problem?

The teacher wants to nudge students to form relationships so that these strategies become more natural. By weighing the merits of the strategies and talking about the relationships used, students may be more inclined to use them.

Paula: I don't normally think to find an equivalent problem, but I wish I did! You always get such an easy problem to solve.

Mika: Yes, constant difference seems like the way to go, but it doesn't always when I'm in the middle of a problem.

Teacher: Which number did they choose to make nicer by shifting the difference between 6.3 and 4.9 to 6.4 and 5?

Mika: They made the 4.9 nice, by getting to 5.

Teacher: Which number in the problem is that? The first or second? And why would I be asking that?

Phil: It's the last number. You want to make the last number nice because then it's really easy to solve.

Teacher: Let's look at the relational thinking problem and see which number in each problem they made nice. Take a minute and look at those. Which number did they make nice every time?

Students work.

Jasmine: In the first one, they turned 3.6 minus 1.9 into 3.7 minus 2, so the last number became nice. And the answer's 1.7.

Clark: The second one made 7.6 subtract 2.7 into 7.9 subtract 3, which is just 7.4. They did the same thing and made the last number friendly.

Rory: It's the same in *c*. It went from 35.2 minus 3.8 to 35.4 minus 4. Easy, the answer's 31.4.

Teacher: What do you think about that, the last number being shifted to something nicer?

Robin: I think that I haven't been paying attention to which number I was trying to make nice. I'll be working to make the last one nice.

Preston: If the last number is really nice, the subtraction problem is easy.

Teacher: Why is that?

Preston: If it's nice, there is usually a lot of zeros and it's easy to subtract those nice zero numbers.

Paula: Like 30 or 2 or 500 — it's nice to subtract those.

Rory: On this page, we subtracted an even 5 for the top problem and then 2, 3, and 4 for the bottom ones. All easy.

Teacher: I wonder if that might help some of you when you are trying to find nicer equivalent problems by shifting the distance up or down the number line. Try to make that second number in the subtraction problem nice and see what happens.

Subtraction Workout 8

1. Four students solved the SAME problem using the different strategies shown below.

   Fill in the blanks.

   What were they all solving? _____

   a.

   b.

   c.
   $$8.8 \quad - \quad \underline{\quad}$$
   $$+0.1 \qquad +0.1$$
   $$8.9 \quad - \quad \underline{\quad} = 1.9$$

   d.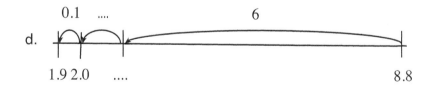

2. Fill in the blanks using relational thinking (do not compute).

   a. $25.3 - 3.9 = \underline{\quad} - 4.0$

   b. $1.902 - 4.97 = \underline{\quad} - 5.00$

   c. $304.52 - 199.98 = 304.54 - \underline{\quad}$

Subtraction Workout 9

Name _____

1. Four students solved the SAME problem using the different strategies shown below.

   Fill in the blanks.

   What were they all solving? _____

   a.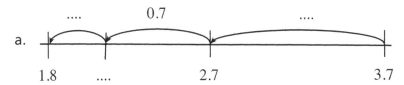

   b.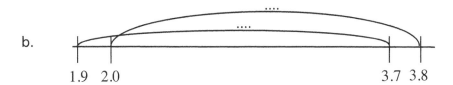

   c.

   d.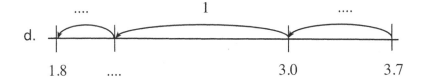

2. Fill in the blanks using relational thinking (do not compute).

   a. $37.63 - 2.98 =$ _____ $- 3.0$

   b. _____ $- 5.89 = 70.33 - 6.0$

   c. $631.06 - 29.95 = 631.11 -$ _____

Subtraction Workout 10

Name _____

1. Alisa and Allison were solving the subtraction problem by keeping the distance constant.

   Fill in the blanks.

   Alisa:

   $$3.70 \; - \; 1.90$$
   $$+ \text{......} \quad + \; 0.10$$
   $$\overline{3.80 \; - \; \text{......}} \; = 1.8$$

   Allison:

   $$3.70 \; - \; 1.90$$
   $$+ \; .30 \quad + \text{......}$$
   $$\overline{\text{......} \; - \; 2.20} \; = \text{......}$$

2. How do their strategies differ; whose do you prefer, and why?

3. Using the constant difference strategy, solve 7.20 − 3.88, showing your work:

©2014 Pamela Weber Harris from *Lessons and Activities for Building Powerful Numeracy*. Portsmouth, NH: Heinemann.

Subtraction Workout 11

Name _____

1. Carlos was solving ¼ − ⅕. The double number lines show his thinking. Fill in the blanks. What answer did he find? _____

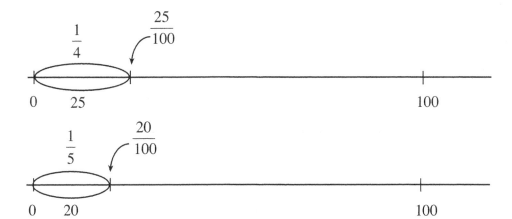

2. Veronica was also solving ¼ − ⅕. The double number line shows her thinking. Fill in the blanks. What answer did she find? _____

3. Julia was also solving ¼ − ⅕. The double number line shows her thinking. Fill in the blanks. What answer did she find? _____

Subtraction Workout 12

Name _____

1. Derek was solving ⅜ − ⅙. The double number lines show his thinking.

    Fill in the blanks.

    What answer did he find? _____

2. Tom was also solving ⅜ − ⅙. The double number line shows his thinking.

    Fill in the blanks.

    What answer did he find? _____

©2014 Pamela Weber Harris from *Lessons and Activities for Building Powerful Numeracy*. Portsmouth, NH: Heinemann.

Subtraction Workout 13

1. Natalie was solving ⁴⁄₅ − ³⁄₇. The double number lines show her thinking. Fill in the blanks. What answer did she find? _____

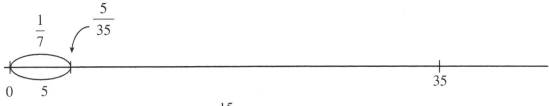

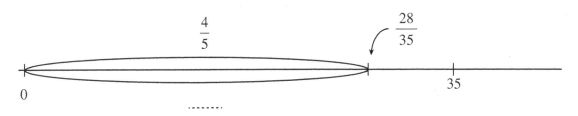

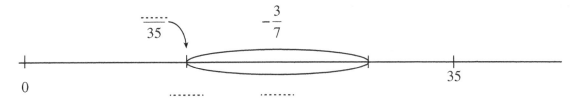

2. James was also solving ⁴⁄₅ − ³⁄₇. The double number line shows his thinking. Fill in the blanks. What answer did he find? _____

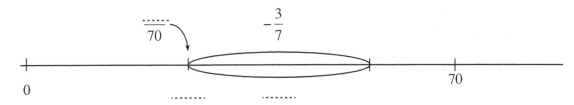

Subtraction Workout 14

Name _____

1. A student used the double number lines below to solve a problem. Fill in the blanks.
   What problem was the student solving? Write the problem and the answer. _____

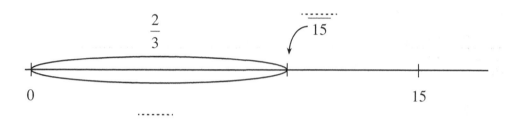

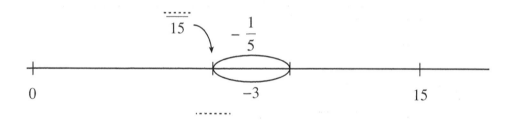

2. If ⅐ of a number is 4, what is

   ½ of that same number? _____

   ¼ of that same number? _____

   ³⁄₇ of that same number? _____

   ⁶⁄₇ of that same number? _____

   ¾ of that same number? _____

Subtraction Workout 15

Name _____

1. A student used the double number lines below to solve a problem. Fill in the blanks.
   What problem was the student solving? Write the problem and the answer. _____

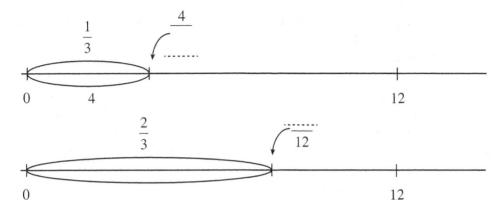

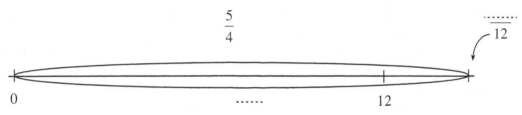

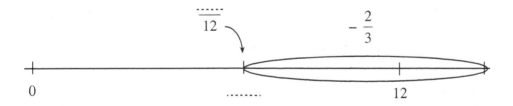

2. If ⅖ of a number is 8, what is

   ⅕ of that same number? _____

   ½ of that same number? _____

   ¼ of that same number? _____

   ¹⁄₁₀ of that same number? _____

Sample Dialog for Subtraction Workout 15

Teacher: How did you know what goes in the first blank on this page?

Angel: Twelve because the total is 12 and $\frac{1}{3}$ of 12 is 4 out of 12, so 12.

Teacher: So, what goes in the denominator is the total?

Molly: Yes, if you are running for 12 miles then $\frac{1}{3}$ of that will be 4 out of those 12.

Teacher: What goes in the next blank, here at the $\frac{2}{3}$ mark?

Roger: If *one*-third is 4, then *two*-thirds is double that, 8.

Teacher: Is $\frac{2}{3}$ always double $\frac{1}{3}$? Mark, you're smiling?

Mark: When you say it like that, of course $\frac{2}{3}$ always double $\frac{1}{3}$, but I don't always think about that when there are other numbers involved. Two of anything is double one of that thing. I'll try to use that more with fractions.

Teacher: Great! What goes in the blank on the third line? What is $\frac{1}{4}$ of 12?

Ginny: The answer is actually there—the 3 below the jump is also the numerator of the fraction, 3 out of the 12 is $\frac{1}{4}$.

Teacher: And what about that fourth line, with the $\frac{5}{4}$ of 12? Tell me about those blanks.

Terrance: If *one*-fourth of 12 is 3, than *five*-fourths of 12 must be 5 times that and 5 times 3 is 15. The 15 goes in both of those blanks. It represents the jump and the number of twelfths.

Teacher: Are you saying that $\frac{5}{4}$ of 12 is 15, which is more than 12?

Terrance: Yes, $\frac{5}{4}$ of anything is going to be more than that thing.

Frank: He's right because $\frac{5}{4}$ is like 125%. That's more than 100%.

Sue: And I thought about it like $1\frac{1}{4}$. The whole is 12 and the $\frac{1}{4}$ is 3, so 12 plus 3 is 15.

Hank: That is why the mark is past the 12 at the end. The 12 represents the whole thing. So more than the whole 12 must be after it.

Teacher: I hear you saying that the unit we are referring to in this problem is 12. And $\frac{5}{4}$ of that 12 is more than 12 so the mark for $\frac{5}{4}$ is after the 12. Great! What is going on in the last number line?

Sara: That's the problem! This student has been working up to this problem, $\frac{5}{4}$ ($\frac{15}{12}$) minus $\frac{2}{3}$.

Teacher: How did they solve it?

Even though Sara has successfully identified the problem, she may have done so without realizing how the student solved the problem.

Sara: They used 12 as their course length. Then found the unit fractions for $\frac{5}{4}$, $\frac{15}{12}$, and for $\frac{2}{3}$, $\frac{8}{12}$. Then $\frac{15}{12}$ minus $\frac{8}{12}$ is $\frac{7}{12}$.

Teacher: Would someone else please summarize this strategy?

Melanie: The original problem was $\frac{5}{4}$ minus $\frac{2}{3}$. Using 12, the person found equivalent unit fractions for $\frac{1}{4}$ and $\frac{1}{3}$ and then scaled up to equivalent fractions to $\frac{5}{4}$ minus $\frac{2}{3}$, $\frac{15}{12}$ minus $\frac{8}{12}$, and that's $\frac{7}{12}$.

Teacher: Nice. Let's talk about the questions at the bottom of the page. If $\frac{2}{5}$ of a number is 8, what is the number? And how did you figure it out?

Alex: I was thinking about $\frac{2}{5}$ as 40%. If 8 is 40%, then 2 is 10%, then 20 is 100%. So the number is 20. So $\frac{1}{5}$ of 20 is 4.

Daniella:	Yeah, but I didn't think percent, I thought that if $\frac{2}{5}$ was 8, then $\frac{4}{5}$ is double that, 16. Then add one more fifth, 4, to get 20. Then I also found $\frac{1}{5}$ of 20 to be 4.
Gabrielle:	I thought about $\frac{2}{5}$ as two $\frac{1}{5}$s and so 2 things. We are looking for 1 thing, so if 2 things is 8, then 1 of them is half of that, 4.
Wes:	Half of $\frac{2}{5}$ is $\frac{1}{5}$ so half of 8 is 4.
Teacher:	I hear that Alex and Daniella found the whole and then found $\frac{1}{5}$. What did Gabrielle and Wes do?
Alex:	They went straight to $\frac{1}{5}$ and never did find the whole. Interesting. I hadn't thought about that.
Teacher:	Could you do that for finding $\frac{1}{2}$ of the number, if you hadn't figured out the whole yet?
Wes:	I didn't do it that way. I found the number 20 and then took half, 10. But I suppose that since you have $\frac{2}{5}$ and you're looking for $\frac{2.5}{5}$, you could find half of the fifth. Since $\frac{1}{5}$ is 4, then half of that $\frac{1}{5}$ is 2, so 8 + 2 is 10.
Teacher:	What did Wes just do?
Melanie:	We're looking for $\frac{1}{2}$ of the number. If you only know $\frac{2}{5}$ of that number is 8, you can find 2½ fifths by finding the half fifth and adding them. Nice. It still might be easier to just find the 20 and take half.
Teacher:	Good point. We don't need to go crazy if there's an easier way, huh? What about the next one, $\frac{1}{4}$ of the number?
Daniella:	I found $\frac{1}{4}$ of 20 since we knew that 20 was the number, but now I am thinking that I could've also figured it out just knowing that half of the number was 10. If half is 10, then a fourth of the number is half of that half, 5.
Teacher:	Nice relationships! And the last problem, $\frac{1}{10}$ of the number?
Nora:	Since the number is 20, $\frac{1}{10}$ of 20 is 2.
Teacher:	I wonder if you could've found that from the very first piece of information, that $\frac{2}{5}$ of the number is 8?
Nora:	Um, so half of $\frac{2}{5}$ is $\frac{1}{5}$ so 4. And $\frac{1}{10}$ is half of $\frac{1}{5}$ so half of 4 is 2. Yep, you can!
Teacher:	Great work.

Subtraction Workout 16

Toni had ¾ of a yard of ribbon. She cut off ⅔ of a yard to put in her hair. How much ribbon was left?

Toni used ratio tables to help her.

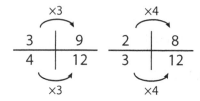

⁹⁄₁₂ − ⁸⁄₁₂ = ¹⁄₁₂ so she had ¹⁄₁₂ of a yard left.

How could Toni's brother, Tony, use ratio tables to find ⅖ − ¼ and ¾ − ⅕?

Fill in the blanks.

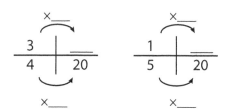

Therefore, ⅖ − ¼ = $\frac{......}{20} - \frac{......}{20}$ = _____ .

Therefore, ¾ − ⅕ = $\frac{......}{20} - \frac{......}{20}$ = _____ .

Subtraction Workout 17

Angel ran ³⁄₁₀ of the race and took a water break. He wanted to run a total of ¾ of the race before he took another break. How much of the race should he run before he stops again? Angel used ratio tables to find the difference. Fill in the blanks.

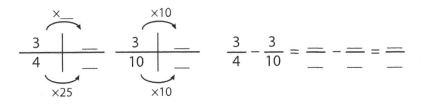

He also used a ratio table to help him simplify ⁴⁵⁄₁₀₀.

Fill in the blanks.

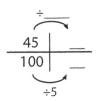

How did Courtney, Natalie, and Haylie use ratio tables to find ⅘ − ¹⁄₁₀?

Fill in the blanks.

Courtney:

Natalie:

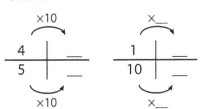

Haylie:

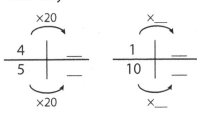

Therefore, ⅘ − ¹⁄₁₀ = _____.

Sample Dialog for Subtraction Workout 17

Teacher: Someone tell me what's going on in this Angel running scenario?

Terry: He wanted to run ¾ of the race before he stops again. He's already run ³⁄₁₀ so how much more is he running before he stops again?

Teacher: Work on these problems and then we'll talk about your work.

Students work.

Teacher: What course length did Angel use?

Ralph: He used 100. That works for fourths and tenths.

Teacher: So how did you fill in the blanks?

Ralph: First, ¾ is equivalent to ⁷⁵⁄₁₀₀ and ³⁄₁₀ to ³⁰⁄₁₀₀.

Lori: Then ⁷⁵⁄₁₀₀ − ³⁰⁄₁₀₀ is ⁴⁵⁄₁₀₀.

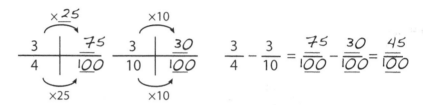

Teacher: And then he simplifies the ⁴⁵⁄₁₀₀ on the ratio table how?

Brad: He divides both by 5 to get ⁹⁄₂₀.

Teacher: That's all pretty straightforward. How else could you do that problem?

Maria: Instead of using a course length of 100, you could use 40.

Teacher: What would that result be?

Maria: You'd have ³⁰⁄₄₀ minus ¹²⁄₄₀ is ¹⁸⁄₄₀. Then that simplifies to ⁹⁄₂₀.

Peter: Or you could go straight to 20. That would be ¹⁵⁄₂₀ minus ⁶⁄₂₀ and that's ⁹⁄₂₀ and you don't have to simplify. You're already there.

Teacher: Great alternatives. I think we see something similar going on here on the bottom of this Workout. Courtney, Natalie, and Haylie also chose different denominators for the same problem. What result would these three ladies get?

Terry: Courtney went to 100 just like the top problem. So she gets ⁸⁰⁄₁₀₀ minus ¹⁰⁄₁₀₀ and that's ⁷⁰⁄₁₀₀ so she must simplify to ⁷⁄₁₀.

Teresa: Natalie used 50 and that gets ⁴⁰⁄₅₀ minus ⁵⁄₅₀ and that is ³⁵⁄₅₀. Divide by 5 and you also get ⁷⁄₁₀.

Louisa: Haylie chose 10 so she didn't even have to change the ¹⁄₁₀. She just changes ⁴⁄₅ to ⁸⁄₁₀ and then subtracts ¹⁄₁₀, so she gets ⁷⁄₁₀ and doesn't have to simplify.

Teacher: I will write these equivalencies: ⁷⁰⁄₁₀₀ = ³⁵⁄₅₀ = ⁷⁄₁₀. So, when you are solving fraction addition and subtraction problems, what is something that this might help you think about?

Ephraim: If you don't want to simplify when you're done, use the smallest course length that you can think of.

Lori: Yeah, find the smallest denominator that works for both of the denominators. Sometimes you still have to simplify but maybe not as much.

Peter: But you don't have to. As long as you keep all the fractions equivalent, you can use the ones that make the most sense to you. You just might have to simplify at the end.

Subtraction Workout 18

Name ______________________________

What is $\frac{3}{4} - \frac{1}{18}$?

Maria used ratio tables. Fill in the blanks:

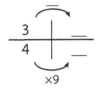

	___	
3	___	
4	___	
	×9	

	___	
1	___	
18	36	
	×2	

Therefore, $\frac{3}{4} - \frac{1}{18}$ = _____.

Use ratio tables to find the following.

Fill in the ratio tables. Simplify your answer.

$\frac{1}{8} - \frac{1}{12}$

8		

12		

Therefore, $\frac{1}{8} - \frac{1}{12}$ = _____.

$\frac{7}{8} - \frac{5}{12}$

8		

12		

Therefore, $\frac{7}{8} - \frac{5}{12}$ = _____.

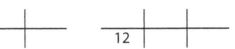

Subtraction Workout 19

What is ⅓ − ¹⁄₁₁?

Estimate a solution: _____

Won used ratio tables. Fill in the blanks:

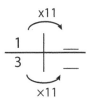 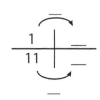

Therefore, ⅓ − ¹⁄₁₁ = _____.

Use ratio tables to find the following.

Fill in the ratio tables. Simplify your answer.

Find ⅖ − ⅙:

Therefore, ⅖ − ⅙ = _____.

Find ⅘ − ⅙:

 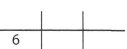

Therefore, ⅘ − ⅙ = _____.

©2014 Pamela Weber Harris from *Lessons and Activities for Building Powerful Numeracy*. Portsmouth, NH: Heinemann.

Subtraction Workout 20

Trent used ratio tables to find ⅞ − ½.

| $\frac{7}{8}$ | $\frac{1}{2}$ | $\frac{6}{6}$ |

So, $\frac{7}{8} - \frac{1}{2} = \frac{6}{6} = 1$

What is Trent's error? Explain:

Lexie used ratio tables to find ⅞ − ½.

| $\frac{1}{2}$ | $\frac{7}{8}$ |

So, $\frac{7}{8} - \frac{1}{2} = \frac{7}{8} - \frac{7}{8} = 0$

What is Lexie's error? Explain:

Find ⅞ − ½.

| $\frac{7}{8}$ | | | | $\frac{1}{2}$ | | |

Therefore, ⅞ − ½ = _____.

Student Workouts for Multiplication and Division

There are forty-five Student Workouts for multiplication and division. Five use strategies modeled on open arrays with whole numbers. The next twenty-five use ratio tables: five with multiplication of whole numbers, five with multiplication of decimals, five that mix multiplication of whole numbers and decimals, five with division of whole numbers, and five with division of decimals. Five use array models with multiplication of fractions, five more mix multiplication and division of fractions using ratio tables, and the last five focus on division of fractions using ratio tables. Each is a five- to ten-minute activity to be completed by individual students or student pairs and then discussed as a class.

Here are some general questions to have handy:

Clarifying Questions

- ▶ What is the question asking?
- ▶ How can you fill in the blanks?
- ▶ What kind of answer is the question expecting (matching, filling in a blank with a number, recording a strategy on an array or ratio table, justifying an answer)?

Scaffolding Questions

- ▶ How would you verbalize the strategy shown on this array/ratio table?
- ▶ How does that strategy differ from this one?
- ▶ So you're dealing with 47s. What multiples of 47 do you know or can find quickly? Are any of those close to your goal?
- ▶ What about half of 47? Then you would have 0.5 in your table to work with. Would that help?

Focusing on "How Much More Do You Need?"

▸ I see that you have gotten to here. What is your goal? About how much do you still need?

▸ How can you find how much more you need?

▸ So, you need that much more. Do you see anything in your ratio table that is near that? Or can get you there?

▸ This is a very important question. How much is left? How much to go? How much is too much?

Class Discussion Questions

▸ Why start with this multiple?

▸ How could you figure out this chunk? Is that reasonable?

▸ Looking at this strategy, how many steps or chunks does it show?

▸ What about these numbers makes these strategies work?

Comparing strategies

▸ Which strategy seems more efficient? Why?

▸ Which strategy seems easier to do mentally?

▸ Which strategy seems more sophisticated or clever?

▸ What about the numbers makes that strategy your favorite for this problem?

▸ How might you change the numbers so that a different strategy would fit better?

The Strategies and Models Used in the Multiplication/Division Workouts

The open array and the ratio table are two primary models for multiplication and division, each bringing important relationships to light. The open array model for multiplication and division builds spatial sense and a sense of the magnitudes involved. The ratio table is a tool that builds proportional reasoning.

The multiplication Workouts and strings use several main strategies: doubling and halving, chunking, over and under, five is half of ten, quarters and other fractions, and combinations of these strategies. The division Workouts and strings use multiplying up to find the quotient (using the same multiplication strategies) and the equivalent ratio division strategy.

Doubling and Halving

I wish I had a better name for the strategy of doubling and halving because it encompasses far more than just doubling and halving. You can also triple and divide by 3, quadruple and quarter, and in general multiply one factor by n and divide the other factor by n. It all involves the associative property working with the multiplicative inverse and multiplicative identity (Figure 3.1).

FIGURE 3.1

$$a \times b$$
$$= a \times (1) \times b \qquad \text{multiplicative identity } m \times 1 = m$$
$$= a \times (c \times \tfrac{1}{c}) \times b \qquad \text{multiplicative inverse } c \times \tfrac{1}{c} = 1$$
$$= (a \times c) \times (\tfrac{1}{c} \times b) \qquad \text{associative property of multiplication}$$
$$\text{And so therefore: } a \times b = (a \times c) \times (\tfrac{1}{c} \times b)$$

Spatially, this property looks like ripping a piece of paper in half and moving one half to double the other dimension. You don't lose any paper! The strategy is constructed and modeled using open arrays (Figure 3.2).

FIGURE 3.2

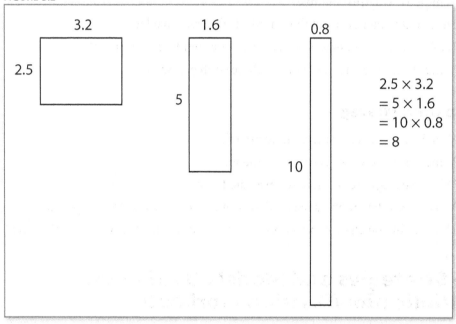

This doubling and halving strategy also leads to a substrategy of factoring to multiply. For example, anytime there are factors of 2 and 5 in the prime factorization, you can reassociate to have an equivalent expression that is 10 times the rest of the factors. Use the associative and the commutative properties of multiplication and a problem like 18×35 can become $(9 \times 2) \times (5 \times 7) = 9 \times (2 \times 5) \times 7 = 63 \times 10 = 630$.

Chunking

The chunking strategy involves chunking the multiplication problem into the fewest, biggest chunks possible and then adding up those chunks. This strategy can be modeled using both open arrays and ratio tables, with the array building the relationships and the ratio table becoming the tool of choice.

The chunking strategy can be justified using the distributive property. For example $35 \times 22 = 35 \times (20 + 2) = (35 \times 20) + (35 \times 2)$ and $4.2 \times 2.3 = (4 + 0.2) \times 2.3 = (4 \times 2.3) + (0.2 \times 2.3)$.

The rest of the multiplication strategies that follow are specialized chunking strategies—using specific chunks to make the problem easier to solve, always aiming toward fewer, bigger chunks (Figure 3.3).

FIGURE 3.3

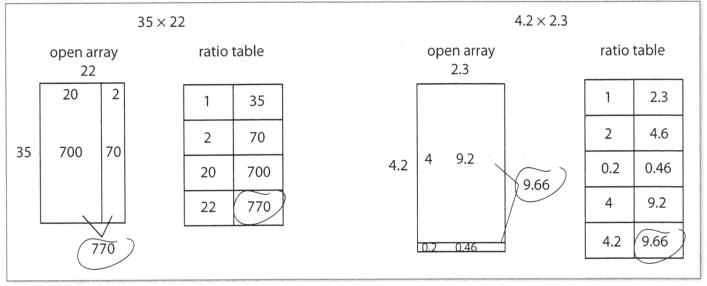

Over and Under

The over and under strategy involves using problems that are easy to compute but are a bit too big or a bit too small and working from there by adjusting a bit down or up as needed. This works well for numbers that are close to landmark numbers and that have easier products, such as multiples of 10. This strategy can be modeled using both open arrays and ratio tables, with the array building the relationships and the ratio table becoming the tool of choice.

The over and under strategy can be justified using the distributive property. For example, $31 \times 29 = 31 \times (30 - 1) = (31 \times 30) - (31 \times 1)$ and $9.9 \times 4.9 = (10 - 0.1) \times 4.9 = (10 \times 4.9) - (0.1 \times 4.9)$ (Figure 3.4).

FIGURE 3.4

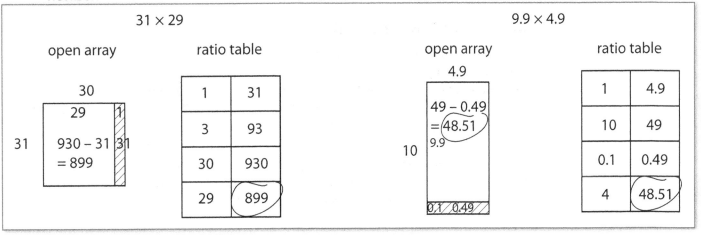

Five Is Half of Ten

The five is half of ten strategy uses the unique role of the number 10 as the base of our number system. To find products dealing with numbers like 5, 50, and 500, we can multiply first by 10, 100, or 1,000, respectively, and then halve. That can be justified using the associative and commutative properties: $5 \times 28 = 10 \times 28 \times \frac{1}{2}$ because $10 \times 28 \times \frac{1}{2} = (10 \times \frac{1}{2}) \times 28 = 5 \times 28$.

Similarly, when students begin to use fraction and decimal relationships, they can rearrange the order by finding half first and then multiplying by 10. In other words, 5×28 can be found by first finding half of 28 and then scaling up by 10: $5 \times 28 = (0.5 \times 10) \times 28 = (0.5 \times 28) \times 10$. With both of the relationships, students can ask, "Do I want to scale up by 10 and then halve to get 5 or do I want to halve first and then scale up by 10?" Sometimes students will choose one over the other depending on the numbers. For example, to find 87×5, a student may choose to scale up by 10 first to 870 and then find half of 870 for 435 because it is easier for that student to find half of 870 than of 87. To find 86×5, the same student may easily halve 86 into 43 and then scale up to 430.

These relationships are very important in the multiplication of decimals (Figure 3.5).

FIGURE 3.5

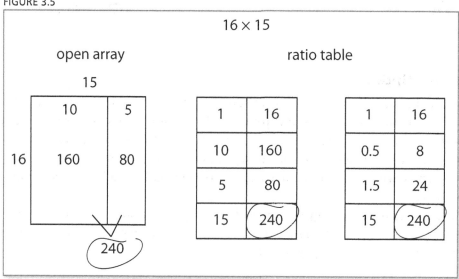

Quarters and Other Fractions

The quarters and other fractions strategy uses the idea of using fractions as operators and then scaling appropriately to find products. Using fractions as operators means that you can think of 0.25×28 as $\frac{1}{4}$ of $28 = 7$. Then to find 25×28, scale up by 100 to get $25 \times 28 = (0.25 \times 28) \times 100 = 7 \times 100 = 700$. You can find 75×28 similarly, by finding $\frac{3}{4}$ of 28 and then scaling up. Since $\frac{1}{4}$ of 28 is 7, then 3 of those one-quarters is $3 \times 7 = 21$. So, $75 \times 28 = (0.75 \times 28) \times 100 = 21 \times 100 = 2,100$. Another example is 375×32. Since $0.375 = \frac{3}{8}$, you can find $(0.375 \times 32) \times 1,000$ by finding $\frac{3}{8}$ of 32 and scaling up. Since $\frac{1}{8}$ of 32 is 4, then $\frac{3}{8}$ is $3 \times 4 = 12$. Then $375 \times 32 = (0.375 \times 32) \times 1,000 = 12 \times 1,000 = 12,000$. These strategies can be modeled on a ratio table (Figure 3.6).

FIGURE 3.6

75 × 28 ratio table	
1	28
0.25	7
0.75	21
75	2,100

375 × 32 ratio table	
1	32
0.125	4
0.375	12
375	12,000

Multiplying Up to Solve Division Problems

A division problem $a \div b$ can be thought of as $b \times$ ___ $= a$. So a problem like $270 \div 18$ can be thought of as $18 \times$ ___ $= 270$. So you can multiply 18 by different factors until you get up to 270. For example, $18 \times 10 = 180$, $18 \times 5 = 90$, so $18 \times (10 + 5) = 270$. Therefore, $18 \times 15 = 270$. In a ratio table, you start with 1:18 and work up until you get to 270. To solve these division problems, you use all of the multiplication strategies as appropriate (Figure 3.7).

FIGURE 3.7

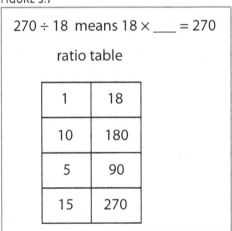

270 ÷ 18 means 18 × ___ = 270 ratio table	
1	18
10	180
5	90
15	270

Finding Equivalent Ratios to Solve Division Problems

A division problem $a \div b$ can be thought of as a/b and then you can find equivalent ratios until you get a unit ratio. The problem $352 \div 16$ can be thought of as $^{352}/_{16}$. Simplifying $^{352}/_{16}$ results in $^{352}/_{16} = {}^{176}/_8 = {}^{88}/_4 = {}^{44}/_2 = {}^{21}/_1 = 21$, so $352 \div 16 = 21$. If it is not possible to find an equivalent unit ratio, you can solve the resulting problem. For example, the problem $238 \div 34$ can be thought of as $^{238}/_{34}$ and $^{238}/_{34} = {}^{119}/_{17}$, and you can now use some other strategy to solve $119 \div 17$. These equivalent ratios are behind the "move the decimal" part of the traditional long division algorithm. When you are moving the decimal in both the divisor and the dividend, you are creating an equivalent ratio and then solving that problem (Figure 3.8).

FIGURE 3.8

$$270 \div 18$$

vertical ratio table

270	18
90	6
45	3
15	1

horizontal ratio table

270	90	45	15
18	6	3	1

equivalent ratios

$$\frac{270}{18} = \frac{90}{6} = \frac{45}{3} = \frac{15}{1}$$

The Progression

Whole Number Multiplication: Workouts 1 Through 5

The first set of Workouts uses open arrays to show four different strategies to solve the same multiplication problem. The intent is for students to compare partial products to bigger chunks and to doubling and halving so that students' intrigue will motivate them to seek more efficient strategies. Because the arrays have missing dimensions and areas, students get practice with both multiplication and division relationships. To find the missing areas, students multiply the given dimensions. To find the missing dimensions, students divide the given area by the given dimension.

Whole Number Multiplication: Workouts 6 Through 10

The second set uses some partially filled-in and some blank ratio tables to nudge students to use proportional relationships to solve multiplication and a few division problems, all with whole numbers. The problems are given in context, like 22 sticks of gum in a pack, 15 candies in a bag, and 18 snack bars in a box.

Decimal Number Multiplication: Workouts 11 Through 15

The third set is similar to the second, Workouts 6 through 10, but uses decimal numbers in context.

Whole Number and Decimal Multiplication: Workouts 16 Through 20

The arrays in Workouts 16 through 20 are similar to the arrays in Workouts 1 through 5 in that students are presented with four or five different strategies to solve the same problem. The strategies are shown in ratio tables where students fill in missing steps. Then students compare the strategies for efficiency and sophistication.

Whole Number Division: Workouts 21 Through 25

The first two Workouts in the fifth set are similar to the multiplication Workouts where the problems are given in context. Up through these Workouts, students have solved division problems by multiplying up to the dividend to find the quotient. The next two Workouts compare this multiplying up strategy with the equivalent ratio strategy. It is important for students to be able to solve problems both in and out of context, so the last Workout lists five decontextualized division problems where students can choose to solve either by multiplying up or by finding equivalent ratios.

Decimal Division: Workouts 26 Through 30

The first Workout is similar to Workouts 23 and 24 where students compare the division strategies of multiplying up and finding equivalent ratios. The rest of the Workouts present students with decontextualized decimal division problems that students can choose to solve either by multiplying up or by finding equivalent ratios.

Fraction Multiplication: Workouts 31 Through 35

The arrays in Workouts 31 through 35 are similar to the arrays in Workouts 1 through 5 and the ratio tables in Workouts 16 through 20 in that students are presented with four different strategies to solve the same problem. These strategies are for solving fraction multiplication problems, with some strategies modeled using arrays and others using decimal or percent language.

Fraction Multiplication: Workouts 36 Through 40

The grouping in Workouts 36 through 40 presents students with fraction multiplication problems to solve using ratio tables. Students can use the same multiplicative strategies they used with whole numbers and decimals to solve fraction multiplication problems. This set is an important lead-up to the next set of Workouts, where the same ratio table format is used to solve fraction division problems.

Fraction Multiplication: Workouts 41 Through 45

The next set is similar to Workouts 26 through 30, using fractions instead of whole numbers or decimals. The first two Workouts compare the division strategies of multiplying up and finding equivalent ratios. The rest of the Workouts present students with decontextualized fraction division problems that students can choose to solve either by multiplying up or by finding equivalent ratios.

Name _____

Below are four different strategies for 18 × 15. Fill in the missing dimensions and areas.

a.

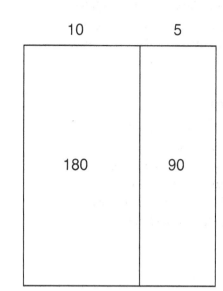

b.

c.

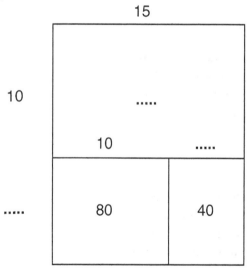

d.

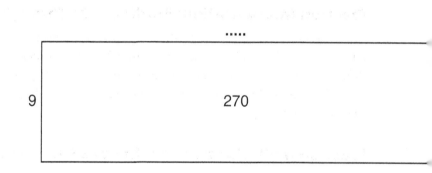

Which strategy do you prefer for this problem? Why?

Sample Dialog from Multiplication/Division Workout 1

Teacher: On this Workout, there are four arrays that each model the same problem, 15 × 18. Fill in the blanks for the missing dimensions or area. When you get the blanks all filled in, look back at the arrays and think about the strategy each represents. Which strategy do you prefer for this problem?

Students work to fill in the blanks.

Teacher: First, let's describe the strategies. Who will start by describing one of the strategies? *Students have filled in the blanks. Now the teacher invites students to describe the strategies so that they can then compare them, discussing efficiency and sophistication.*

Penny: For *a*, they split the 15 into 10 and 5. They just broke the problem into 2 chunks.

Teacher: Do you think it's reasonable that students would just know the chunk on the right, that 18 × 5 is 90?

Leo: They don't have to, because they already have ten 18s, so they can just find half of 180 to get 5 × 18.

Teacher: Nice. That 5 is half of 10 is handy. The other strategies?

Amy: The person in *c* broke up the 18 into 10 and 8. Then when they tried to multiply 8 times 15, they didn't know it so they found it by breaking the 15 into 10 and 5.

Teacher: How many chunks in *c*?

Amy: Three.

Teacher: So, 2 nice chunks in *a* and 3 in *c*. Others?

Raj: The strategy in *b* is like place-value chunking. They split both numbers, 18 into 10 and 8 and 15 into 10 and 5. Then they find the area of all chunks.

Teacher: The last one, *d*, what's up with that? Where is the original problem, 18 × 15? *If students haven't done so already, the teacher wants them to consider why the strange-looking array fits on the same page as the others.*

Howard: It's doubling and halving. Or in this case, halving and doubling. Halve the 18 to get 9 and double the 15 to get 30. Then 9 × 30 is easy.

Lesley: Oh, right. I hadn't seen that.

Teacher: What do you see?

Lesley: The height is half of the others and the width is twice. So the area stays the same.

Teacher: So, looking at all of these, which strategy do prefer for these numbers?

Raj: I like *a*. It reminds me of geometry and angles. It's easy to get 180 and half of that is 90. Then you just add 2 chunks together. That's a lot less work than *b* and *d*.

Howard: I didn't think about finding 18 × 5 by halving 18 × 10, so *a* didn't look too easy to me. I like *d*. It's easy to double 15 and halve 18. Then 9 × 30 is easy, too.

Amy: All of the pieces are easy to find in *b*, but I think for these numbers, it's quicker to do any of the other three strategies, *a*, *c*, or *d*.

Teacher: Some of you always use the traditional algorithm to multiply, no matter what the numbers. How many steps would it take to use the traditional algorithm with this problem?

Penny: Lots! Hmmm . . . it doesn't take much thought for me to do the algorithm, but it takes a whole lot more steps. For problems like this one, I could look for friendly chunks or double and halve.

Lesley: One advantage of *a* and *d* is that it's easy to check your work because there are just a few things to check.

Teacher: I wonder what other numbers might lend themselves to nice strategies like these. . . .

Multiplication/Division Workout 2

Name _____

Below are four different strategies for 12 × 35. Fill in the missing dimensions and areas.

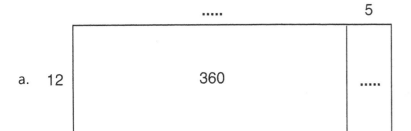

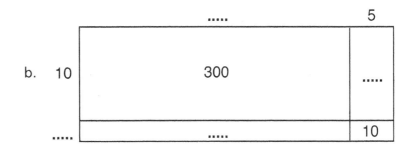

Which strategy do you prefer for this problem? Why?

Multiplication/Division Workout 3

Name _____

Below are four different strategies for a multiplication problem. Fill in the missing dimensions and area

1. What is the problem? _____

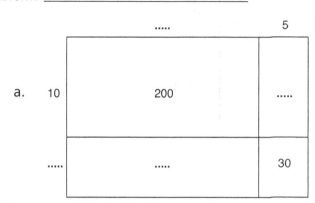

2. Which strategy do you prefer for this problem? Why?

©2014 Pamela Weber Harris from *Lessons and Activities for Building Powerful Numeracy*. Portsmouth, NH: Heinemann.

Sample Dialog from Multiplication/Division Workout 3

Teacher: In this Workout, we see four different strategies for figuring out a multiplication problem, but this time, we do not know what the problem is. So, after you fill in the blanks and examine the strategies, decide what the original problem is. Don't forget to decide which strategy you prefer and why.

Students work.

Teacher: What problem is represented by all of these arrays?

Kaelyn: I think it's 16 × 25.

Teacher: Why?

Kaelyn: When you fill in the blanks for 3 of the arrays, you get 16 × 25.

Kade: Yeah, *a* is 10 and 6 by 20 and 5. *C* is 10 and 6 by 25 and *d* is 16 by 20 and 5.

Teacher: Does anyone agree or disagree?

Braden: I agree. Strategy *a* broke up both the 16 and the 25 into place-value pieces. Strategy *c* broke up the 16 into place-value but left the 25 alone. Strategy *d* broke up the 25 and left the 16 alone.

Teacher: Which of those strategies do you prefer?

Reba: I like *c* — just two easy pieces.

Lena: And those pieces are easy to find because of quarters. Ten by 25 is easy and 6 × 25 is just 6 quarters, that's 150.

Teacher: What is going on with strategy *b*?

Kaelyn: That's the doubling/halving strategy. Half of 16 is 8 and double 25 is 50.

Cameron: Then 8 times 50 is like 4 times 100, and that's obviously 400.

Reba: Ah, right. That's why there is just one long array, because it shows doubling and halving. I can fill in the blank ok because I just find 8 times 50, but I don't think about doubling and halving as being the strategy that gets that array. How are you guys seeing that?

Christine: After I have filled in the dimensions for one of the other arrays, I look to see what the relationship is. Since we know that they are all the strategies to figure out the same multiplication problem, so there has to be a relationship.

Tori: And since the others are all 16 by 25 and that one is 8 by 50, you halved the 16 to get 8 and doubled the 25 to get 50. But like Cameron said, I wouldn't stop there. I would double and halve again to get 4 by 100 because then you don't even have to think. It's just 400.

Reed: I think I wish that I thought about doubling and halving when I have to multiply. I bet it would make a lot of problems easier.

Kaelyn: And really, if I just had to find 16 × 25, I would fourth and quadruple to go straight to 4 × 100.

Teacher: That's really nice thinking. Good work.

Multiplication/Division Workout 4

Name _____

Below are four different strategies for a multiplication problem. Fill in the missing dimensions and area

1. What is the problem? _____

a.

15
····· 60
····· 60
····· 60
····· 60

b.
	·····	5
16	160	·····

c.

30
8   ·····

d.

	10	·····
·····	100	·····
6	60	30

Which strategy do you prefer for this problem? Why?

Multiplication/Division Workout 5

Name _____

Below are four different strategies for a multiplication problem. Fill in the missing dimensions and areas.

1. What is the problem? _____

a.

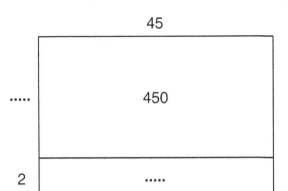

	45
.....	450
2	.....

b.

	40	5
.....	400	.....
2	.....	.....

c.   12

	.....	5
	480	.....

d.

	90
.....	540

Which strategy do you prefer for this problem? Why?

Multiplication/Division Workout 6

Name _____

Chew gum packs contain 22 sticks. Use the following ratio tables to find how many sticks there are in different numbers of packs.

1. 8 packs

Packs	1	2	3	4	8	
Sticks	22					

Eight packs have _____ sticks.

2. 6 packs

Packs	1	2	3	6		
Sticks	22					

Six packs have _____ sticks.

3. 15 packs

Packs	1	10	5	15		
Sticks	22					

Fifteen packs have _____ sticks.

4. 9 packs, 11 packs

Packs	1					
Sticks	22					

Nine packs have _____ sticks.

Eleven packs have _____ sticks.

Sample Dialog from Multiplication/Division Workout 6

Teacher: In this Workout, we've got gum — 22 sticks in every pack. What is item 1 asking?

Deborah: How many sticks are in 8 packs?

Teacher: So this first ratio table is giving you some hints about how you might do that. Work for a minute and then we'll share. *Students work.*

I am going to model what you did by writing on the ratio table. For example, how do you know how many sticks are in 2 packs?

Avery: I just doubled 22, that's 44.

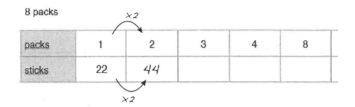

Teacher: How about 3 packs? How did you find how many sticks are in 3 packs?

Ray: Since you have 1 pack and 2 packs, you can add the 22 and 44, 66 sticks.

Lily: You could multiply 22 × 3.

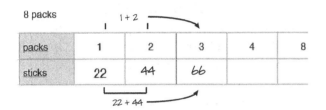

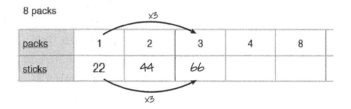

Teacher: What about 4 packs? How many sticks for 4 packs?

June: You could add 66 and 22 because that's 3 packs plus 1 pack, so 88.

May: Or you could double 2 packs.

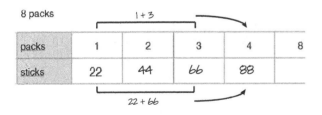

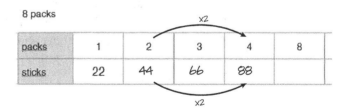

Teacher: So, there are a couple of ways to think about these so far. How about 8 packs? How many sticks are in 8 packs?

Rose: You could double the 4 packs. *The teacher draws arrows and "× 2."*

Teacher: To get? *By focusing on the result, the teacher helps students consider how easy it is to do each move. He wants students to realize that no matter how nice a strategy seems, if it results in unwieldy chunks, then it makes sense to consider other strategies.*

Rose: Double 88 sticks is 176 sticks. *The teacher fills in the 176.*

Teacher:	Those are easy numbers to work with. What else?
Terrance:	Or quadruple the 2 packs, 4 times 44 isn't too bad. It's 4 × 40 = 160 plus 4 × 4 = 16, 160 + 16 = 176.
Teacher:	Anything else?
Zach:	I don't know that I would want to, but you could add 1, 3, and 4 packs. I guess that's not too bad, 22 and 66 is 88 and 88 more is 176. So, you end up doubling 88 anyway. I think I'd rather double the 4 packs to start with.

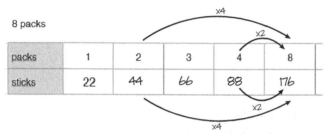 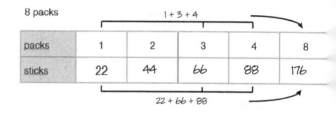

The dialog continues similarly for item 2.

Teacher:	Let's talk about item 3. What are we looking for this time?
Lily:	The number of sticks in 15 packs. First, 10 times 22 is easy, 220. Then you could use the 4 packs we already found, 88 sticks. Then add 1 pack to get the 5 packs, to get 110. To find 15, just add the 10 and 5 packs, 220 plus 110 is 330.
Ray:	Or since you've already got the 10, you can just divide it by 2 to get 5 packs. Half of 220 is 110.
Teacher:	How did Ray just find 5 packs? *He knows that some students may not have followed the move to get 5 packs by finding ½ of 10 packs, so he asks for students to repeat Ray's thinking.*
Lily:	I get it. He just found half of the 10 packs, so half of 220.
Teacher:	What if you don't know half of 220? *This not only helps students connect dividing 220 by 2 with finding ½ of 220, but it gives students a chance to compare strategies to do that.*
Ray:	You can think about half of 22, 11. So half of 220 is 110.
Avery:	You could also think about ½ of 200, that's 100, and then half of 20, that's 10. So 100 plus 10 is 110.
Teacher:	Nice thinking!

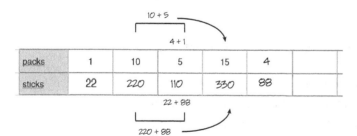 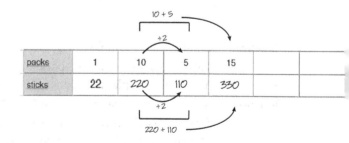

Teacher:	Tell me about your thinking for item 4.
May:	You had to find 2 answers, 9 and 11.

Teacher:	Which one do you want to tell us about?
May:	Actually, both. You can just subtract 1 to get 9 and add 1 to get 11.
Teacher:	What do you mean by subtract 1? Subtract 1 what? *The conversation has the potential to get abstract and hard to follow, so the teacher helps the students focus on what groups are being removed and added. Staying in context is helpful.*
May:	Since we already have 10 packs, you just subtract the sticks in 1 pack. So 220 minus 22.
Teacher:	It's 220 what? *Again, focusing on the context helps students justify steps in a ratio table.*
May:	It's 220 sticks in the 10 packs minus 22 sticks in 1 pack. That gives you 198 sticks in 9 packs.
Avery:	So, then you could just add 1 pack to 10 packs to get 11 packs. That is 220 + 22 = 242.
Teacher:	I'm going to record that in the ratio table and also write these equations:

$$22 \times 9 = 22 \, (10 - 1) = (22 \times 10) - (22 \times 1) = 220 - 22 = 198$$
$$22 \times 11 = 22 \, (10 + 1) = (22 \times 10) + (22 \times 1) = 220 + 22 = 242$$

9 packs, 11 packs

		×10	10 − 1	10 + 1
packs	1	10	9	11
sticks	22	220	198	242
		×10	220 − 22	220 + 22

Teacher:	Let's look at this whole page. Who would summarize the strategies that we've been talking about?
Zach:	We used some problems to put together to answer other problems.
Terrance:	Yeah, to find bigger chunks, we used smaller chunks we knew.
Rose:	We kind of worked up or down from problems that were easy to figure out to find others that were not so easy to figure out.
Teacher:	Chunking products into smaller products and then bringing those chunks together—that's using the distributive property of multiplication. When you added chunks, like to find $22 \times 11 = (22 \times 10) + (22 \times 1)$, that is using the distributive property of multiplication over addition. When you found a bit too much and removed a chunk, like to find $22 \times 9 = (22 \times 10) - (22 \times 1)$, that is using the distributive property of multiplication over subtraction.

Multiplication/Division Workout 7

Name _____

Chew gum packs contain 22 sticks. Use the following ratio tables to find how many sticks there are in different numbers of packs.

1. 99 packs

Packs	1					
Sticks	22					

99 packs have _____ sticks. 99 × 22 = _____

2. 999 packs

Packs	1					
Sticks	22					

999 packs have _____ sticks. 999 × 22 = _____

3. 49 packs

Packs	1					
Sticks	22					

49 packs have _____ sticks. Write an equation: _____.

4. Juan wants 440 sticks of gum. Use the following ratio table to determine how many packs he needs to order.

Packs	1					
Sticks	22					

Juan wants to buy _____ packs. Write an equation: _____.

Sample Dialog from Multiplication/Division Workout 7

Teacher: In this workout, we are still dealing with packs of gum that have 22 sticks each. How did you find the number of sticks in 99 packs?

Charlie: I remembered how we found the sticks in 9 packs. First I found the sticks in 10, that's 220. Then 9 packs would have 22 less.

Teacher: Twenty-two less what? *This helps the students keep all the numbers in the problem in context.*

Charlie: Twenty-two less sticks than 220. That's 198. So, then 90 would be 10 times 198, so 1,980. Then I have 90 and 9 and I added them together.

Teacher: And what is 1,980 sticks and 198 sticks?

Charlie: It's 2,178.

Teacher: So, that's 2,178 sticks of gum in 99 packs. *The teacher continues to stress the context.* James, it looks like you used fewer steps. What did you do? *It's not just about comparing strategies. It's also about efficiency.*

James: I went straight to 100 packs, that's 2,200 sticks. Then I just subtracted 1 pack, so that's 2,200 minus 22 and I got the same answer.

99 packs		×10		×10		99 + 9		99 packs		×100		100 − 1		
packs	1		10	9	90	99		packs	1		100	99		
sticks	22		220	198	1,980	2,178		sticks	22		2,200	2,178		
		×10		×10	1,980 + 198					×100		2,200 − 22		

Teacher: What equation could we write for this problem? What are we doing when we are finding the number of sticks in 99 packs?

Sarah: Ninety-nine 22s.

Teacher: An equation to represent that is 99 × 22 = 2,178. *The teacher knows that students may have found an answer but not realize what arithmetic problem they had solved. Writing the equation has the potential to help students connect their actions in the ratio table to a multiplication question. They can draw on this when they encounter multiplication problems that are not already set up in a ratio table.*

Teacher: Let's talk about item 3. How can you find the number of sticks in 49 packs?

David: First I found 100 packs. That's easy. It's 2,200. Then I divided the 100 packs in half. Half of 2,200 is 1,100 so that's 50 packs. Forty-nine packs is 1 less pack, so 1,100 minus 22 is 1,078.

Ty: I found 50 packs too, but a little differently. Since I already had 10 packs for 220 sticks, I halved that to get 5 packs for 110 sticks. So 50 packs is 10 times that, 1,100. Then I subtracted the 1 pack like David and got the same answer, 1,078.

Nygen: I also found 50 packs, but first I found half of a pack, that's 11. So 0.5 packs have 11 sticks. I multiplied the 0.5 and the 11 by 100 and got 50 packs for 1,100. Then I did the same thing and got rid of 1 pack of 22.

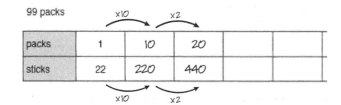

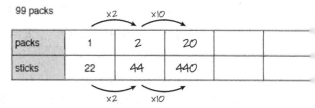

Teacher: So, on item 4, wow, you had to find 440! That's a ton. How did you do that? *Since this is the first division problem these students have solved in a ratio table, the teacher suggests that students are to find the sticks in 440 packs in order to get the students to rethink what they have done and to justify their reasoning.*

Brittany: But we're not finding 440 packs. Juan has 440 sticks and we have to find the number of packs.

John: Yeah, and I know that 10 packs have 220 sticks. And so double that means that 20 packs have 440 sticks.

Ty: I doubled first to get 44 sticks in 2 packs, then times 10 is 440.

Teacher: So how many packs have 440 sticks?

John: Twenty packs.

Teacher: I will model this question with an equation: *440 ÷ 22 = 20.*

LESSONS AND ACTIVITIES FOR BUILDING POWERFUL NUMERACY

Multiplication/Division Workout 8

Name _____

Bags of candies hold 15 candies. Use the following ratio tables to find how many candies there are in different numbers of bags.

1. 21 bags

Candies	15					
Bags	1					

21 bags have _____ candies. 21 × _____ = _____

2. 91 bags

Candies	15					
Bags	1					

91 bags have _____ candies. _____ × 15 = _____

3. 51 bags

Candies	15					
Bags	1					

51 bags have _____ candies. Write an equation: _____.

4. 99 bags, 101 bags

Candies	15					
Bags	1					

99 bags have _____ candies. Write an equation: _____.

101 bags have _____ candies. Write an equation: _____.

Multiplication/Division Workout 9

Name _____

Bags of candies hold 15 candies. Use the following ratio tables to find how many candies there are in different numbers of bags.

1. 24 bags

Candies	15					
Bags	1					

24 bags have _____ candies. 24 × _____ = _____

2. 31 bags

Candies	15					
Bags	1					

31 bags have _____ candies. _____ × 15 = _____

3. How many bags should you order if you need 330 candies?

Candies	15					
Bags	1					

There are 330 candies in _____ bags. 330 ÷ 15 = _____

4. How many bags should you order if you need 735 candies?

Candies	15					
Bags	1					

There are 735 candies in _____ bags. Write an equation: _____.

Multiplication/Division Workout 10

Name _____

A box of *Munch* snack bars contains 18 bars. Use the following ratio tables to find how many bars there are in different numbers of boxes.

1. 15 boxes

Bars						
Boxes						

15 boxes contain _____ bars. Write an equation: _____.

2. 49 boxes

Bars						
Boxes						

49 boxes contain _____ bars. Write an equation: _____.

3. How many boxes should you order if you need 468 bars?

Bars						
Boxes						

There are 468 bars in _____ boxes. Write an equation: _____.

4. 89 boxes

Bars						
Boxes						

89 boxes contain _____ bars. Write an equation: _____.

Sample Dialog from Multiplication/Division Workout 10

Teacher: OK, now that you've had a chance to solve the problems, let's discuss your thinking. Mika, what strategies did you use to find the number of bars in 15 boxes? *The teacher states the problem in context.*

Mika: Ten times 18 is 180. Five 18s is half of that, 90. That's 270 bars.

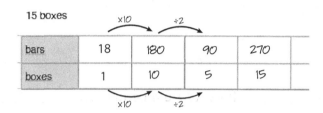

Shannon: I decided to find 1.5 times 18 and then scale up. Half of 18 is 9 and 18 + 9 is 27. So 1.5 times 18 is 27. But we want 15 times 18 so that is 10 times 27, and that's 270.

The teacher knows this strategy is new to her students and so encourages a conversation around it.

Teacher: What do you mean, you wanted 1 and a half 18s? I don't see any 1 and a half in this problem. I only see 15 and 18. Help?

Shannon: I know I am looking for 15, and 15 is 10 times 1 and a half. So, if I can find 1.5 then I can scale up.

Teacher: Who can repeat Shannon's strategy?

As students repeat each other's strategies, they are held accountable to listening in the first place and they also continue to parse out what their fellow student was explaining.

Mark: Most of the time, I start with the numbers in the problem and multiply up until I find what I need. Shannon made the problem smaller and then scaled up. I don't usually think about 1.5 when I see 15. I guess you can!

Renn: I don't either, Mark. Since 1.5 times 10 is 15, Shannon found 1.5 18s and then could multiply by 10 to get fifteen 18s.

Teacher: Look at Shannon's strategy next to Mika's. How do they compare?

15 boxes		×10	÷ 2	
bars	18	180	90	270
boxes	1	10	5	15

15 boxes		÷ 2	×10	
bars	18	9	27	270
boxes	1	0.5	1.5	15

Renn: Yeah, you can see that Mika multiplied by 10 first and then cut it in half. Shannon cut it in half and then multiplied by 10.

Teacher: What else could 1.5 help you find?

This is a moment for students to begin to generalize an important relationship.

Silva: You could multiply by 100 to get 150 or by 1,000 to get 1,500.

Trey: Or by a tenth to get 15 percent.

Mika: Whoa, 15 percent?

Trey:	If you multiply 1.5 by a tenth, you get 0.15. That's like 15 percent.
Teacher:	Great connections! Let's talk about strategies for item 3, how many boxes for 468 bars.
Silva:	I started with 2 boxes, that's 36 bars. So 20 boxes are 360 bars. Then I still need 108 bars. Since 10 times 18 is 180, then 5 times 18 is 90. So far, I've got 25 boxes for 450. Then I still need 18 bars and that's one more box, so 26 boxes.
Teacher:	I heard you say something really key. Twice while you were discussing your thinking, you said, "Then I still need . . . ." Why is that an important question to ask as you are solving?
Silva:	If you know where you are, how much you have built up, then you can find out how much more you need.
Trey:	That's like helping you see your goal—how much you have left.
Mika:	You had 450 but you needed 468 so you still needed to get 18 more—that tells you that you need one more box.
Teacher:	I wonder if that might help some of you when you get stuck—to ask yourself how much you have left? That might help you decided what to do next. Let's end with item 4. Did anyone go a little over with this problem and then have to back up?
Trey:	I know that if I find one hundred 18s, then I can subtract ten 18s and then subtract 1 more 18. That's eighty-nine 18s.
Teacher:	What do you think about Trey's chunks? Which of them are easy to find? Hard to find?
Samuel:	They are all easy—100, 10, and 1!

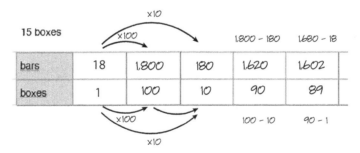

Multiplication/Division Workout 11   Name _____

Bananas are $0.38 per pound. How much will it cost to buy the following?

1. 1.5 pounds

Bananas (lbs.)	1					
Cost ($)	0.38					

1.5 pounds cost _____. 1.5 × 0.38 = _____

2. 4.2 pounds

Bananas (lbs.)	1					
Cost ($)	0.38					

4.2 pounds cost _____. _____ × 4.2 = _____

3. 5.1 pounds

Bananas (lbs.)	1					
Cost ($)	0.38					

5.1 pounds cost _____. 0.38 × _____ = _____

4. 9.9 pounds

Bananas (lbs.)	1					
Cost ($)	0.38					

9.9 pounds cost _____. Write an equation: _____.

Sample Dialog from Multiplication/Division Workout 11

Teacher: Let's talk about your thinking. What did you get for item 1? How much does 1 and a half pounds cost if 1 pound costs $0.38?

Archie: Since half of $0.38 is $0.19, I can think about one and a half as 38 plus 19, and that's 57.

Teacher: Fifty-seven what?

Students may use whole number strategies to add numbers together, but the teacher wants to help clarify if the student has lost the place values involved or if the student just needs to use more precise language.

Archie: Cents, it's $0.57.

Teacher: Great, how about problem 2? How much does 4.2 pounds of bananas cost?

Caleb: I love 4.2 because with just a couple of pieces, you have an answer.

Sarah: What do you mean?

Caleb: I think about times four as double, double. So, if I need to figure out 4 times 38 cents, that's just double 38 to get 76 and then double it again to get 152.

Teacher: 152 what?

Caleb: 152 cents. $1.52. And the cool thing is, you can use some of that to figure out the 0.2 times 38 cents that is still left.

Teacher: OK . . . can you say more?

Caleb: Sure. When I doubled 38 to get 76, that was the total for two pounds of bananas. And I know that I can use that to figure out 0.2 pounds — it's just a place-value shift. So instead of 76 cents, or 0.76, it's really 0.076. So, by thinking about doubles, I got the 4 and the 0.2. Then I can just add those together.

bananas (lbs)	1	0.5	1.5	
cost ($)	0.38	0.19	0.57	

×0.5 ↱   1 + 0.5
×0.5 ↲   0.38 + 0.19

bananas (lbs)	1	2	4	0.2	4.2
cost ($)	0.38	0.76	1.52	0.076	1.596

×2 ↱   1 + 0.5
×2 ↲   0.38 + 0.19

Teacher: Would someone explain what Caleb said about 4.2 being nice?

Annie: Four point 2 is nice because once you've doubled and doubled again, you've got the 4. Then shift 2 to 0.2 and add them together.

Joan: Yeah, so I think that 2.4 would be nice for the same reason.

Teacher: Nice connection! Now let's look at the next one. What relationships did you use for item 3?

Arthur: I started with 10 pounds is $3.80, and cut that in half to get $1.90 for 5 pounds. But I still had to figure out the price of 0.1 pounds. That's pretty easy because it's $\frac{1}{10}$ of 38 cents, which is $.038. When you add $1.90 and $.038, you get $1.938. You need to round it up because it's money, so $1.94.

Teacher: Arthur, that was a nice explanation. Henry, can you tell us about your thinking?

Henry: I thought about ½ first. So, instead of finding 10 pounds to get 5 pounds, I was thinking ½ of a pound is $0.19.

Teacher: I'm not clear on that. Why you were thinking about ½? *This is an important idea that needs attention.*

Henry: Well, since ½ is 0.5, I could use that to figure out 5 pounds. It's just ten times bigger! That's how I got the 1.9. Then I added the 0.1 the same way Arthur did.

bananas (lbs)	1	10	5	0.1	5.1
cost ($)	0.38	3.8	1.9	0.038	1.938

x10   x05   5 + 0.1
x10   x05   1.9 + 0.038

	1	0.5	5	0.1	5.1
	0.38	0.19	1.9	0.038	1.938

x05   x10   5 + 0.1
x05   x10   1.9 + 0.038

Teacher: What do Arthur and Henry's strategies have in common? How are they different?

Jay: It's like they are just doing it in different orders. Arthur scaled up by 10 first then took ½. Henry found ½ first, then scaled up by 10.

Teacher: Do you like one strategy better? Why? *The teacher wants students to seek for efficiency. Their initial strategies are places to begin, not end.*

Jay: I think it might depend on the numbers. If the number is easy to halve, I think I would do it first. If not, then I'd multiply by 10 first and then find ½.

Teacher: Let's keep those ideas in mind for future problems. Last, how about item 4, 9.9 pounds?

Annie: Its kinda like, how 99 is close to 100 so we can use that to make the problem easier? This time, since we had 9.9, I thought about 10.

Teacher: You used 10 to think about 9.9?

Annie: Yes, 9.9 is only one-tenth away from 10 and 10 times anything is easy to find.

Teacher: What is 10 times 0.38?

Annie: It is a place-value shift to 3.8. Then you can just remove one-tenth of 0.38, and that's 0.038. So 3.8 minus 0.038 is 3.762.

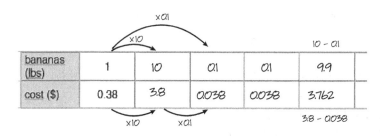

bananas (lbs)	1	10	0.1	0.1	9.9
cost ($)	0.38	3.8	0.038	0.038	3.762

x0.1
x10   10 − 0.1
x10   x0.1   3.8 − 0.038

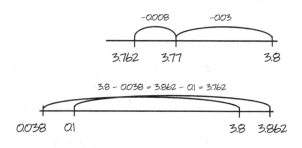

Multiplication/Division Workout 12   Name _____

Kiwi costs $0.44 per pound. How much will it cost to buy the following?

1. 2.5 pounds

Kiwi (lbs.)	1					
Cost ($)	0.44					

2.5 pounds cost _____. Write an equation: _____.

2. 4.9 pounds

Kiwi (lbs.)	1					
Cost ($)	0.44					

4.9 pounds cost _____. Write an equation: _____.

3. 9.1 pounds, 11.1 pounds

Kiwi (lbs.)	1					
Cost ($)	0.44					

9.1 pounds cost _____. Write an equation: _____.

11.1 pounds cost _____. Write an equation: _____.

4. Michelle paid $6.60. How many pounds of kiwi did she buy?

Kiwi (lbs.)	1					
Cost ($)	0.44					

$6.60 bought _____ pounds of kiwi. Write an equation: _____.

Multiplication/Division Workout 13   Name _____

Tangerines cost $0.74 per pound. How much will it cost to buy the following?

1. 1.6 pounds

Tangerines (lbs.)	1					
Cost ($)	0.74					

   1.6 pounds cost _____. Write an equation: _____.

2. 2.5 pounds

Tangerines (lbs.)	1					
Cost ($)	0.74					

   2.5 pounds cost _____. Write an equation: _____.

3. 5.5 pounds

Tangerines (lbs.)	1					
Cost ($)	0.74					

   5.5 pounds cost _____. Write an equation: _____.

4. How many pounds of tangerines can you buy for $112.48?

Tangerines (lbs.)	1					
Cost ($)	0.74					

   $112.48 buys _____ pounds of tangerines. Write an equation: _____.

Multiplication/Division Workout 14   Name _____

Apples are $1.29 per pound. How much will it cost to buy the following?

1. 9 pounds

Apples (lbs.)	1					
Cost ($)	1.29					

   9 pounds cost _____. Write an equation: _____.

2. 8.9 pounds

Apples (lbs.)	1					
Cost ($)	1.29					

   8.9 pounds cost _____. Write an equation: _____.

3. 5 pounds, 6.5 pounds

Apples (lbs.)	1					
Cost ($)	1.29					

   5 pounds cost _____, and 6.5 pounds cost _____.

4. How many pounds of apples can you buy for $5.16? For $10.32?

Apples (lbs.)	1					
Cost ($)	1.29					

   You can buy _____ pounds of apples for $5.16, and _____ for $10.32.

Sample Dialog from Multiplication/Division Workout 14

Teacher: Did anyone use the relationships in problem 1 to find problem 2, the cost for 8.9 pounds of apples?

Shea: I did. Nine pounds cost $11.61. So, I just subtracted one-tenth of 1.29 from 11.61.

Teacher: What is one-tenth of 1.29? *This question helps all students focus on what Shea did, even if they used different relationships.*

Shea: It is 0.129. And when I subtracted it from 11.61, I got 11.481.

apples (lbs)	1	9	0.1	8.9
cost ($)	1.29	11.61	0.129	11.481

(9 − 0.1 above the 8.9 column; 11.61 − 0.129 below the 11.481 column)

Teacher: Great. How were you all thinking about item 3, 5 pounds and 6.5 pounds? It's kind of odd that you are asked to find both of those numbers since they are not very related. Hummm . . .

Brandon: Actually, once I found the 5 pounds, I used that to find both 6 pounds and 0.5 pounds.

Teacher: Really? How?

Even though the teacher is clear how one could use the 5 pounds to find both values, this is an opportunity for others to experience the relationships involved. As he explains, Brandon has the opportunity to cement the relationships for himself and clarify his thinking for others.

Brandon: Well, first to find the 5 pounds, I found 10 pounds, $12.90, and then half of that is 5 pounds, $6.45. Add 1 more pound, and 6 pounds is $6.45 plus $1.29, which is $7.74. Then I did a place value shift to find 0.5 pounds by shifting the 6.45 to 0.645. So, 6.5 is the 6 pounds plus 0.5 pounds, $7.74 + 0.645 and that's $8.385. Because it's money, that rounds to $8.39.

apples (lbs)	1	10	5	6	0.5	6.5
cost ($)	1.29	12.9	6.45	7.74	0.645	8.385

(×0.5 arrows between 10 and 5; 5 + 1 above 6; 6 + 0.5 above 6.5; 6.45 + 1.29 below 7.74; 7.74 + 0.645 below 8.385; ×0.5 below)

Teacher: Can someone repeat the big ideas Brandon used? *Repeating the big ideas can help other students make connections.*

Elizabeth: Sure, 0.5, ½ and 5 are all related and can be used to find each other.

Teacher: Let's talk about the last problem, finding the number of pounds for $5.16 and $10.32. Tom?

Tom: Since 10 pounds is $12.90 and 5 is $6.45, it has to be less than 5 pounds. So, I doubled $1.29 to get $2.58 for 2 pounds. Double that and I got $5.16 for 4 pounds.

Anne: I also knew it was less than the 5 pounds for $6.45. It is exactly $1.29 less so it must be 1 pound less, for 4 pounds.

apples (lbs)	1	10	5	2	4
cost ($)	1.29	12.9	6.45	2.58	5.12

(arrows labeled ×2, ×2 above and below)

5 − 1

apples (lbs)	1	10	5	4
cost ($)	1.29	12.9	6.45	5.12

6.45 − 1.29

Teacher: What about the $10.32?

Tom: It's just double the $5.16, which is 4 pounds, so it's 8 pounds.

Anne: I like how Tom keeps doubling. I went a little over again. It's just $1.29 less than the $11.61 that we got earlier for 9 pounds, so that would also be 8 pounds.

Tom: I like the way Anne keeps thinking a little over. I wonder if next time I might look at $10.32 and notice that it is $2.58 under the 10-pound price of $12.90. That would be a nice way to find 8 pounds too.

Teacher: Would someone talk about Tom's and Anne's strategies in a general way? *Asking students to generalize strategies invites them to think outside of the problems at hand and make mental connections that students can use for other situations.*

Elizabeth: Tom is doubling. That's nice for numbers like 2, 4, 8. Anne is using friendly numbers that are a bit too big, like 10 times and 5 times. Those are easy to find and can be used to find 4, 6, 9, and 11 times.

Maggie: And with place-value shifts, you can find numbers like 0.2, 20, or 200 once you double.

Martin: Yeah, and with those nice over numbers, you could find 0.9, 90, 900 times the number.

Teacher: Great generalizations — let's see if we can use some of these relationships in future problems!

Multiplication/Division Workout 15

Name _____

Gasoline is $2.53 a gallon. How much will it cost to buy the following?

1. 1.5 gallons

Gas (gallons)	1					
Cost ($)	2.53					

1.5 gallons cost _____. Write an equation: _____.

2. 4.2 gallons

Gas (gallons)	1					
Cost ($)	2.53					

4.2 gallons cost _____. Write an equation: _____.

3. 5.1 gallons

Gas (gallons)	1					
Cost ($)	2.53					

5.1 gallons cost _____. Write an equation: _____.

4. 9.9 gallons

Gas (gallons)	1					
Cost ($)	2.53					

9.9 gallons cost _____. Write an equation: _____.

Multiplication/Division Workout 16   Name _____

Five students solved a multiplication problem. Fill in the blanks. What problem were they all solving?

1.

1	2		40		50	49
18		360		180		

Describe this strategy:

2.

1		50	49			
18	1,800					

Describe this strategy:

3.

1		50	49			
18	9					

Describe this strategy:

4.

1		5	15	3	18	
49	9					

Describe this strategy:

5.

1	2		18			
49	98	980				

Describe this strategy:

6. What problem did they all solve? (Write an equation with the problem and the answer.)

Sample Dialog from Multiplication/Division Workout 16

Teacher:	Before you start on this Workout, let's talk about the format. Here we have five different solutions for the same multiplication problem. You need to fill in the cells with the missing relationships and then figure out what the multiplication problem is that the five students solved. Who thinks they've got it?
Sam:	It's like those array problems we did where we had to figure out what the problem is that they were all solving.
Teacher:	Correct. Fill in the empty cells first. Let's do the first couple together. For item 1, what do you think belongs in the cell under 2? *The teacher points to the empty cell and circles the 2 in the cell above.*
Charlie:	Double 18, so 36. *The teacher writes in the 36.*
Teacher:	Then what about in the next cell, above 360? *The teacher points to the cell above the 360.*
Josi:	That's 10 times 36 so 10 times 2 is 20. *The teacher writes in the 20.*
Teacher:	Great! Keep filling out the missing cells and then we'll talk about what the problem is that they are all solving.

The teacher begins the discussion after students have filled in the workout.

Teacher:	How would you describe the strategy in 1?
Abigail:	They worked up to 50 by doubling and adding 10 and then back to 49 from 50.
Teacher:	And 2?
Brad:	They got to 49 from 50 also, but they got to 50 from 100.
Zoe:	The strategy in 3 also got to 49 from 50 but they used the ½ thing to get to 50. Find ½ first and then scale up to 50.
Teacher:	What did these first three strategies all have in common? How were they different?
Allison:	They all got to forty-nine 18s by getting to 50 first.
Sam:	They got to 50 in different ways. The first was lots of smaller chunks, the other two used 100 or 0.5 to get to 50. I really like the third strategy of finding ½ of 18 and then scaling up to 50 from there.
Teacher:	What about the last two? Are they even describing solving the same problem?
Abigail:	Well, they are not finding forty-nine 18s. They are finding eighteen 49s.
Brad:	The fourth strategy worked up to eighteen 49s by finding 10 and 5, that's 15 and then 3 more to get to eighteen 49s. The last strategy got there faster, by finding twenty 49s and then taking off two 49s.
Teacher:	What is the problem that all five of these strategies solved?
Will:	Eighteen times 49.
Kristin:	Or 49 times 18.
Teacher:	Which of these strategies do you like the best? If you were hit by this problem, which strategy do you wish came naturally to you?
Sam:	I like the twenty 49s and then take off two 49s. All of those numbers are easy for me to deal with.
Zoe:	I think the half of 18 to find fifty 18s is slick. Then you can subtract one 18, minus 20 plus 2.
Allison:	Yeah, that 0.5 of 18 is 9 and scale up to 900 for fifty 18s is pretty clever.

Multiplication/Division Workout 17

Four students solved a multiplication problem. Fill in the blanks. What problem were they all solving?

1.

76	152			760			
1		3	30		5	35	36

Describe this strategy:

2.

76		304	3,040	760			
1	2		40		5	35	36

Describe this strategy:

3.

36				900			
1	10	5	50		75	76	

Describe this strategy:

4.

36	9						
1	0.25	0.75	75	76			

Describe this strategy:

5. What problem did they all solve? (Write an equation with the problem and the answer.)

Multiplication/Division Workout 18   Name

Five students solved a multiplication problem. Fill in the blanks. What problem were they all solving?

1.

1		9			0.89	
42	420		37.8	0.42		

Describe this strategy:

2.

1	100		90		0.89	
42		420		3,738		

Describe this strategy:

3.

1		0.9	0.01	0.89		
42	4.2					

Describe this strategy:

4.

1	2		40	42		
0.89		3.56				

Describe this strategy:

5.

1		20	40		42	
0.89	8.9			1.78		

Describe this strategy:

6. What problem did they all solve? (Write an equation with the problem and the answer.)

Multiplication/Division Workout 19   Name _____

Four students solved a multiplication problem. Fill in the blanks. What problem were they all solving?

1.

1		5		25	75	74	
0.26	2.6		13				

Describe this strategy:

2.

0.26		13				
1	100		25	75	74	

Describe this strategy:

3.

1	0.5	0.25	0.75		74		
0.26				19.5			

Describe this strategy:

4.

74	37	18.5					
1			0.01	0.26			

Describe this strategy:

5. What problem did they all solve? (Write an equation with the problem and the answer.)

Multiplication/Division Workout 20

Name _____

Five students solved a multiplication problem. Fill in the blanks. What problem were they all solving?

1.

7.4	14.8			0.74		
1		4	5		4.9	

Describe this strategy:

2.

1	0.5			4.9		
7.4		37	0.74			

Describe this strategy:

3.

7.4	740					
1		50	49	4.9		

Describe this strategy:

4.

1		4	6			7.4
4.9	9.8			34.3	1.96	

Describe this strategy:

5.

4.9	2.45			36.75		
1		0.25	0.75		7.4	

Describe this strategy:

6. What problem did they all solve? (Write an equation with the problem and the answer.)

Sample Dialog from Multiplication/Division Workout 20

The teacher begins the discussion after students have filled in the workout.

Teacher: How would you describe the strategy in 1?

Margaret: Start with 7.4. Double, double and add 1 to get to 5 — that's 37. Then subtract one-tenth of 7.4, which is 0.74 and get 36.26.

Toby: Basically, get up to 5 by doubling and then subtract one-tenth to get to 4.9.

Teacher: Great, how about in item 2?

Katy: They also got up to 5 and subtracted one-tenth.

Mark: But they got up to 5 by first finding ½ of 7.4 and then scaling up.

Teacher: And why does ½ work?

Mark: Because ½ is 0.5 and then scale 0.5 up to 5 by shifting the place value once. Since half of 7.4 is 3.7, then 5 times 7.4 is 37.

Teacher: And item 3? What is that person's strategy?

Donna: They found one hundred 7.4s and then halved that to get fifty 7.4s. Then subtract 7.4 to get forty-nine 7.4s and that's 362.6. Divide by 10 to get 4.9 of the 7.4s.

Josh: The first strategy worked up to 5, the second worked down and then up to 5, and the third worked way up to 49 and then scaled down to 4.9.

Teacher: That's a nice comparison of those three strategies. What about item 4?

Danny: The last two started with 4.9s. Number 4 worked up by doubling and adding to get 7 of the 4.9s. Then since you already had 4 of them as 19.6, you could shift the place value to get 0.4 of them as 1.96. Then add the 0.4 to 7 to get 7.4.

Mandy: Lots of little steps.

Teacher: Why do you say that?

Mandy: Well, they are all doable, but there are lot's of them and lots of adding. I think if I was going to deal with the 4.9s, I'd use the last strategy.

Teacher: Tell us about the last strategy.

Mandy: Find half of 4.9 and then half again so you have ¼ of 4.9. Then add those together to get ¾ of 4.9. Then multiply by 10 to get 7.5 of the 4.9s. Now you just get rid of one-tenth so you end up with 7.4 of the 4.9s.

Danny: I can see that it's fewer steps then strategy 4, but you are still adding too much for my taste.

Teacher: Before we move on, tell me — what problem are we solving here?

Josh: 4.9 times 7.4 or 7.4 times 4.9.

Teacher: Which strategy do you like the most?

Danny: I like strategy 3, starting with the 7.4s and finding 50 of them, then back one 7.4 to 49 of them. Then shift the place value. It is easy for me to find half of 740 and to subtract the 7.4.

Mark: I think I like the half of 7.4 first to then scale up to the five 7.4s in strategy 2. Finding half of 7.4 is easier for me than half of 740.

Josh: I am really thinking about these strategies that use ½ to get at 5 or 50. It doesn't occur to me to think about finding a half in order to find 5 or 50 of something, but I am going to try to use that strategy from now on.

Teacher: Great!

Multiplication/Division Workout 21   Name _____

A bag of frozen juice pops contains 36 pops. Use the following ratio tables to find out how many bags are needed for different numbers of pops.

1. 864 pops

Pops	36					
Bags	1					

There are 864 pops in _____ bags. 864 ÷ 36 = _____

2. 1,764 pops

Pops	36					
Bags	1					

There are 1,764 pops in _____ bags. 1,764 ÷ 36 = _____

3. 540 pops

Pops	36					
Bags	1					

There are 540 pops in _____ bags. Write an equation: _____.

4. 3,276 pops

Pops	36					
Bags	1					

There are 3,276 pops in _____ bags. Write an equation: _____.

Multiplication/Division Workout 22

Name _____

A package of mints holds 47 mints. Use the following ratio tables to find out how many packages are needed for different numbers of mints.

1. 235 mints

Packages	1					
Mints	47					

There are 235 mints in _____ packages. 235 ÷ 47 = _____

2. 705 mints

There are 705 mints in _____ packages. 705 ÷ 47 = _____

3. 1,175 mints

There are 1,175 mints in _____ packages. Write an equation: _____.

4. 4,606 mints

There are 4,606 mints in _____ packages. Write an equation: _____.

Sample Dialog from Multiplication/Division Workout 22

Teacher: Today we are dealing with mints in packages, 47 mints per package. What is your job?

Nathan: We have to find a lot of mints!

Kate: Wait, I don't think so. I think we need to find how many packages the lots of mints are in.

Nathan: Ah. Yes, I think you're right.

Teacher: Does anyone not agree with Nathan and Kate? No? OK, then go package those mints.

As the students worked, the teacher found three strategies to have students share in a discussion of strategies. The first to be shared is an entry point for most of the students. The next two strategies will stretch some students to consider more sophisticated strategies.

Teacher: Lannie, will you tell us what you did in item 1?

Lannie: I doubled the 47 to get 94, doubled again to get 188. So, that's 4. Then I added 1 more 47 to get 235.

Teacher: So your answer is 235?

Lannie: No, I was trying to find the number of packages for 235 mints, so the answer is 5 packages.

Teacher: Great. Javier, what did you do?

Javier: I found ten 47s first, that's 470. Then halve that to get 235, so half of 10 is 5.

Teacher: Nice — and 470 isn't too hard to halve, is it? Victoria, what did you do?

Victoria: I found half of 47 first. That's 23.5. Then I scaled up by 10 to get 5 packages holding 235 mints.

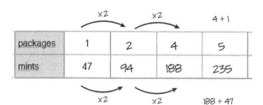 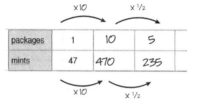 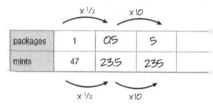

Teacher: So, we can fill in the equation with 435 ÷ 47 = 5. Let's talk about item 2. How did you fill in the headers of the ratio table?

Kate: Oh, I didn't even notice that they weren't filled in. I just assumed they were the same as the first one.

Teacher: Does it work if you assume that the labels are the same? Yes? Could you switch the labels so that mints are on the top and packages are on the bottom?

Lannie: Sure, as long as you are consistent and keep the 1 with the packages and the 47 with the mints.

Teacher: OK, so now tell us how you found the number of packages for 705 mints. Javier?

Javier: Since I already had the 10 and the 5 from the first problem, 470 and 235 mints, I just added them together to get 15 packages.

Teacher: Victoria, I am wondering if you did something different? Like you did with item 1?

Victoria: I did, but I can see now how nice Javier's strategy was because he already knew the 10 and 5. I had already found ½, so 0.5. I added that to the 1 package to get 1.5 packages, 70.5 mints. Multiply both by 10 to get the 705 mints, and that's 15 packages.

packages	1	10	5	15
mints	47	470	235	705

packages	1	0.5	1.5	15
mints	47	23.5	70.5	705

Lannie: That ½ strategy keeps showing up. Victoria, how do you even think to try that?

Victoria: Well, I look at the target number, like 705 and I think about double and 10 times, but neither of those were very close. Then I try ½ to see if it gets me something that looks the same, but is just place-value shifts off. Like this time 23.5 and 47 got me to 70.5, which is ⅒ of 705, which was the goal. I don't know . . . Does that make sense?

Lannie: You're saying that you try a few things, double, times 10, and also ½ to see if it gets you something you can work with. I think I'll add those to my list of things to try.

Teacher: I wonder if we could try something similar with the next one. Does 23.5 or 70.5 feel like it would help with 1,175?

Lannie: Well, 11 from the 11 hundred is about half of 23. Let's see, what is half of 23.5? Hey, it's 11.75!

Teacher: Let me record what you've got so far so everyone can follow you.

packages	1	0.5	0.25	
mints	47	23.5	11.75	

Lannie: Now I just need to make 11.75 into 1,175. That's 2 place-value shifts or times 100. So, it must be 24 packages. Cool!

packages	1	0.5	0.25	24
mints	47	23.5	11.75	1,175

Teacher: And what about for the last problem?

Kate: 4,606 is 94 away from 4,700. So 100 times 47 is 4,700. Two less 47s is 4,606 so the answer is 98 packages.

Name _____

The teacher brought 456 candies for the 24 students in her class. If the students share the candies even
how many does each student get?

1. Kim thought, "There are 24 students times some amount of candies and that total is 456 candies. So
   24 × ____ = 456." Fill in the ratio table to show a way that Kim might have solved the problem.

1	2	20				
24						

The 24 students each get _____ candies. 456 ÷ 24 = ____

2. Bo thought, "There are 456 candies divided among 24 students."

Candies	456					
Students	24	12				

456 candies divided among 24 students is _____ candies per student. 456 ÷ 24 = ____

3. Now there are 1,488 candies for the 24 students to share. Complete the strategy below.

Candies	1,488	744				
Students	24					

1,488 candies divided among 24 students is ____ candies per student. 1,488 ÷ 24 = ____

4. If a student solved the problem using a strategy similar to Kim's, where 24 × ____ = 1,488, fill in
   the table.

24						
1	100	50	10			

The 24 students each get _____ candies. 1,488 ÷ 24 = ____

Sample Dialog from Multiplication/Division Workout 23

Teacher: The format for this workout is a little different from earlier ones. I am noticing that some of the ratio tables have labels and some do not. Also, the first two ratio tables are solving the same problem, but using different strategies. Let's talk about this first problem. The teacher has 456 candies for her 24 students. Read over what Kim is thinking about how to evenly share those candies. *Students read.* Juan, what's Kim thinking?

Juan: She is thinking that the 24 kids each get some candy and if she multiplied that amount of candy per kid times the 24 kids that is the total of 456 candies.

Teacher: Great. What do you notice about the ratio table that she used to solve the problem?

Juan: She's got the 24 that she's going to multiply up to get to the 456.

Maryanne: It also suggests the first 2 moves that Kim makes, 2 and 20. So that would be 48 and 480. Ah, then that's a bit too much.

Teacher: How much too much?

This is a very important question. How much left? How much to go? How much too much? If students can focus on how much is left, they may be able to find it in less steps—fewer, bigger chunks.

Maryanne: Let's see, 480 minus 456 is the same as 484 minus 460, so, 24. Right, that's just one of them, so each kid gets 19 candies.

1	2	20	19
24	48	480	456

Teacher: Fabulous. And this looks like the way that we have solved similar division problems in these Workouts, by multiplying up until we get to the goal number. So, what's going on with Bo in number 2? Charlie?

Charlie: His ratio table has labels. He's looking at 456 candies per 24 students. Then he is looking at 12 students.

Teacher: I wonder how that can help? *It's a good noticing, but so what? The teacher pushes for relevance.*

Brittany: If there are 456 for the 24 kids, then there would be half of that candy for half of the kids, right?

Teacher: Is that right? *This is getting right at the idea of equivalent ratios.*

Carlos: Yes, that is an equivalent amount per kid. Half the kids get half the candy.

Teacher: How does that help?

Brittany: Well, you can keep going. That would be 228 candies for 12 kids and 114 candies for 6 kids. Then 57 candies for 3 kids. Umm . . .

Charlie: And I just know that 3 times 19 is 57.

		×½	×½	×½	×⅓
candies	456	228	114	57	19
students	24	12	6	3	1
		×½	×½	×½	×⅓

Teacher:	What if you didn't just know that?
Carlos:	I know that 60 candies for 3 kids would be 20 per kid, but there are 3 less candies, so 1 less candy per kid. That means each kid gets the 19 candies, the same as Kim found.
Teacher:	So, both Kim and Bo found out how many candies each student gets when they are evenly shared. Would someone please compare Kim and Bo's strategies? *As students restate and compare the strategies, they begin to own the relationships and work to describe and generalize the strategies.*
Jacob:	Kim thought about multiplication and multiplied up. Bo thought about the ratio and found equivalent ratios.
Penny:	I think that Kim's strategy was more efficient for these numbers.
Charlie:	I wonder what numbers would be easier for Bo's equivalent ratio strategy?
Teacher:	Those are excellent thoughts. Keep asking them as you work the rest of the page.

Multiplication/Division Workout 24

Name _____

The 280 volunteers from the club were planting donated flowers around town. How many flowers did each volunteer plant at the different parks if they each planted the same number of flowers?

1. One park received 2,520 donated flowers. Luke thought, "How many flowers did each of the 280 volunteers plant?" So, _____ × 280 = 2,520.

1						
280						

So, _____ plants for each of 280 volunteers is 2,520 flowers. 2,520 ÷ 280 = _____

2. Cooper thought, "There are 2,520 flowers divided among 280 volunteers."

Flower	2,520					
Volunteers	280					

2,520 flowers divided among 280 volunteers is _____. 2,520 ÷ 280 = _____

3. A bigger park had 9,800 flowers donated. Fill in the table with a strategy like Cooper's. Complete the strategy below.

Flower	9,800					
Volunteers	280					

9,800 flowers divided among 280 volunteers is _____. 9,800 ÷ 280 = _____

4. If a student solved the problem using a strategy similar to Luke's, where 280 × _____ = 9,800, fill in the table.

280						
1						

The 280 volunteers each planted _____ of the 9,800 flowers. 9,800 ÷ 280 = _____

Multiplication/Division 25

Name _____

Solve these division problems:

1. 672 ÷ 112

Describe your strategy:

2. 1,364 ÷ 31

Describe your strategy:

3. 9,660 ÷ 420

Describe your strategy:

4. 775 ÷ 5

Describe your strategy:

5. 1,539 ÷ 9

Describe your strategy:

©2014 Pamela Weber Harris from *Lessons and Activities for Building Powerful Numeracy*. Portsmouth, NH: Heinemann.

Sample Dialog from Multiplication/Division Workout 25

Teacher: Now that you've had a chance to work these, let's compare strategies. What did you do for 672 divided by 112?

Kelly: I wrote it as a ratio and then found equivalent ratios until I got to 6 to 1, so the answer is 6. All of the halving was pretty easy but it took a few steps.

Samantha: I multiplied 112 by ½ to find 5 and then added 1 more, so I also got 6.

Sharon: I just looked at 112 and thought about 672. Six times 100 is 600 and 6 times 12 is 72. So, the answer is 6.

1. 672 ÷ 112

672	336	168	84	42	6
112	56	28	14	7	1

equivalent ratio

1. 672 ÷ 112

112	56	560	672
1	0S	5	6

multiply up

100 × 6 + 12 × 6

1. 672 ÷ 112

112	672
1	6

×6

multiply up

John David: You just looked at 112 and could see that 112 times 6 is 672. Man, I have got to remember to look at the numbers!

Teacher: Well put, John David. Let's talk about item 2, 1,364 ÷ 31. How many of you think that finding equivalent ratios is the best strategy for this problem? No takers? Why not?

Tyler: You can't divide 31 by anything. I mean, 31 doesn't have any factors.

Kirsten: So you can't find equivalent ratios because 31 is prime.

Teacher: Nice. Did you all multiply up in some way? Who thinks they have a particularly nice strategy?

Shanalla: I don't know if it's the best, but it was pretty straightforward. I doubled and doubled and got 124. Times 10 is 1,240.

Teacher: Let me interrupt you, please. What did you ask yourself at that point, when you had 1,240?

Shanalla: I knew I needed 1,364, so I wanted to know how much more I needed to get from 1,240 to 1,364 and it was 124.

Teacher: That is a really important point. You asked yourself how much more you needed and when you figured out it was 124, it was right there in the table for you. Nice. *The teacher points out the step of finding out how much more you need.*

2. 1,364 ÷ 31

1,240 + 124

31	62	124	1,240	1,364
1	2	4	40	44

40 + 4

Teacher: What about item 3, 9,660 ÷ 420? Did anyone think of finding equivalent ratios for this one?

Tyler: I did because both of them end in 0 so you can divide out a 10 right away. That is equivalent to 966 ÷ 42. But I am not sure that it goes so well after that.

Teacher: What could you do after that?

Kirsten: You can keep going. That's equivalent to 483 ÷ 21. And that's not very nice.

John David: It's nicer than 9,660 ÷ 420.

Teacher: Say more about that, please. *It might seem obvious to John David, but the teacher wants to make the reasoning explicit.*

John David: Well, now you can solve 483 ÷ 21 however you want.

Teacher: What did you do?

John David: I doubled 21 and multiplied by 10 to get 420. Then I just need 63 more. That's three 21s. So, the answer is 23.

3. 9660 ÷ 420

9,660	966	483	
420	42	21	

3. 9660 ÷ 420

1	2	20	3	23
21	42	420	63	483

Teacher: So, you used a mixture of finding equivalent ratios and then multiplying up to solve the simpler problem. Did anyone just multiply up?

Kelly: I did. Double 420 is 840, then times 10 is 8,400. Add those together to get 9,240. Now you're just one 420 short, so that's 23.

3. 9660 ÷ 420

1	2	20	22	23		
420	840	8,400	9,240	9,660		

Teacher: Which strategy do you prefer and why? *The teacher ends the conversation asking students to justify which strategy they like.*

Multiplication/Division Workout 26   Name _____

To find 435 ÷ 25, Matthew thought about 25 × ___ = 435.

1.

1	16	17	4			
25						

435 ÷ 25 = _____

To find 435 ÷ 25, Craig thought about equivalent ratios.

2.

435	870					
25						

435 ÷ 25 = _____

Which of the strategies, Matthew's multiplying up or Craig's equivalent ratios, do you prefer?

To find 6.4 ÷ 0.5, Eboni thought about 0.5 × ___ = 6.4.

3.

1	2					
0.5						

6.4 ÷ 0.5 = _____

To find 6.4 ÷ 0.5, Brianna thought about equivalent ratios.

4.

6.4						
0.5						

6.4 ÷ 0.5 = _____

Sample Dialog from Multiplication/Division Workout 26

Teacher: Let's take a look at items 1 and 2 together. What is Matthew thinking about solving 435 ÷ 25?

The teacher knows that students might need to hear the two different strategies described aloud to make sense of what is happening in this workout.

Latisha: He is thinking about twenty-fives and working up to 435.

Greg: Yeah, he's thinking about multiplying 25 by something to get to 435.

Teacher: What about Craig? How is he thinking about solving 435 ÷ 25?

Scott: Ratios. He is going to try to simplify the ratio of 435 to 25. I can see right now that they have a common factor of 5 so that might be a good idea.

Teacher: Good thoughts. Work on this page and we'll talk about your thinking in a few minutes.

Students work.

Teacher: Let's talk about some possibilities for Matthew's strategy.

Michelle: I think he used quarters to get to sixteen 25s. Since there are 4 quarters in a dollar, 16 quarters is 4 bucks, so 400.

Caleb: And then he added those together to get 425.

Teacher: What are you thinking now?

Caleb: Since he is working up to 435, we still need 10 more.

Teacher: Finding out how much you have left is important, isn't it? Ten more. That's an interesting amount to still need considering we're talking about 25s. How do you get 10 from 25 times something?

Latisha: Well, we got a good hint! He had a 4 so that would correspond to 100. Now you can divide by 10 to get 10.

Greg: And then add that 10 to get the 435.

1	16	17	4	.4	17.4
25	400	425	100	10	435

Teacher: So, then we have Craig solving the same problem but by thinking about equivalent ratios. Scott, you had mentioned that 435 and 25 have common factors. Is that where you went?

Scott: Actually, no. Craig gave a nice hint, too. He has that 870 next to the 435. So that's twice so I doubled the 25 to 50. Then I decided to continue his trend and got 1,700 divided by 100. That's sweet! Shift the place value twice and you get the same 17.4.

435	870	1,740	17.4
25	50	100	1

Teacher: What do you think about Craig's strategy of finding equivalent ratios?

Kate: I was surprised that he wasn't simplifying the ratio. He was sort of un-simplifying and it worked!

Teacher: What do you mean, it worked?

Kate: Once you get to a number divided by 100, the problem is easy. I just hadn't thought about doing that.

Greg: I hadn't either, but it makes sense and look how quickly he got that answer.

Teacher: What about the numbers in the problem made finding those equivalent ratios so nice?

Sarah: The 25 multiplies up to the 100. So, I am thinking any numbers that multiply to 100.

Gene: Or maybe 10 or even 1. Like in the next problem, 6.4 divided by 0.5. You can just double both the numerator and the denominator and get 12.8 divided by 1!

6.4	12.8
0.5	1

Kate: Again, he was finding an equivalent ratio by scaling up instead of simplifying by scaling down. And this time the denominator is 1. I like it.

Teacher: So, did you like that better for 6.4 divided by 0.5 than the multiplying up strategy?

Kate: Yes, it took a lot more steps to multiply up to 6.4 from 0.5. It was much faster to just find the equivalent ratio.

Teacher: Maybe you'll look for those nice divisors in future problems.

Multiplication Workout 27

Name _____

Three students solved a division problem. Fill in the blanks.

1.

1	0.5		0.2	0.7	0.8		0.81	6		
2.5		0.25				0.025			0.015	2.04

Describe this strategy:

2.

1		80		1.6	0.016	
2.5	25		2			2.04

Describe this strategy:

3.

2.04		8.16			
2.5	5		1		

Describe this strategy:

4. What problem did they all solve? (Write an equation with the problem and the answer.)

Two students solved a division problem. Fill in the blanks.

5.

0.79	1.58					
5		1				

Describe this strategy:

6.

5		0.25	0.75		0.04	0.79
1	0.1			8		

Describe this strategy:

7. What problem did they all solve? (Write an equation with the problem and the answer.)

Multiplication/Division Workout 28   Name _____

Three students solved a division problem. Fill in the blanks.

1.

1	10	2			7	.7	
0.5			1.5	6.5			6.85

Describe this strategy:

2.

1		20		14	3	.3	
0.5	5		3				6.85

Describe this strategy:

3.

6.85					
0.5	1				

Describe this strategy:

4. What problem did they all solve? (Write an equation with the problem and the answer.)

Two students solved a division problem. Fill in the blanks.

5.

1.4	2.8					
1.75		7	1			

Describe this strategy:

6.

1	2	4				
1.75			14	1.4		

Describe this strategy:

7. What problem did they all solve? (Write an equation with the problem and the answer.)

Multiplication/Division Workout 29   Name _____

Solve these division problems:

1. 468 ÷ 24

    Describe your strategy:

2. 636 ÷ 16

    Describe your strategy:

3. 5.7 ÷ 2.5

    Describe your strategy:

4. 24.15 ÷ 3.5

    Describe your strategy:

5. What makes a divisor a "nice divisor" to use the equivalent ratio strategy?

Multiplication/Division Workout 30   Name _____

Solve these division problems:

1. 1.44 ÷ 0.8

Describe your strategy:

2. 1.92 ÷ 3.84

Describe your strategy:

3. 10.9326 ÷ 2.74

Describe your strategy:

4. 1.8352 ÷ 0.31

Describe your strategy:

5. What makes a problem nice to use the equivalent ratio strategy? What makes a problem nice to use a multiplying up strategy?

Sample Dialog from Multiplication/Division Workout 30

Teacher: OK, some fun problems today! Let's share some strategies. What about item 1? Terri, let's put your work under the document camera and then you can explain what you did.

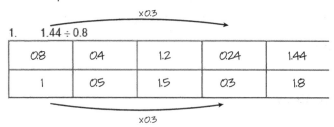

1. $1.\overline{44} \div 0.8$

0.8	0.4	1.2	0.24	1.44
1	0.5	1.5	0.3	1.8

Terri: That one wasn't too bad. I worked up from 0.8 to 1.44. I started with half of 0.8, that's 0.4. Then I added them together to get 1.5 to 1.2. Now I just needed 0.24 more. That's 0.3 more 0.8s. So, the answer is 1.8.

Teacher: Does anyone have any questions or comments for Terri?

Ryan: I did almost the same thing, but I thought about it as 14.4 divided by 8. It was easier for me to deal with the bigger numbers.

Teacher: Is everyone clear why Ryan can do that?

Carrie: It's because $^{1.44}\!/_{0.8}$ is equivalent to $^{14.4}\!/_{8}$. You just multiply both by 10.

Teacher: Great. Let's move on to the second problem, 1.92 divided by 3.84. Jenna, would you show us your strategy and talk us through it?

2. $1.92 \div 3.84$

1.92	1	0.5
3.84	2	1

Jenna: Well, I am not sure how to explain but I thought about 19 and 38 and 19 is half of 38 so I checked and sure enough 19.2 is half of 38.4, so that means that 1.92 is half of 3.84. The answer is 0.5.

Teacher: So, even though you didn't write down 19.2 and 38.4, they were helpful in your thinking? Nice job.

John: Boy, that was tons easier than what I tried to do. I'll look for that next time!

Teacher: What about problem 3? Josh, would you please put your work under the camera and tell us about it?

3. $10.9326 \div 2.74$

1	2	4	0.01	3.99		
2.74	5.48	10.96	2.74	1,093.26		

1,096 − 1,093.26 = 1,096.74 − 1,094 = 2.74

Josh: I decided to think about 274 and make my goal be 1,093.26. It's easier for me to think about the numbers that way. Then I doubled and doubled again and that was close. It took me a minute to find out how much more I needed.

I knew I needed the difference between 1,093.26 and 1,096. I was happy to find that was exactly 2.74. So I only needed to subtract 0.01 to get 3.99.

Teacher: Does anyone have any questions or comments for Josh?

Remy: How did you know how much more you needed once you got to 1,096?

Josh: I shifted both numbers up 0.74 to get 1096.74 minus 1,094 and that was just 2.74. I wrote that here, under the table.

Remy: Right. Thanks.

Teacher: Fabulous work. Let's look at the last problem. Kelli and Rhonda, let's compare your strategies.

4. $1.8352 \div 0.31 \qquad \dfrac{1.8352}{.31} = \dfrac{183.52}{31}$

1	10	5	6	0.1	5.9	0.02	5.92
31	310	155	186	3.1	182.9	0.62	183.52

4. $1.8352 \div 0.31 \qquad \dfrac{1.8352}{.31} = \dfrac{183.52}{31}$

1	10	5	9	0.9	5.9	0.02	5.92
31	310	155	27.9	27.9	182.9	0.62	183.52

Teacher: It looks like you're thinking along the same lines in some places. Everyone, turn and talk to a partner about how they approached it differently and then we'll talk.

Below are five different strategies for ⅖ × ¾. Fill in the missing values in the boxes.

Strategy a

1/5 × 1/4 = ☐

2/5 × 1/4 = 2 (1/5 × 1/4)

= 2 (☐) = ☐

2/5 × 3/4 = 3(2/20) = ☐

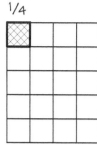

1/4

1/5

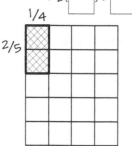

1/4

2/5

3/4

2/5

Strategy b

one dimension of 2/5

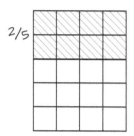

2/5

one dimension of 3/4

☐ ← Fill in the dimension

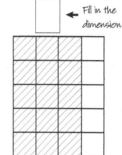

area of a 2/5 × 3/4 = ☐

3/4

2/5

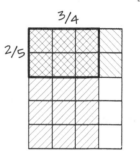

Strategy c

I think about 2/5 as 40% so

2/5 × 3/4 is 40% of 3/4. Since

10% of 0.75 is 0.075, then

40% is ☐ which is = ☐/10.

Strategy d

2/5 × 3/4 = ☐/5 × ☐/4 = 3/5 × 1/2 = 1/2 × 3/5 = ☐/10

☐/4

3/4

2/5

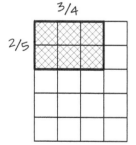

☐/5

☐/4

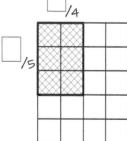

Strategy e

I think about 2/5 × 3/4 as

3/4 × 2/5. Then 3/4 of 2 is

☐ , so 3/4 of 2/5 is 1.5/5

and 1.5/5 = ☐/10.

Which strategy do you prefer for this problem? Why?

Sample Dialog from Multiplication/Division Workout 31

Teacher: First thing, please find $\frac{2}{5} \times \frac{3}{4}$.

Students work. The teacher knows it is important for students to have thought about the relationships first before examining other strategies.

Teacher: Now, let's talk through this new Workout together. First of all, what do you see?

Jennifer: It's about multiplication and division.

Ike: Of fractions.

Norma: There are lots of arrays.

Teacher: There are five different strategies shown, *a*, *b*, *c*, *d*, and *e*, and they all solve the same problem, $\frac{2}{5}$ times $\frac{3}{4}$. Now that you've worked on the problem, look at the strategies. Fill in the blanks and then figure out what the person was doing to solve the problem using each strategy. Talk with your partner and compare ideas.

The teacher circulates and asks scaffolding questions. Then the class has a whole-group discussion where students defend their ideas.

Teacher: What's going on in strategy *a*?

Stuart: I think the strategy is using unit fractions first. They know that they are dealing with fifths and fourths, so they found $\frac{1}{5}$ of $\frac{1}{4}$ and that's $\frac{1}{20}$.

Teacher: How does that help?

Monica: Because now you can scale up. In the middle, if you know $\frac{1}{5}$ of $\frac{1}{4}$ is $\frac{1}{20}$, then $\frac{2}{5}$ of $\frac{1}{4}$ is twice that. So $\frac{2}{20}$.

Harry: The next step stumped me a bit, but I think they are doing the same scaling up, this time by 3 because it's not just $\frac{1}{4}$ it's $\frac{3}{4}$.

Teacher: What is Harry talking about here?

Norma: Just like they scaled up from $\frac{1}{5}$ of $\frac{1}{4}$ to twice that to get $\frac{2}{5}$ of $\frac{1}{4}$, they can scale up to get $\frac{3}{4}$ by 3.

Teacher: You mean, since they know $\frac{2}{5}$ of $\frac{1}{4}$ is $\frac{2}{20}$ then that means that $\frac{1}{4}$ of $\frac{2}{5}$ is $\frac{2}{20}$ but they don't want $\frac{1}{4}$ of $\frac{2}{5}$, they want $\frac{3}{4}$ of $\frac{2}{5}$, or three times what they had? Ah, nice thinking. And what is 3 times $\frac{2}{20}$?

Harry: It's $\frac{6}{20}$.

Teacher: What about strategy *b*? What's going on here?

Ike: The factors are the dimensions. The answer is the double shaded part out of the total.

Jennifer: One dimension is $\frac{2}{5}$, so you split the array into fifths one way and shade 2 of the fifths. Then the other dimension is $\frac{3}{4}$ so you split the array into fourths and shade 3 of those sections.

Ike: Then you count the doubled shaded parts—that's 6 out of the total 20, so $\frac{6}{20}$.

Teacher: What relationship is there between the denominators of the factors and the inside array—the 6 double-shaded parts?

Harry: The denominators tell you how many total little pieces you'll have—the 4 by 5 makes the 20 pieces.

Teacher: Why is that? *Harry has given a spot-on answer, but the teacher knows that not all the students have made the connection and they need this connection to understand what is happening in strategy d.*

Ellen:	Because the denominators tell you that you're dealing with fourths and fifths, so fourths in one dimension and fifths in the other will always give you 20 total pieces. It would be the same if it was thirds and fourths—you'd have 12 total pieces.
Teacher:	What do the numerators tell you?
Norma:	The numerators tell you how many of those total pieces are double-shaded. This time a 2 by 3 was double-shaded, so you have 6 pieces. If the numerators were something like 5 and 8, then you'd have a 5 by 8 double-shaded, or 40 pieces.
Teacher:	Someone put that all together for us.
Stuart:	The product of the numerators is the inside array and the product of the denominators is the outside array.
Teacher:	And how does that relate to strategy *d*?
Sue:	Since you are multiplying the numerators and the denominators, you can rotate the inner array and get the same answer.
Ike:	How's that?
Wes:	Because if you rotate the inner array, you still have the same ratio of the pieces in the small array and the pieces in the big array.
Sue:	And it can make the problem easier. This time the problem becomes $\frac{2}{4}$ times $\frac{3}{5}$ and that's just $\frac{1}{2}$ of $\frac{3}{5}$ which $\frac{3}{10}$.
Teacher:	How do you know what $\frac{1}{2}$ of $\frac{3}{5}$ is?
Sue:	Because half of a fifth is a tenth, so half of $\frac{3}{5}$ is $\frac{3}{10}$.
Teacher:	How about strategy *e*?
Ellen:	This strategy used $\frac{3}{4}$. They were thinking about $\frac{3}{4}$ of $\frac{2}{5}$ by finding $\frac{3}{4}$ of 2 and then it's that many fifths.
Teacher:	So, first they switched the problem around, from $\frac{2}{5}$ of $\frac{3}{4}$ to $\frac{3}{4}$ of $\frac{2}{5}$?
Ellen:	Yes, then $\frac{3}{4}$ of 2 is 1.5 so $\frac{3}{4}$ of $\frac{2}{5}$ is 1.5 fifths $(\frac{1.5}{5})$.
Thomas:	And 1 and a half fifths is $\frac{3}{10}$.
Teacher:	Strategy *c* has all of these percents and decimals. What's going on?
Stuart:	Since $\frac{2}{5}$ is 40%, they thought about percents. I didn't really like it until I realized that they used 10%—that's easy.
Sam:	Yeah, because 10% of 75 is easy, that's just 7.5, but since you need 40%, you have to find 4 of the 7.5s.
Wes:	And 2 times 7.5 is 15. Double again is 30, so that's 0.30 or $\frac{3}{10}$.
Teacher:	Sam, I heard you say 7.5, not 0.075.
Sam:	It is easier for me to think about 7.5 and double up to 30 and then remember that it's percents to get 30%.
Teacher:	Nice!

Multiplication/Division Workout 32

Name _____

Below are four different strategies for $\frac{8}{11} \times \frac{3}{4}$. Fill in the missing values in the boxes.

Strategy a

$\frac{1}{11} \times \frac{1}{4} = \frac{1}{44}$ $\frac{8}{11} \times \frac{1}{4} = 8(\boxed{}) = \frac{8}{44}$ $\frac{8}{11} \times \frac{3}{4} = \boxed{} (\frac{8}{44}) = \boxed{}$

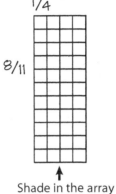

Shade in the array

Strategy b

one dimension of $\frac{8}{11}$ one dimension of $\frac{3}{4}$ $\frac{8}{11} \times \frac{3}{4} = \boxed{}$

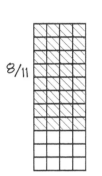   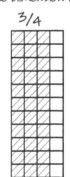   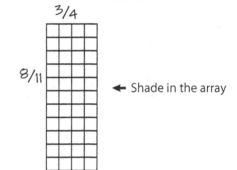

← Shade in the array

Strategy c

$\frac{8}{11} \times \frac{3}{4} \quad = \quad \frac{3}{11} \times \frac{8}{4} = \frac{3}{11} \times 2 = \boxed{}$

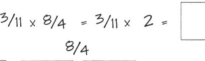

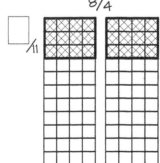

Strategy d

Since $\frac{8}{11} \times \frac{3}{4} = \frac{3}{4} \times \frac{8}{11}$

I can think about $\frac{3}{4}$ of 8

and $\frac{3}{4}$ of 8 is $\boxed{}$.

So, $\frac{3}{4}$ of $\frac{8}{11} = \frac{\boxed{}}{11}$.

Which strategy do you prefer for this problem? Why?

Multiplication/Division Workout 33   Name _____

Below are four different strategies for $5/6 \times 3/10$. Fill in the missing values in the boxes.

Strategy a

$1/6 \times 1/10 = 1/60$ $5/6 \times 1/10 = \boxed{} (1/60)$ $5/6 \times 3/10 = 3(1/12) = \boxed{}$

$= 5/60 = 1/12$

$\boxed{}$ ← Fill in the dimension

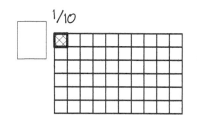
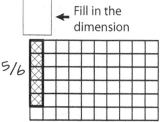
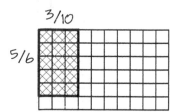

Strategy b

one dimension of $\boxed{}$ one dimension of $3/10$ $5/6 \times 3/10 = \boxed{}$

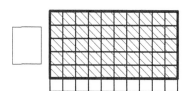
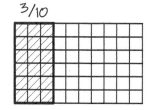
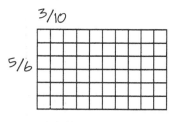

 Shade in the array

Strategy c

$5/6 \times 3/10$ $= 3/6 \times 5/10 = 1/2 \times 1/2 = 1/4$

Fill in the dimensions → $\boxed{}$

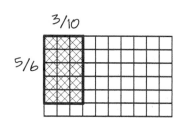
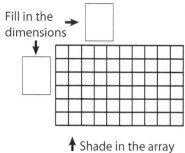

↑ Shade in the array

Strategy d

If I think of $3/10$ as money, 0.30, then 1/6 of 0.30 is 0.05, so $5/6$ is 0.25 so 1/4.

Which strategy do you prefer for this problem? Why?

Multiplication/Division Workout 34

Below are four different strategies for $\frac{9}{10} \times \frac{2}{3}$. Fill in the missing values in the boxes.

Strategy a

$1/10 \times 1/3 = 1/30$ $9/10 \times 1/3 = 9(\boxed{}) = 9/30$ $9/10 \times 2/3 = \boxed{}(9/30) = \boxed{}$

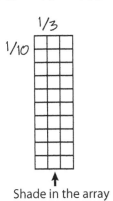

1/10   1/3

Shade in the array

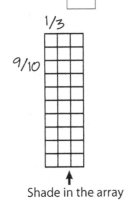

9/10   1/3

Shade in the array

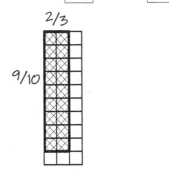

9/10   2/3

Strategy b

one dimension of 9/10   one dimension of 2/3 $9/10 \times 2/3 = \boxed{}$

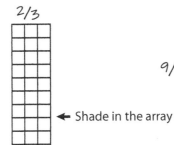

9/10   ← Shade in the array

2/3   9/10   ← Shade in the array

2/3   9/10   ← Shade in the array

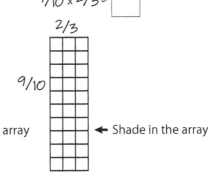

Strategy c

$9/10 \times 2/3$ = $2/10 \times 9/3 = 2/10 \times 3 = \boxed{}$

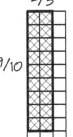

2/3   9/10

$\boxed{}$/10   9/3

Strategy d

Since $9/10 \times 2/3 = 2/3 \times 9/10$

I can think about 2/3 of 9

and 2/3 of 9 is $\boxed{}$.

So, 2/3 of 9/10 = $\boxed{}$/10

Which strategy do you prefer for this problem? Why?

Below are four different strategies for $5/12 \times 3/5$. Fill in the missing values in the boxes.

Strategy a

$1/12 \times 1/5 = 1/60$ $5/12 \times 1/5 = 5(\boxed{}) = 5/60$ $5/12 \times 3/5 = \boxed{}(5/60) = \boxed{}$

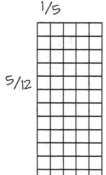

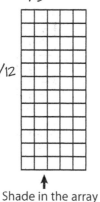

Shade in the array

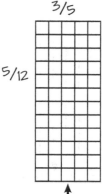

Shade in the array

Strategy b

one dimension of $5/12$ one dimension of $3/5$ $5/12 \times 3/5 = \boxed{}$

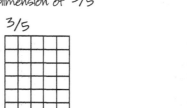

← Shade in the array   ← Shade in the array   ← Shade in the array

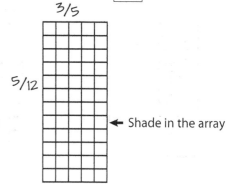

Strategy c

$5/12 \times 3/5 \quad = \quad 3/12 \times 5/5 = 3/12 \times 1 = \boxed{}$

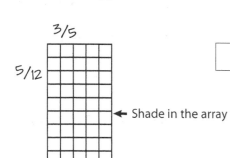

← Shade in the array

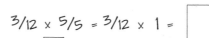

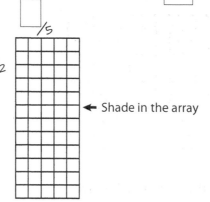

← Shade in the array

Strategy d

Since $5/12 \times 3/5 = 3/5 \times 5/12$

I can think about $3/5$ of 5

and $3/5$ of 5 is $\boxed{}$.

So, $3/5$ of $5/12 = \boxed{}/12$

Which strategy do you prefer for this problem? Why?

Sample Dialog from Multiplication/Division Workout 35

Teacher:	Let's talk about these strategies for $\frac{5}{12}$ times $\frac{3}{5}$. First, tell me how you are doing all of this shading. What in the fractions tells you what should be shaded?
Danny:	It's always the denominators that tell you how many total pieces there are.
Lyn:	The denominators make the outside, the big array.
Peter:	Because they are the dimensions of the outer array, the product of the denominators is the area of the whole array.
Silvia:	The numerators make the small array, the inside one.
Danny:	So when you multiply the numerators, you get the area of the inside array. So, that's the number of pieces in the numerator of the answer because it's like that many pieces out of the total.
Russel:	Each of the fractions in the problem are one of the dimensions of the array.
Teacher:	Those were great descriptions. Let's focus on the strategies. Which do you like for this problem?
Donna:	I really like the scaling-up one—*a*. I used to try to remember what to do with multiplying fractions and now it reminds me that if you start with the unit fractions, you multiply the denominators to get the 1 little piece, the $\frac{1}{60}$. Then you scale up by each numerator and that is essentially like multiplying the denominators and the numerators to get the answer.
Reg:	I can see that, but I really like *d* because finding $\frac{3}{5}$ of 5 is so slick. It's just 3! So the answer is just $\frac{3}{12}$ or $\frac{1}{4}$.
Teacher:	Tell me how you're thinking about $\frac{3}{5}$ of 5?
Reg:	To find $\frac{3}{5}$ of anything, you need 5 parts and then keep 3 of them. So, $\frac{5}{12}$ is 5 one-twelfths. So I just think about $\frac{3}{5}$ of 5 and that's just 3. But since it was $\frac{5}{12}$ I am taking $\frac{3}{5}$ of, then it becomes 3 one-twelfths, $\frac{3}{12}$.
Teacher:	So, are you saying that $\frac{3}{5}$ of 5 anythings can be thought of as 3 of those things?
Reg:	Yes, and in this case, the thing is $\frac{1}{12}$.
Teacher:	Does anyone have any questions for Reg? *The teacher knows that this discussion is all without a model to reference and that can make it difficult to follow for students.*
Maribel:	Are you saying that you just kind of ignored the twelfths? And just thought about the 5?
Reg:	Yes, sort of. Five twelfths is like 5 one-twelfths. So it could be, like, 5 sodas. I know it's easy to find $\frac{3}{5}$ of 5 sodas.
Maribel:	That is just 3 sodas? So, since it was 5 one-twelfths, then $\frac{3}{5}$ of that 5 is 3 one-twelfths. Got it.
Teacher:	Anyone else?
Robert:	I like strategy *c*—the swapping one.
Teacher:	What do you mean, the swapping one?
Robert:	If you know that you can rotate the inner array and still get the same answer, that means that you can swap the numerators. So, instead of the problem being the original $\frac{5}{12}$ times $\frac{3}{5}$, it can be $\frac{3}{12}$ times $\frac{5}{5}$ and that's just $\frac{1}{4}$ times 1. Done!

Sue:	I think that in order to understand Robert's strategy, you have to first understand either *a* or *b* because they get you to the array and then you know you can rotate the inner array so you can swap.
Teacher:	Does swapping the numerators always help?
Robert:	Um, I hadn't thought of that. Wait, no, not always. It only helps if it makes nice fractions.
Sue:	Yes, like in this example, it makes $\frac{5}{5}$ which is just 1! That is nice. But you could have fractions like, um . . . $\frac{2}{3}$ times $\frac{4}{5}$. Then it doesn't matter because you would end up with fractions that don't simplify to anything nicer than you already have.
Robert:	Wait, let me try those. Let's see . . . $\frac{2}{5}$ times $\frac{4}{3}$ or $\frac{4}{3}$ of $\frac{2}{5}$. Yeah, you're right. Those aren't really any nicer than the original.
Teacher:	So, let's get general. What would be true about the numbers in a fraction multiplication problem so that you would want to swap by rotating that inner array? *The teacher wants the students to generalize when to use the strategy.*
Maribel:	When one of the resulting fractions will simplify to something nice.
Silvia:	Like if they have the same factors.
Teacher:	What do you mean, the same factors? *The teacher knows what she means, but wants to help all students construct this idea.*
Silvia:	If a numerator has the same factor as the other fraction's denominator, then swap the numerators so that the numerator and denominator that have the same common factor are in the same fraction. Then you can simplify that fraction and see if it turns into something nicer.
Russel:	Like the $\frac{5}{5}$ in this problem — that is very nice — it's just 1. But it could be something like $\frac{1}{2}$ or $\frac{1}{4}$ because those are easy to figure.
Teacher:	So, what will you look for to see if rotating the inner array, which means you swap the numerators, will be an efficient strategy? Someone besides Robert.
Maribel:	The numerator of one fraction and the denominator of another, having common factors.
Ted:	And then checking to see if that simplified fraction makes the problem easier.
Teacher:	Great work today!

Multiplication/Division Workout 36

Name _____

It takes ⅓ cup of chopped pepperoni to make Sarah's all-meat pizza. Use the ratio tables to find out how many cups of chopped pepperoni are needed for different numbers of pizzas.

1. 5 pizzas

Pizzas	1	2	3			
Pepperoni (C)	⅓					

It takes _____ cups of pepperoni to make 5 pizzas. ⅓ × 5 = _____

2. 3½ pizzas

Pizzas	1	3	½			
Pepperoni (C)	⅓					

It takes _____ cups of pepperoni to make 3½ pizzas. ⅓ × 3½ = _____

3. 6¼ pizzas

Pizzas	1	½	¼			
Pepperoni (C)	⅓					

It takes _____ cups of pepperoni to make 6¼ pizzas. ⅓ × 6¼ = _____

4. How many pizzas can you make with 8⅔ cups of pepperoni?

Pizzas	1					
Pepperoni (C)	⅓					

You can make _____ pizzas with 8⅔ cups of pepperoni. 8⅔ ÷ ⅓ = _____

Multiplication/Division Workout 37

Name _____

It takes ¾ cup of sausage to make Sarah's all-meat pizza. Use the ratio tables to find out how many cup of sausage are needed for different numbers of pizzas.

1. 5 pizzas

Sausage (C)	¾					
Pizzas	1					

It takes _____ cups of sausage to make 5 pizzas. ¾ × 5 = _____

2. 4½ pizzas

Sausage (C)	¾					
Pizzas	1					

It takes _____ cups of sausage to make 4½ pizzas. ¾ × 4½ = _____

3. 2⅓ pizzas

Sausage (C)	¾					
Pizzas	1					

It takes _____ cups of sausage to make 2⅓ pizzas. ¾ × 2⅓ = _____

4. How many pizzas can you make with 8¼ cups of sausage?

Sausage (C)	¾					
Pizzas	1					

You can make _____ pizzas with 8¼ cups of sausage. 8¼ ÷ ¾ = _____

Sample Dialog from Multiplication/Division Workout 37

Teacher: Let's make some pizza! Thomas, how did you find the amount of sausage we need to make 5 of these pizzas that take ¾ of a cup of sausage per pizza?

Thomas: I doubled to get 1 and a half cups of sausage for 2 pizzas. Then doubled again to get 3 cups of sausage for 4 pizzas. Then I just need one more pizza, which is ¾ of a cup, so it's 3 and ¾ cups of sausage.

Teacher: Shari, what did you do?

Shari: I know that since it's ¾ of a cup, that if you have 4 of them, it will be 3 cups, because 4 times ¾ is 3.

Teacher: How do you know that?

Shari: Well, if it's fourths, you need 4 of them to get a whole number. Four ¼s is 1, so four ¾s is 3.

Teacher: Does anyone get that? Can you repeat what Shari is doing? *The teacher knows that this relationship is important and wants to help all students construct it, that $\frac{a}{b} \times b = a$, because $\frac{1}{b} \times b = 1$.*

Larry: She knows that ¼ four times is 1. So 3 times that is 3.

Teacher: Do you think that would work for another fraction, like ⅚? How many of them would we need to make a whole number?

Shari: You'd need 6 of them. Six one-sixths is 1, so 6 five-sixths is 5 times that 1, or 5.

Teacher: I wonder if that might come in handy.

		x2	x2	3 + ¾
sausage (c.)	¾	1.5	3	3 ¾
pizzas	1	2	4	5
		x2	x2	1 + 4

		x4	3 + ¾	
sausage (c.)	¾	3	3 ¾	
pizzas	1	4	5	
		x4	1 + 4	

Teacher: So, now that we've got the amount of cheese for 4 pizzas, let's just talk about finding the ½ of a pizza.

Zoe: It's just ½ of ¾. Half of a fourth is an eighth, so it's ⅜.

Maddy: I think about it as one-and-a-half fourths, which is also ⅜.

½ of ¼ is ⅛, so ½ of ¾ = 3(⅛) = ⅜   ½ of ¾ = 1.5/4 = ⅜

Teacher: Let's talk about the next one, 2 and ⅓ pizzas. How much sausage do we need and how do you know?

Anna: I got 1¾ cups. Finding 2 pizzas was easy, just double ¾ to 1 and a half. Finding ⅓ of ¾ was trickier. I know that ⅓ of ¼ is 1/12, so it would be 3 times that, 3 times 1/12 is 3/12, which is ¼.

Thomas: I thought about ⅓ of 3 because ¾ is three ¼s. One-third of 3 anythings is 1, so ⅓ of ¾ is just one of those fourths, ¼.

⅓ x ¼ is 1/12, so ⅓ of ¾ = 3(1/12) = 3/12 = ¼   ⅓ of 3 things is 1, so ⅓ of ¾ = ¼

Teacher: So, once you had 2 pizzas and ⅓ of a pizza . . .

Anna: Then you just add them together to get 1 and a half and ¼ and that's 1¾.

	x2 →		x ⅓ →	1½ + ¼
sausage (c.)	¾	1.5	¼	1 ¾
pizzas	1	2	⅓	2 ⅓
		x2 →	x ⅓ →	2 + ⅓

Teacher: For the last one, 8¼ cups of sausage, how did you do that?

Kristin: I doubled, doubled, doubled, and that is 6 cups of sausage for 8 pizzas. Then I added 2 pizzas and 1.5 cups of sausage. Then I just needed 1 more pizza because I needed ¾ cups of sausage more to get 8¼ cups of sausage making 11 pizzas.

Teacher: Terri, tell us about your thinking? *The teacher wants to bring in the connection with decimals and times 10.*

Terri: I was thinking about ¾ as decimals, 0.75. So 10 pizzas gets me straight to 7.5 cups of sausage and then I added the 1 more pizza to get 11 pizzas.

	x2 →	x2 →	x2 →	6 + 1½	7½ + ¾
sausage (c.)	¾	1.5	3	6	7 ½	8 ¼
pizzas	1	2	4	8	10	11
	x2 →	x2 →	x2 →	8 + 2	10 + 1

	x10 →	7½ + ¾
sausage (c.)	¾	7.5	8 ¼
pizzas	1	10	11
	x10 →	10 + 1

Multiplication/Division Workout 38

Name _____

It takes $\frac{1}{6}$ of an onion to make Sarah's all-meat pizza. Use the ratio tables to find out how many onions are needed for different numbers of pizzas.

1. 6 pizzas

Onions	$\frac{1}{6}$					
Pizzas	1					

It takes _____ onions to make 6 pizzas. $\frac{1}{6} \times 6 =$ _____

2. 2½ pizzas

Onions	$\frac{1}{6}$					
Pizzas	1					

It takes _____ onions to make 2½ pizzas. $\frac{1}{6} \times 2\frac{1}{2} =$ _____

3. 3⅓ pizzas

Onions	$\frac{1}{6}$					
Pizzas	1					

It takes _____ onions to make 3⅓ pizzas. $\frac{1}{6} \times 3\frac{1}{3} =$ _____

4. How many pizzas can you make with 8⅔ onions?

Onions	$\frac{1}{6}$					
Pizzas	1					

You can make _____ pizzas with 8⅔ onions. $8\frac{2}{3} \div \frac{1}{6} =$ _____

©2014 Pamela Weber Harris from *Lessons and Activities for Building Powerful Numeracy*. Portsmouth, NH: Heinemann.

Multiplication/Division Workout 39   Name _____

It takes ⁵⁄₄ cup of cheese to make Sarah's all-meat pizza. Use the ratio tables to find out how many cups of cheese are needed for different numbers of pizzas.

1. 4 pizzas

Pizzas	1					
Cheese (C)	⁵⁄₄					

It takes _____ cups of cheese to make 4 pizzas. ⁵⁄₄ × 4 = _____

2. 8½ pizzas

Pizzas	1					
Cheese (C)	⁵⁄₄					

It takes _____ cups of cheese to make 8½ pizzas. Write an equation: _____

3. 1⅓ pizzas

Pizzas	1					
Cheese (C)	⁵⁄₄					

It takes _____ cups of cheese to make 1⅓ pizzas. Write an equation: _____

4. How many pizzas can you make with 6¼ cups of cheese?

Pizzas	1					
Cheese (C)	⁵⁄₄					

You can make _____ pizzas with 6¼ cups of cheese. Write an equation: _____

Sample Dialog from Multiplication/Division Workout 39

Teacher: Anyone noticing a pattern for the first problems of these latest Workouts? In one, we found the onions we needed if it takes ⅙ cup of onions for 6 pizzas and in this one we found the amount of cheese we needed if it takes 5/4 cups of cheese to make 4 pizzas. I'm going to record what we found. Do you think this will always happen? Why?

$$\tfrac{1}{6} \times 6 = 6 \qquad \tfrac{5}{4} \times 4 = 5 \qquad \text{Is it true that } a/b \times b = a?$$

Kyle: I think it will always happen because whatever is in the denominator means you have that many pieces, fourths, fifths, whatever. And if you have that many of them, 4 fourths, 5 fifths, then you have a whole thing.

Allie: And if you think about it like multiplication, then ⅕ times 5 is like 5 divided by 5, which is 1.

Wes: Even if the numerator isn't 1, like ⅔ times 3 is 2 times 3 divided by 3 and the threes divide out. So you're just left with the denominator.

Teacher: That seems like an important idea. I will model it on the board with equations.

$$\tfrac{2}{3} \times 3 = \frac{2 \times 3}{3} = 2 \times \frac{3}{3} = 2 \times 1 = 2 \qquad \text{So, } a/b \times b = \frac{a \times b}{b} = a \times \frac{b}{b} = a \times 1 = a$$

Teacher: For the next problem, 8½ pizzas, I saw many of you find the amount of cheese for 8 pizzas by doubling and then finding the amount of cheese for ½ of a pizza. Let's focus on how you found the ½ of a pizza. Marcus?

Marcus: Since it takes 1¼ cups of cheese for 1 pizza, then we need half of 1¼. Half of 1 is ½ and half of ¼ is ⅛, so ½ and ⅛.

Teacher: What is ½ and ⅛?

Marcus: It's ⅝, because 4/8 and ⅛ is ⅝.

Teacher: Anyone find half of 1¼ differently? *Marcus' strategy is fine, but the teacher wants to pull out more proportional reasoning.*

Trevor: I thought about it as 5/4, and half of a fourth is an eighth. So it's ⅝.

Margaret: I also thought about 5/4. Since half of 5 is 2 and a half, it's ²·⁵/4 and that's equivalent to ⅝.

Teacher What did you get for the whole 8½ pizzas, how much cheese do you need?

Trevor: I got 10⅝.

Teacher: Larry, I noticed that you did something different. Tell us what you did.

Larry: I didn't split up the 8 and the ½. I thought about 5/4 × 8½ as 1.25 × 8½.

Teacher: How did that help?

Larry: I found 1 × 8½ and then added that to a quarter of 8½. To find a quarter of 8½, I know ¼ × 8 = 2 and ¼ × ½ = ⅛.

Teacher: Does this model your thinking?

$$\tfrac{5}{4} \times 8\tfrac{1}{2} = 1\tfrac{1}{4} \times 8\tfrac{1}{4}$$
$$= (1 \times 8\tfrac{1}{2}) + (\tfrac{1}{4} \times 8\tfrac{1}{2})$$
$$= 8\tfrac{1}{2} + (\tfrac{1}{4} \times 8) + (\tfrac{1}{4} \times \tfrac{1}{2})$$
$$= 8\tfrac{1}{2} + 2 + \tfrac{1}{8}$$
$$= 10\tfrac{5}{8}$$

Teacher: Great. Let's talk about the next one, 1 ⅓ pizzas. The 1 pizza isn't hard, right? Tell me about your thinking for ⅓ of a pizza.

Marcus: I didn't do it this way, but I am thinking now that you could think about a third of a fourth, that's $\frac{1}{12}$. So ⅓ of $\frac{5}{4}$ must be 5 times that, $\frac{5}{12}$.

Teacher: Cool. Then what's $\frac{5}{4}$, the amount of cheese for 1 pizza, and $\frac{5}{12}$, the amount of cheese for ⅓ of a pizza?

Kyle: I think about it like $\frac{15}{12}$ and $\frac{5}{12}$, that's $\frac{20}{12}$ or $\frac{5}{3}$.

Teacher: Let's talk about all three of these — what equations are you writing? Let's see: $\frac{5}{4} \times 4 = 1$, $\frac{5}{4} \times 8\frac{1}{2} = 10\frac{5}{8}$, $\frac{5}{4} \times 1\frac{1}{3} = 1\frac{2}{3}$. Is the same relationship happening in the last problem?

Jose: No, because this time you're asking for the number of pizzas. The other ones are asking for the amount of cheese.

Maria: This one is division, how many $\frac{5}{4}$ are in $5\frac{1}{4}$? So $5\frac{1}{4} \div \frac{5}{4}$.

Martin: Instead of working up in the ratio table until you have the correct numbers of pizzas, this time you're working up to get the correct amount of cheese, so I think about it like $\frac{5}{4} \times \underline{\quad} = 5$.

Teacher: Either one of those work. Can everyone see how they are related? How did you find the number of pizzas for 5¼ cups of cheese? Elizabeth and Samantha, will you both please bring your papers up here and we'll compare your strategies?

		4 + 1	
pizzas	1	4	5
cheese (c.)	⁵⁄₄	5	6 ¼

5 + 5/4

			÷ 2 →	
pizzas	1	10	5	
cheese (c.)	⁵⁄₄	12.5	6 ¼	

÷ 2

Teacher: Who can explain these two strategies?

Multiplication/Division Workout 40

Name _____

It takes ⅔ cup of sauce to make Sarah's all-meat pizza. Use the ratio tables to find out how many cups of sauce are needed for different numbers of pizzas.

1. 3 pizzas

Sauce (C)	⅔					
Pizzas	1					

It takes _____ cups of sauce to make 3 pizzas. 3 × ⅔ = _____

2. ³⁄₂ pizzas

Sauce (C)	⅔					
Pizzas	1					

It takes _____ cups of sauce to make ³⁄₂ pizzas. Write an equation: _____

3. ¾ pizza

Sauce (C)	⅔					
Pizzas	1					

It takes _____ cups of sauce to make ¾ pizza. Write an equation: _____

4. How many pizzas can you make with 1⅓ cups of sauce?

Sauce (C)	⅔					
Pizzas	1					

You can make _____ pizzas with 1⅓ cups of sauce. Write an equation: _____

Multiplication/Division Workout 41   Name _____

The school club is making posters to advertise the upcoming fundraiser. From $\frac{5}{6}$ of a bottle of yellow paint, they were able to make $\frac{1}{6}$ of a poster. How much paint do they need for a whole poster so they can plan how much paint to buy?

1. Clarence thought, "The number of posters ($\frac{1}{6}$) times the rate (paint per poster) is the amount of paint ($\frac{5}{6}$ of a bottle)." So, $\frac{1}{6} \times$ _____ $= \frac{5}{6}$. Fill in the ratio table to show a way that could solve the problem.

1						
$\frac{1}{6}$						

So, $\frac{1}{6}$ times _____ is $\frac{5}{6}$. $\frac{5}{6} \div \frac{1}{6} =$ _____

2. Ruth thought, "We need to find the amount of paint per poster, so I'll find an equivalent amount of yellow paint for 1 poster."

Yellow paint (bottle)	$\frac{5}{6}$					
Poster	$\frac{1}{6}$	1				

The ratio of $\frac{5}{6}$ of a bottle of paint to $\frac{1}{6}$ of a poster is equivalent to _____ bottles of paint per poster. $\frac{5}{6} \div \frac{1}{6} =$ _____

3. They made $\frac{2}{5}$ of a poster with $\frac{4}{5}$ of a bottle of orange paint. Fill in the table with a strategy like Ruth's. Complete the strategy below.

Orange paint (bottle)	$\frac{4}{5}$					
Poster	$\frac{2}{5}$	1				

The ratio of $\frac{4}{5}$ of a bottle of orange paint to $\frac{2}{5}$ of a poster is equivalent to _____ bottles of orange paint per poster. $\frac{4}{5} \div \frac{2}{5} =$ _____

4. If a student solved the problem using a strategy similar to Clarence's, where $\frac{2}{5} \times$ _____ $= \frac{4}{5}$, fill in the table.

$\frac{2}{5}$						
1						

So, $\frac{2}{5}$ times _____ is $\frac{4}{5}$. $\frac{4}{5} \div \frac{2}{5} =$ _____

Sample Dialog from Multiplication/Division Workout 41

Teacher:	OK, so what is going on in this scenario? Something about posters?
Melinda:	They need to know how much paint to buy so they make posters with the leftover paint to see how many they can make.
Teacher:	How many can they make?
Melinda:	Not even a whole one. They made ⅙ of a poster from ⅚ of a bottle.
Teacher:	How is Clarence thinking about this problem?
Val:	He is trying to find the rate of yellow paint per poster by finding the missing factor.
Steve:	Yeah, I don't get that. Why multiplication?
Val:	If you know how much paint you need per poster, then you can multiply that by the paint you have to get the number of posters. But he doesn't have that. He needs to find it.
Steve:	Ah, so that is why he puts the ⅙ in the ratio table. He is multiplying up by ⅙ with the goal of multiplying to ⅚?
Val:	Yes, though I wonder if, really, once he knew he was thinking about ⅙ times what is ⅚, if he just knew that ⅙ times 5 is ⅚ without really doing any work.

So, ⅙ × __5__ = ⅚.

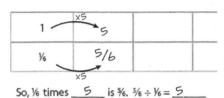

So, ⅙ times __5__ is ⅚. ⅚ ÷ ⅙ = __5__

Steve:	That makes sense. But it was easier for me to understand the second strategy, Ruth's. She is just simplifying the ratio to get to a ratio of paint to 1 poster — that's the rate she's looking for.
Teacher:	Once she set up that ratio of ⅚ to ⅙, how do you think she found the unit ratio?
Peter:	She's trying to get to a ratio of paint per 1 poster, right? So to get from ⅙ to 1, you multiply by 6. It's like we've been talking about in the other fraction multiplication workouts, that $1/b$ times b is 1.
Teacher:	And so if you multiply the ⅙ by 6, you multiply the ⅚ by 6 also? I'll write that down.

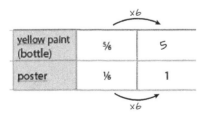

Teacher:	Now they've got orange paint. How does that change the story?
Patricia:	They were able to make more of a poster with less paint. It took ⅘ of a bottle of orange paint to make ⅖ of a poster.
Teacher:	So how might Ruth find the amount of paint for 1 whole poster? Martin?

Martin:	To simplify that ratio, first I multiplied both of the fractions by 5 and that gave me a 4 to 2 ratio and that's just 2.
Norma:	I just looked at the ratio of 4 fifths to 2 fifths. That's like the ratio of 4 things to 2 things—it's just 2 to 1, which is what we wanted 2 bottles of orange paint to 1 poster. Those must be small bottles.
Teacher:	And what about the last strategy? What is Clarence thinking here?
Frank:	He's going to multiply up from ⅖ to ⅘. And that's pretty easy, just 2.

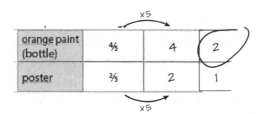 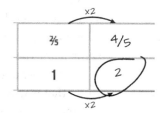

Frank:	This almost seemed too easy. Did I miss something?
Teacher:	We are setting the stage for some more complicated fractions. Today we looked at ⅚ ÷ ⅙ and ⅘ ÷ ⅖. Those are pretty easy when you are thinking about them. In the next few Workouts, we'll apply the same ideas with some less friendly problems. What made today's problems so friendly?
Frank:	In each of the problems, both numbers had the same denominator.
Sue:	And it was easy to divide the numerators. Five divided by 1 and 4 divided by 2.

Multiplication/Division Workout 42   Name _____

Wendell is washing windows. He is able to wash ¼ of the windows on the building with ⅔ of a bottle of glass cleaner. How much glass cleaner does he need to wash all the windows?

1. Callie thought, "The part of the building (¼) times the rate (bottles of cleaner per building) is the amount of cleaner (⅔ of a bottle)." So ¼ × _____ = ⅔. Fill in the ratio table to show a way that could solve the problem.

1						
¼						

So, ¼ times _____ is ⅔. ⅔ ÷ ¼ = _____

2. Randy thought, "We need to find the amount of cleaner per building, so I'll find an equivalent amount of cleaner for 1 building."

Glass cleaner (bottle)	⅔					
Building	¼	1				

The ratio of ⅔ of a bottle of cleaner to ¼ of a building is equivalent to _____ bottles of cleaner per building. ⅔ ÷ ¼ = _____

3. Wendell washed ¾ of a building with ⅖ of a bottle of cleaner. Fill in the table with a strategy like Randy's. Complete the strategy below.

Glass cleaner (bottle)	⅖					
Building	¾	1				

The ratio of ⅖ of a bottle of cleaner to ¾ of a building is equivalent to _____ bottles of cleaner per building. ⅖ ÷ ¾ = _____

4. If a student solved the problem using a strategy similar to Callie, where ¾ × ____ = ⅖, fill in the table.

¾						
1						

So, ¾ times _____ is ⅖. ⅖ ÷ ¾ = _____

To find $6/7 \div 2/7$, Macie thought about $2/7 \times$ _____ $= 6/7$.

1.

1						
$2/7$	$6/7$					

$6/7 \div 2/7 =$ _____

To find $6/7 \div 2/7$, Carter thought about equivalent ratios.

2.

$6/7$						
$2/7$						

$6/7 \div 2/7 =$ _____

Which of the strategies, Macie's multiplying up or Carter's equivalent ratios, do you prefer for this problem?

To find $7/9 \div 11/21$, Nariko thought about $11/21 \times$ _____ $= 7/9$.

3.

1						
$11/21$	1	$7/9$				

$7/9 \div 11/21 =$ _____

To find $7/9 \div 11/21$, Michelle thought about equivalent ratios.

3.

$7/9$						
$11/21$	11	1				

$7/9 \div 11/21 =$ _____

Which of the strategies, Nariko's multiplying up or Michelle's equivalent ratios, do you prefer for this problem?

Multiplication/Division Workout 44

Name _____

Solve these division problems:

1. $\frac{3}{5} \div \frac{3}{10}$

Describe your strategy:

2. $\frac{1}{5} \div \frac{5}{2}$

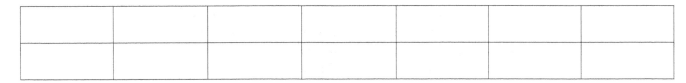

Describe your strategy:

3. $\frac{2}{5} \div \frac{3}{4}$

Describe your strategy:

4. $\frac{3}{9} \div \frac{1}{9}$

Describe your strategy:

5. What makes a divisor a "nice divisor" to use the equivalent ratio strategy?

Sample Dialog from Multiplication/Division Workout 44

Teacher: How did you solve the first problem, $\frac{3}{5} \div \frac{3}{10}$?

Kyle: Since it's fifth and tenths, I thought about $\frac{6}{10} \div \frac{3}{10}$. That's easy. It's just like 6 ÷ 3 and that's 2.

Teacher: What do the rest of you think?

Natalie: I found an equivalent ratio and it wasn't too bad, but I think that $\frac{6}{10} \div \frac{3}{10}$ is easier.

Teacher: Let's talk about the second problem, $\frac{1}{5} \div \frac{5}{2}$.

Christina: I couldn't think of a nice way to do this one so I set up a ratio. Since I want a divisor of 1, I multiplied both fractions by $\frac{2}{5}$. That got me 2 /25 divided by 1, so the answer is $\frac{2}{25}$.

Henry: Why did you multiply by $\frac{2}{5}$?

Christina: When you set up the ratio, you want to find an equivalent ratio so that the bottom fraction is 1, then it's just whatever the numerator is divided by 1.

Henry: OK, but why did you multiply by $\frac{2}{5}$?

Rob: I think I can help. I multiplied first by 2 so that the $\frac{5}{2}$ became 5. Then the $\frac{1}{5}$ is now $\frac{2}{5}$.

$^{x2}\nearrow$			
1/5	2/5		
5/2	5		
	$\underset{x2}{\nearrow}$		

Rob: Now, to make the 5 into a 1, you divide both of them by 5. Does that make sense? Christina multiplied by $\frac{2}{5}$ and I did the same thing but a part at a time, first multiply by 2 and then by $\frac{1}{5}$.

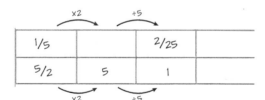 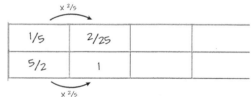

Henry: OK, I get it. Can you always do that? Multiply by the fraction by itself upside down?

Teacher: We call that the reciprocal. The reciprocal of $\frac{5}{2}$ is $\frac{2}{5}$. That's a great question, Henry. Does that always work? What do you all think? *The name of the reciprocal is social knowledge, decided by convention, and it is appropriate for the teacher to tag the concept with the correct vocabulary term. This is in contrast to logical-mathematical knowledge, which needs to be constructed.*

Christina: Yes, it always works. When you multiply by a fraction's reciprocal you get a 1.

Craig:	Yeah, it's like it undoes the fraction. The reciprocal divides the numerator by itself and multiplies the denominator by itself, so you just get 1.
Henry:	And you want to do that because then you do the same thing to the other fraction . . .
Teacher:	To the dividend . . .
Henry:	Yeah, the dividend and so then that result divided by 1 is just the answer to the problem. OK.
Teacher:	Nicely said. How about problem 3, ⅖ divided by ¾? Could you do something similar?
Henry:	Let's see. So, multiply both the ⅖ and ¾ by, um, 4/3. That gets 8/15 divided by 1. Cool. So the answer is just 8/15.
Teacher:	Great work. Did anyone do anything different for that problem?
Ky:	No, nothing hit me as any quicker.
Teacher:	What about problem 4, 3/9 divided by 1/9? Samantha?
Samantha:	You can just think about it. It's like 3 things divided by 1 thing. Three divided by 1 is just 3. So it's just 3.
Teacher:	Henry, would the reciprocal strategy work here?
Henry:	Let's see. You want to get a 1 in the divisor, so you'd multiply both fractions by 9. That leaves 3 divided by 1. Yep, it's 3. It works, but I think Samantha's strategy is more efficient for these numbers.
Teacher:	What is it about these numbers that makes Samantha's strategy more efficient? *The teacher takes this opportunity to help students generalize when to use a strategy, what relationships lend themselves to the strategy.*
Craig:	The two fractions, the 3/9 and 1/9, have the same denominator, so you can just think about the 3 divided by 1.
Christina:	Yeah, if the denominators are the same, then you can just think through the problem.

Solve these division problems:

1. ⁶/₅ ÷ ³/₆

Describe your strategy:

2. ⁹/₆ ÷ ⅓

Describe your strategy:

3. ⁷/₃ ÷ ⅖

Describe your strategy:

4. ³/₂ ÷ ⁵/₆

Describe your strategy:

5. What makes a problem nice to use the equivalent ratio strategy? What makes a problem nice to use a multiplying up strategy?

Student Workouts for Proportions and Percents

There are twenty-five Student Workouts for proportions and percents: fifteen for solving proportions and ten for solving percent problems. The fifteen proportion Workouts are all solved in ratio tables: five are with whole number, non-unit ratios where the ratio is given and students find many other equivalent ratios, five with less friendly non-unit ratios, and five where students solve proportions choosing to use *within* or *between* relationships. The percent problems are solved using percent bars: five where students find the percent of a number and five where the unknown varies. Each is a five- to ten-minute activity to be completed by individual students or student pairs and then discussed as a class.

Here are some general questions to have handy:

Clarifying Questions

- ► What is the question asking?
- ► What is the given information?
- ► Where does that given information go in the ratio table? On the percent bar?
- ► How can you fill in the blanks?

Scaffolding Questions

- ► How would you verbalize the strategy shown on this ratio table? The percent bar?
- ► How does that strategy differ from this one?
- ► So you're trying to get from 2 to 5, can you get close and then work on what's left?
- ► You are using this ratio to work up to the missing number. Could you try the other ratio in the proportion?

▸ Can you multiply or divide this percent by something to get a factor of the number you're trying for?

Focusing on "Which Ratio Are You Using?"

▸ What are the different ratios you could use?

▸ Why choose that ratio? Is there an obvious or nice place to go from here?

▸ Would another ratio be more friendly?

▸ What is the proportion you are solving?

Class Discussion Questions

▸ Why start with this ratio/percent?

▸ How could you figure out part of your goal? Is that reasonable?

▸ Looking at this strategy, can you see any other relationships that would work?

▸ What about these numbers make these strategies work?

Comparing strategies

▸ Which strategy seems more efficient? Why?

▸ Which strategy seems easier to do mentally?

▸ Which strategy seems more sophisticated or clever?

▸ What about the numbers makes that strategy your favorite for this problem?

▸ How might you change the numbers so that a different strategy would fit better?

The Strategies and Models Used in the Proportions and Percents Workouts

The model for solving proportions is the ratio table, where students reason proportionally using equivalent ratios. The model for solving percent problems is the percent bar, where students reason proportionally using percents (a percentage is a ratio of a number to 100).

The proportion Workouts and strings use the same strategies found in the multiplication/division chapter (Chapter 3) with the added consideration of which ratio in the proportion to use, the *within* or the *between*.

Choosing the *Within* or the *Between* Ratio

This strategy involves deciding which relationships to build from in a proportion. In the triangles shown in Figure 4.1, two different and equivalent proportions can be written:

FIGURE 4.1

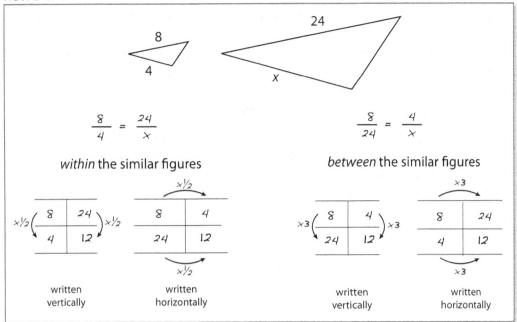

For this problem, using either relationship is arguably easy. Students can use the *within* relationship that 4 is half 8 so the missing length must be half of 24, which is therefore 12. Students can also use the *between* relationship and reason that 8 times 3 is 24 so 4 times 3 is 12. In the Workouts, we write all the ratios in horizontal ratio tables for print purposes.

When solving different proportions, it may be advantageous to choose one relationship over the others. For example, the problem in Figure 4.2 can be solved by using either relationship shown. Which do you find easier to use?

FIGURE 4.2

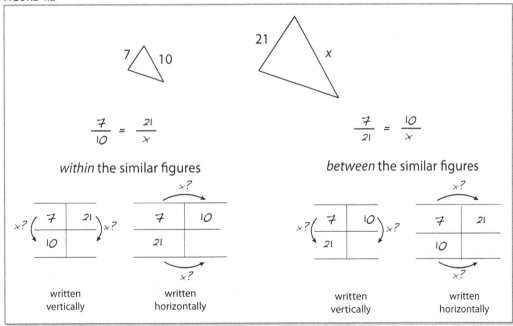

Choosing which proportion to solve based on the relationships of the numbers takes some experience. The Workouts give students experience discussing and comparing both options.

In solving proportion problems, sometimes the strategy of finding the unit rate is helpful and sometimes it is more helpful to use the non-unit rate.

Finding the Unit Rate and Scaling

When solving proportional situations, sometimes it can be helpful to find the unit rate and then scale up or down to find the desired equivalent ratio. For example, given the problem of finding the cost for 2 pounds of nachos when the price for 1.2 pounds is $8.40, it is helpful to find the unit rate, which is the price for 1 pound, and then double to get the price for 2 pounds (Figure 4.3).

FIGURE 4.3

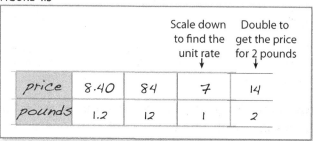

Finding the unit rate can be accomplished by either finding equivalent ratios or by multiplying up (see the division strategies in Chapter 3).

Using the Non-unit Rate

Other times when solving proportional situations, it can be helpful to use the non-unit rate. For example, given the problem of finding the cost for 4.8 pounds of nachos when the price for 1.2 pounds is $8.40, it is helpful to scale up from the non-unit rate, not finding the unit rate at all (Figure 4.4).

FIGURE 4.4

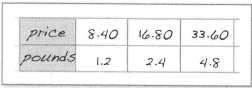

Chunking Percents

When finding the percent of a number, find friendly percents and add them together. To find the friendly percents, take advantage of all of the multiplication strategies such as over and under, using fractions, and so on. For example, to find 49% of 28, find 50% and 1% and then find the corresponding 50% − 1%. So 50% of 28 is 14 and 1% of 28 is 0.28. So 49% is 14 − 0.28 = 13.72 (Figure 4.5).

FIGURE 4.5
To find 49% of 28:

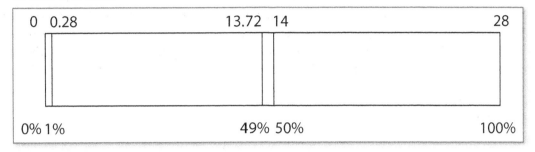

Using the Commutative Property (Swapping the Start and the Percent)

When given the starting number and the percent, it can be helpful to swap them when finding the result. This is because a% of b is equivalent to b% of a. For example, it is easier to find 50% of 72 than 72% of 50, and they both yield the result of 36.

Finding a Friendly Factor of the Given

When given a problem like "36 is 45% of what number?" it can be helpful to find a friendly common factor of the given (in this case, 36) and the percent that, when divided into the percent, results in a new percent that is a factor of 100. In this case, since 45 is not a factor of 100, we search to divide both the 45 and the 36 by something that results in a percent that is a factor of 100. So, divide both by 9 (common factor of both 36 and 45) to get corresponding values of 4 and 5%. Since 5% is a factor of 100, multiply both the 4 and the 5% by 20 and therefore 30 is 15% of 200 (Figure 4.6).

FIGURE 4.6
To find 36 is 45% of _____:

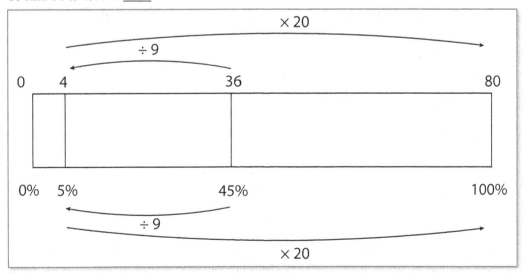

When given a starting number and a result and asked to find the percentage, it can be helpful to find a common factor of the result and 100 such that after dividing the result by the factor, you have a factor of the starting number. For example, to find the percent that 36 is of 45, put them both on the percent bar and find a common factor of 45 and 100%, like 5. Divide the 45 and 100 by 5 to get the corresponding results of 9 and 20%. Multiply the 9 and 20% by 4 to get to the 36 and it's corresponding answer of 80% (Figure 4.7).

FIGURE 4.7

To find 36 is _____% of 45:

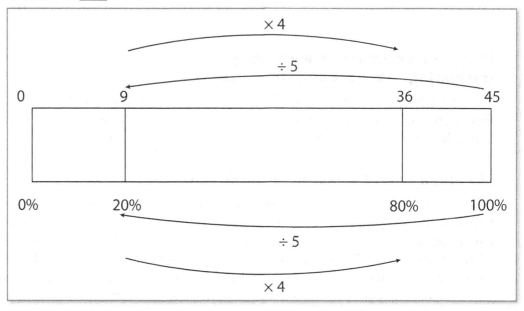

The Progression

Proportions, Non-unit Ratios: Workouts 1 Through 5

The first set of five Workouts uses non-unit ratios, such as pears costing $8 for 5 pounds, to have students find the cost for weights and lengths of various items for different money amounts. The beginning non-unit ratios use all whole numbers: 8:5, 3:4, 2:3, 4:5, 2:5. Students use these ratios to solve proportions involving decimals. For example, Find the feet of ribbon Craig can buy for $63.75 if the ribbon costs $5 for 4 feet. In effect, students solve the proportion 63.75:x = 5:4.

Proportions, Non-unit Ratios: Workouts 6 Through 10:

The second set of five Workouts uses less friendly non-unit ratios: 300:16, 301:14, 3.5:1.25, 5.5:2.2, 1.2:8.4. Students solve problems given contexts such as miles per gallon and finding the cost of food given sample prices (not unit rates). For example, Henry bought bulk peanut butter and the tag reports he spent $3.50 for 1.25 pounds. Students find the cost of different amounts of peanut butter and the different amounts he could buy for certain costs.

Proportions, Similar Triangles, and Decontextualized Proportions: Workouts 11 Through 15

The third set uses similar triangles and decontextualized proportions to ask students to consider all the ratios in the proportion, within and between, in order to choose the one that works the best for the particular numbers.

Percent Problems: Workouts 16 Through 20

In the fourth set, students are given the start number and the percent and asked to fill in the blanks and analyze strategies for finding the result. The last problem of Workout 18 sets up the use of the commutative property seen in Workouts 19 and 20, where students fill in blanks to solve the same problem four different ways and compare strategies.

Percent Problems: Workouts 21 Through 25

The fifth set asks students to find either the starting number or the percent. Students fill in the blanks, using common factors to work up and down in the percent bar to find the unknown.

Proportions/Percents Workout 1

Name _____

Pears are on sale for 5 pounds for $8.00. Use the following ratio tables to find out how many pounds of pears you can buy for different amounts of money.

1. 10 pounds and 1 pound

Price	$8					
Pounds of pears	5					

10 pounds cost _____. 1 pound costs _____.

2. 3 pounds and 20 pounds

Price	$8					
Pounds of pears	5					

3 pounds cost _____. 20 pounds cost _____.

3. How many pounds can you buy for $2? For $1? Use the following ratio table to determine how many pounds of pears you can buy.

Price	$8					
Pounds of pears	5					

You can buy _____ pounds for $2. You can buy _____ pounds for $1.

4. Saul has $41.60. Use the following ratio table to determine how many pounds of pears he can buy.

Price	$8					
Pounds of pears	5					

Saul can buy _____ pounds of pears for $41.60.

Sample Dialog from Proportion/Percents Workout 1

Teacher: Pears, anyone? We've done many Workouts like this one before, right? Anything different here?

Pete: I think they have all been just 1 box that had things in it or 1 bag or 1 package. This is 5 pounds for $8.

Meredith: But you can do the same kinds of things, right? I mean, you can still double the price and double the pounds and the ratio stays the same.

Teacher: I hear you saying that the previous scenarios have dealt with unit ratios, where one of the numbers is 1. And that the same rules apply here. If you double the pounds of pears, it will cost twice as much. So, let's talk about your strategies for finding the cost for 10 pounds and 1 pound. I am curious; how many of you found the cost for 10 pounds first?

Sal: Ten pounds were really easy to find. Just double the 5 pounds and so double the $8 to $16.

Teacher: Did anyone find the cost for 10 pounds a different way? No? OK. How did you find the cost for 1 pound?

Sal: I started thinking about dividing by 5 to get 1 pound. So then I need to divide $8 by 5. I know that's at least 1. Now I've got $3 divided by 5. I thought about 30 divided by 5 and that's 6, so 300 cents divided by 5 is 60 cents. So, 0.6.

Pete: When I divide by 5, I divide by 10 first and then multiply by 2. So 8 divided by 10 is 0.8 and times 2 is 1.6.

Teacher: I'll write that down. Now why can Pete divide by 10 and then multiply by 2 when what he wants is to divide by 5?

Sarah: Two divided by 10 is ⅕ and that's what you're doing, 8 divided by 5 is like 8 times ⅕.

Joe: I get the same result but I just find an equivalent fraction by doubling both the 8 and 5 to get ¹⁶⁄₁₀, which is $1.60 a pound.

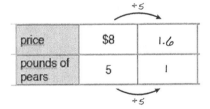

price	$8	1.6
pounds of pears	5	1

$8/5 = 5/5 + 3/5 = 1 + 0.6 = 1.6$

$8/5 = 8/10 \times 2 = 0.8 \times 2 = 1.6$ because $8 \times (1/5) = 8 \times (2/10)$

or $8/5 = 16/10 = 1.6$

Teacher: Nice ways of thinking about 8 divided by 5. But some of you didn't find the cost for 1 pound of pears that way.

Zach: I found the price for 10 pounds first. That's $16 for 10 pounds by just doubling. And it's actually what Joe did to find the price for one pound. When he found the equivalent ratio of $16 per 10 pounds he found the 10 pounds and then the 1 pound.

Ralph: So, to find the price for 1 pound, find the 10 pounds first and then just shift the place value. I'll try that next time.

Teacher: Good work. For the second problem, both 3 pounds and 20 pounds seemed pretty easy. Craig, tell us quickly what you did.

Craig:	I noticed that we needed 20 and 3 pounds so I decided to get 2 first. I doubled $1.60 and that's $3.20. There's 2 pounds. Now I can either add 1 more pound to get 3 pounds for $4.80 or scale up by 10 to get 20 pounds for $32.00.
Teacher:	Now the third problem — how many pounds can you buy for $2 or $1? How did you do that?
Ralph:	I halved to get $4 for 2.5 pounds and then $2 for 1.25 pounds and then $1 for 0.625 pounds.
Craig:	I started to find 5 pounds divided by $8 so I would get the pounds per dollar rate. But then I noticed I could do what Ralph did.
Teacher:	That's the hallmark of numeracy! Weighing different options and choosing the one that feels the most efficient or sophisticated. Nice.

The teacher wants students to understand that it is not about always knowing the best strategy off the bat, but it is choosing relationships that work best for the numbers in the particular problem.

Teacher:	What about the last problem?
Hank:	I looked at what we already had. Twenty pounds cost $32.00. So I added $8 to get $40 and we already decided the price for 1 pound was $1.60, so 25 + 1 = 26 pounds.
Teacher:	And Sheri, what did you do? *The teacher asks for another strategy, hoping to find one that is less dependent on previous relationships explored on the page and easier to find if students found this problem without any helpers.*
Sheri:	I know that $8 times 5 is 40 so that just leaves $1.60 and, so 25 + 1 = 26 pounds.

price	$8	32	40	1.16	41.6
pounds of pears	5	20	25	1	26

price	$8	40	1.16	41.6
pounds of pears	5	25	1	26

Teacher:	That is great use of the fact 8 times 5. Nice big chunk. What would a proportion look like for this last problem?
Zach:	Eight to 5 equals 41.5 to *x*.

$$\frac{8}{5} = \frac{41.5}{x}$$

Teacher:	So, I wonder: if you were just asked to solve this proportion, could you set it up in a ratio table and use the same relationships? *Students need to be able to work from a word problem like the one given in this Workout, but they also need to be able to work problems that have no context. By modeling the problem as a proportion and calling attention to it, the teacher hopes students make connections between the word problems and the proportion representation.*

Proportions/Percents Workout 2

Name _____

The price for bulk pretzels is $3 for 4 pounds. Use the following ratio tables to find out how much different amounts of pretzels cost.

1. 10 pounds and 1 pound

Price	$3					
Pounds of pretzels	4					

10 pounds cost _____. 1 pound costs _____.

2. 9 pounds

Price	$3					
Pounds of pretzels	4					

9 pounds cost _____.

3. How many pounds of pretzels can you buy for a dollar?

Price	$3					
Pounds of pretzels	4					

You can buy _____ pounds for a dollar.

4. Abigail has $39. Craig has $42. Use the following ratio table to determine how many pounds of pretzels each can buy.

Price	$3					
Pounds of pretzels	4					

Abigail can buy _____ and Craig can buy _____ pounds of pretzels.

Proportions/Percents Workout 3

Name _____

Maribel found 2 pounds of mixed nuts for $3. Use the following ratio tables to find the cost for differer amounts of mixed nuts.

1. 10 pounds and 1 pound

Pounds of mixed nuts					
Price					

10 pounds cost _____. 1 pound costs _____.

2. 9 pounds and 4 pounds

9 pounds cost _____. 4 pounds cost _____.

3. How many pounds of mixed nuts can you buy for a dollar?

You can buy _____ pounds for a dollar.

4. Kristin has $22.50. Anna has $28.50. Use the following ratio table to determine how many pounds of mixed nuts each can buy.

Kristin can buy _____ and Anna can buy _____ pounds of mixed nuts.

Proportions/Percents Workout 4

Name _____

Sheila can buy 4 feet of ribbon for $5. Use the following ratio tables to find out how much different lengths of ribbon cost. Label the ratio tables.

1. 10 feet and 1 foot

10 feet cost _____. 1 foot costs _____.

2. 9 feet and 5 feet

9 feet cost _____. 5 feet cost _____.

3. How many feet of ribbon can you buy for $1?

You can buy _____ feet for $1.

4. Abigail has $61.25. Craig has $63.75. Use the following ratio table to determine how many feet of ribbon each can buy.

Abigail can buy _____ and Craig can buy _____ feet of ribbon.

Proportions/Percents Workout 5

Name _____

The price is $2 for 5 pounds of watermelon. Use the following ratio tables to find out how much different amounts of watermelon cost.

1. 9 pounds

      9 pounds cost _____.

2. 3 pounds

      3 pounds cost _____.

3. How many pounds of watermelon can you buy for $1.60?

      You can buy _____ pounds for $1.60.

4. Abigail spent $19.60. Craig spent $42.40. Use the following ratio table to determine how many pounds of watermelon each bought.

      Abigail bought _____ and Craig bought _____ pounds of watermelon.

Sample Dialog from Proportion/Percents Workout 5

Teacher: What proportion did you solve for problem 1, finding the price for 9 pounds? And how did you do it?

Stuart: Two to 5 is equal to x to 9. I thought that 9 is close to 10 and 10 is easy to find from 5, just double. So 10 pounds cost $4. Then I found the price for 1 pound by dividing $2 by 5. I thought about 200 cents divided by 5, that's 40 cents, so $2 divided by 5 is 0.4. Then 10 pounds minus 1 pound is 9 pounds, so $4 minus 40 cents is $3.60.

Mary: Once you had that 10 pounds cost $4, I just did a place-value shift to find 1 pound by dividing both by 10.

Stuart: Oh, right, that would've worked. That didn't occur to me. I didn't even see the connection between $4 and 40 cents until right now. Well, I will next time. I'll be looking for it.

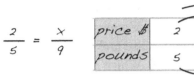
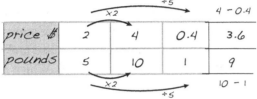
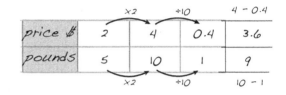

Teacher: So, even though this workout didn't ask you to find 10 pounds and 1 pound, you did anyway because they were both helpful in this problem. Great. Let's talk about problem 2, finding the cost for 3 pounds.

Ben: Since we already have 9 pounds, we could divide $3.60 by 3, that's $1.20.

Martha: Or we already have the price for 1 pound, $0.40, so multiply by 3 to get the $1.20.

Teacher: Do you think that either of those strategies would always work when given a ratio and you're trying to get from 5 to 3?

Yasmine: What do you mean?

Teacher: This ratio is $2 for 5 pounds and we are trying to get from the 5 pounds to 3 pounds. What if the ratio was different? Could you still use Ben's find 9 and divide by 3 strategy or Martha's find 1 and multiply by 3 strategy?

Mary: Yes, you could use either. I suppose it would depend on the numbers which one I would try.

Teacher: Say more about that.

Mary: Let's see, if it was easy to find the unit rate, then I'd find that and multiply by 3. If it wasn't, I might find 10, that's easy. Oh wait. Once I had 10, I could quickly have 1 and I'd be back to multiplying by 3. Humm . . .

Ben: Yeah, I wonder if the only time you would use the 9 to get to 3 is if we already had the 9 like we did here.

Teacher: That was a nice discussion of strategy. Let's talk about the third problem, finding the number of pounds that cost $1.60.

Darren: Since 1 pound is 40 cents, then 4 pounds would cost $1.60, so, 4 pounds.

Sally: I thought about the relationship between $1.60 and $2.00. That's like 0.8 to 1 or 80%. So then I wondered what was 80% of 5 and that's 4.

Teacher: I am going to model that in a ratio table. I think you are using the table a little differently that we have been. We have been considering the ratio of cost to pounds but you were looking at the ratio between the costs.

$$\frac{2}{5} = \frac{1.60}{x}$$

price $	2	0.40	1.60
pounds	5	1	(4)

$$\frac{1.60}{2} = \frac{x}{5}$$

1.60	0.8	8	(4)
2	1	10	5

Louise: That's kind of like some of the other proportions we solved in class, where you can look at the ratio between the costs to help and not just at the ratio between the price and the pounds.

Teacher: Do you think you can always do that?

Louise: Yes, and I am wondering if there are other proportions I have solved that might have been easier to solve if I had switched things around.

Teacher: Let's keep that strategy in mind — considering all the relationships before deciding which one to use. Take a couple of minutes and look at the last problem, finding the amount that cost $19.60 and $42.40. Which relationship do you want to use?

Proportions/Percents Workout 6

Name _____

Daniel filled up his tank and then drove 300 miles. When he filled up his tank, it took 16 gallons. How many miles per gallon is Daniel averaging?

1. Ted thought, "It took 16 gallons times the mileage rate to go 300 miles. So, 16 × ___ = 300." Fill in the ratio table to show a way that Ted might have solved the problem.

1						?
16						300

So, Daniel got _____ miles to the gallon. 300 ÷ 16 = _____

2. Gabriella thought, "That's 16 gallons for 300 miles. I'll use equivalent ratios." Fill in the ratio table to show a way that Gabriella might have solved the problem.

Miles	300					?
Gallons	16					1

16 miles per 300 gallons is _____ miles per gallon. So $\frac{300}{16} = \frac{\ldots}{1}$.

3. How many gallons does Daniel need to drive 450 miles? 75 miles?

450 miles takes _____ gallons. Write the proportion:

75 miles takes _____ gallons. Write the proportion:

4. How many miles can Daniel drive with 12 gallons?

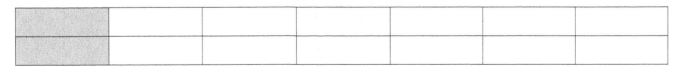

He can drive _____ miles with 12 gallons. Write the proportion:

Sample Dialog from Proportion/Percents Workout 6

Teacher: Take a brief look at this workout. What do you see?

Ralph: It looks like other division stuff we've done, with the two ways to divide, by multiplying or finding equivalent ratios.

Remi: Yeah, but I notice that further down the page are some proportions.

Teacher: Is this a proportional situation?

Pete: Yes, because the ratio is miles per gallon and they are talking about averages, so it's like finding a car's average mileage with different miles and gallons. They should all be equal.

Teacher: Would everyone please work on the first two problems and then we'll talk.

Students work.

Teacher: What were both of these problems asking you to find, just using different strategies?

Ephraim: The miles per gallon.

Ronda: The unit rate, how many miles per 1 gallon.

Teacher: I have noticed that often many of you find the unit rate first whenever given any kind of rate problem. That can be a good strategy. Work on the next problem and then we'll discuss.

Students work.

Teacher: How did you find how many gallons he needs to drive 450 miles? Did anyone use the unit rate of 18.75 miles per 1 gallon?

Sarah: I did. Since he is getting 18.75 miles per gallon, I multiplied 18.75 until I got 450. I started with 18.75 times 10, then doubled that to get 20, which is 375. I still needed 75 more, so I found 2 from the 20 by a place-value shift to 37.5, then doubled to get 4, which is 75, and then added the 20 and the 4 together to get 450 miles with 24 gallons. Whew!

miles	18.75	187.5	375	37.5	75	450
gallon	1	10	20	2	4	24

Teacher: Did anyone use the non-unit rate we were given, 300 miles per 16 gallons?

Mike: Yes, I noticed that the 450 was just 1 and a half three hundreds. So, I cut the 300 in half to get 150 miles for 8 gallons, and then added them together. That's 450 miles for 24 gallons.

miles	300	150	450
gallon	16	8	24

Teacher: Wow! That was efficient. Turn to the person next to you and talk about these two different approaches, using the unit rate and using the non-unit rate.

Students talk to a partner. The teacher knows that there are moments of disequilibrium that can be capitalized on by having students say out loud what they are thinking and work out their noticings.

Teacher:	What do you think? Can Mike do that? Why or why not?
Ephraim:	I wish I would have thought of that! Yes, he can because he is using an equivalent ratio.
Sarah:	Yeah, wow. That is certainly faster. I'm thinking about the next one, the 75 miles . . .
Teacher:	Before you say anything about the 75 miles, let's let everyone think about it. In fact, go ahead and finish the rest of the problems and then we'll talk. *The teacher wants to give everyone a chance to consider the implications for the rest of the problems.*

Students work.

Teacher:	What did you find for these particular numbers, unit rate or the non-unit rate of 300 to 16?
Harvey:	Non-unit rate all the way!
Teacher:	Anyone disagree? Agree?
Jessica:	I agree. All the numbers in those problems were too nice to do anything else.
Rachel:	Yeah, the numbers were easy to get from either the 300 or the 16.
Teacher:	So, what is a message that these problems are sending?
Mike:	Look to the numbers first before you decide to find and use the unit rate. The non-unit rate might be easier.

Proportions/Percents Workout 7

Name _____

Theo filled up his tank and then drove 301 miles. When he filled up his tank, it took 14 gallons. How many miles per gallon is Theo averaging?

1. Ted thought, "It took 14 gallons times the mileage rate to go 301 miles. So, 14 × ___ = 301." Fill in the ratio table to show a way that Ted might have solved the problem.

1						301
16						?

So, Theo got _____ miles to the gallon.

2. Gabriella thought, "That's 14 gallons for 301 miles. I'll use equivalent ratios." Fill in the ratio table to show a way that Gabriella might have solved the problem.

Miles	301					?
Gallons	14					1

14 miles per 301 gallons is _____ miles per gallon. So $\frac{301}{14} = \frac{......}{1}$.

3. How many gallons does Theo need to drive 602 miles? 75.25 miles?

602 miles takes _____ gallons. Write the proportion:

75.25 miles takes _____ gallons. Write the proportion:

4. How many miles can Theo drive with 7 gallons?

He can drive _____ miles with 7 gallons. Write the proportion:

Proportions/Percents Workout 8

Name _____

Henry bought peanut butter. When he got home, he noticed that the tag said that he paid $3.50 for 1.25 pounds of peanut butter. Use the following ratio tables to find the cost for different amounts of peanut butter.

1. 5 pounds

5 pounds cost _____. Write the proportion:

2. 15 pounds, 30 pounds

15 pounds cost _____. Write the proportion:

30 pounds cost _____. Write the proportion:

3. How much peanut butter can you buy for $1.75?

You can buy _____ pounds of peanut butter. Write the proportion:

4. Rick bought some of the same peanut butter. His tag said $10.50. How many pounds of peanut butter did he buy?

Rick bought _____ pounds of peanut butter. Write the proportion:

Proportions/Percents Workout 9

Name _____

Sylvia likes gummy candy. She bought some and saw that the tag said she paid $5.50 for 2.2 pounds of candy. Use the following ratio tables to find the cost for different amounts of candy.

1. 22 pounds

 22 pounds cost _____. Write the proportion:

2. 1 pound, 5 pounds

 1 pound costs _____. Write the proportion:

 5 pounds cost _____. Write the proportion:

3. How much candy can you buy for $1.25?

 You can buy _____ pounds of candy. Write the proportion:

4. Here is a proportion that represents a question in this candy scenario.
   What problem does it represent?
   Find the answer.

$$\frac{5.50}{2.2} = \frac{18.50}{x}$$

Proportions/Percents Workout 10

Name _____

Nachos at the concessions stand sell by the pound. Naomi bought 1.2 pounds for $8.40. Use the following ratio tables to find the cost for different amounts of nachos.

1. 5 pounds

5 pounds cost _____. Write the proportion:

2. 2 pounds, 2.4 pounds

2 pounds cost _____. Write the proportion:

2.4 pounds cost _____. Write the proportion:

3. How many pounds of nachos can you buy for $50.40?

You can buy _____ pounds of nachos. Write the proportion:

4. Here is a proportion that represents a question in this nachos scenario.
    What problem does it represent?
    Find the answer.

$$\frac{1.2}{8.40} = \frac{x}{33.60}$$

Sample Dialog from Proportion/Percents Workout 10

Teacher: You've had a chance to work on these. Let's share some strategies. Ross, kick us off.

Ross: For number 1, I tried a bunch of things, but I ended up using equivalent ratios. So 8.4 to 1.2 is equal to 84 to 12 and that's 42 to 6 and 42 divided by 6 is 7. So, it's $7 for 1 pound.

Shannon: Whoa, what did you do?

Teacher: Let me represent those ratios you were talking about.

$$\frac{8.40}{1.2} = \frac{84}{12} = \frac{42}{6} = \frac{7}{1}$$

Shannon: Ah, that helps to see the 7 to 1, so it's $7 per 1 pound. OK. But weren't you supposed to find 5 pounds?

Ross: Yes, so $7 times 5 pounds is $35.

Shannon: And now that you have the unit rate, you can find the cost for 2 pounds, that's 14. I didn't need the unit rate to find the cost for 2.4 pounds.

Teacher: Tell us about that.

Shannon: I just scaled up the 1.2 pounds for $8.40 by doubling and got that 2.4 pounds cost $16.80.

Teacher: So, we have two problems here, finding the cost for 2 pounds and 2.4 pounds and you each used different strategies. What did you do to find 2 pounds versus the 2.4 pounds?

Jennifer: For the 2 pounds, we used the unit rate, doubled the unit rate of 7. For the 2.4 pounds, we could just double the given non-unit rate, double the 8.4.

Teacher: Why? What is it about the numbers that would have you use the unit rate on one of them and the non-unit rate on the other? Turn and talk to your partner about that.

Students talk in partners.

Teacher: Before we share out about that, let's talk about the last two problems. First, finding the amount of nachos for $50.40. Sherry?

Sherry: I used the non-unit rate of 8.40 to 1.2. I know that 5 times 8 is 40, so I found that 5 times 8.4 is 42. Then I just had $8.40 left, which is another 1.2 pounds. And 6 pounds and 1.2 pounds is 7.2 pounds.

Mark: I used both the non-unit rate and the unit rate of $7 per pound. Since 7 times 6 is 42, I still needed 8.40 more. I knew that to get $8.40 more, I needed 1.2 pounds, so I added them to get $50.40 for 7.2 pounds.

Teacher: And what proportion did you write?

Sherry: 8.4 to 1.2 equals 50.40 to x.

Teacher: And for the last problem, what's your thinking? First, tell us what you think the problem is.

Ava: It was a little weird that the first ratio looks upside down to me, but then I figured that as long as the ratios were equal, it was OK. So the problem is, if 1.2 pounds cost $8.40, how many pounds can you buy for $33.60?

Mark: I agree. I solved it using the 1.2 to 8.4. I know that 8 times 4 is 32 so I checked to see what 8.4 times 4 is, and it's 33.6. So, 4 pounds.

Ava: I kind of did the same thing, except I doubled to get 2.4 pounds for $16.80. Then I doubled again to get 4.8 pounds for $33.60. I think, Mark, that you forgot to multiply the 1.2 times 4, you just left it at 4.

Mark: Ah! Sure enough. Got it.

Teacher: Great work today!

Proportions/Percents Workout 11

Name _____

1. Given 2 similar triangles, find *a*:

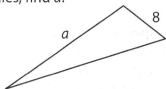 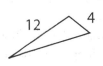

Kyle's strategy:

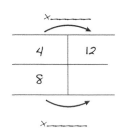

Kayla's strategy:

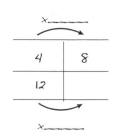

Clark's strategy:

Since the 4 is half
of 8, then 12 is
half of _____.

2. Given 2 similar triangles, find *a*:

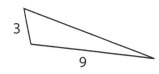 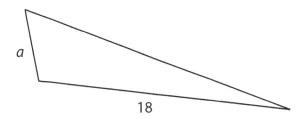

Kyle's strategy:

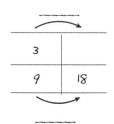

Kayla's strategy:

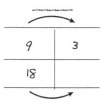

Clark's strategy:

I know that 9 is half
of 18 and 3 is half of
_____.

3. Given 2 similar triangles, find *a*:

 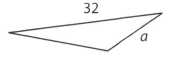

Show the relationships you used to find *a*:

Proportions/Percents Workout 12

Name _____

1. Given 2 similar triangles, find *n*:

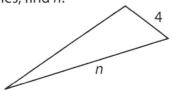 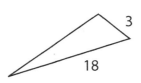

Andy's strategy:

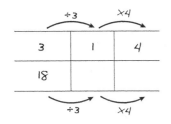

Anne's strategy:

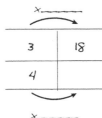

Allison's strategy:

Since the 3 is 75% of 4, the 18 must be 75% of something. There are three 6's in 18 and four 6's in _____. So the answer is _____.

2. Given 2 similar triangles, find *n*:

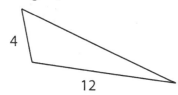 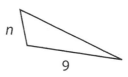

Andy's strategy:

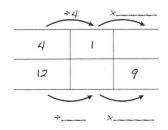

Anne's strategy:

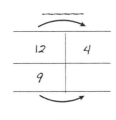

Allison's strategy:

I know that 4 is 1/3 of 12, so the n must be 1/3 of 9. And 1/3 of 9 is _____. So the answer is _____.

3. Given 2 similar triangles, find *n*:

 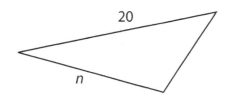

Proportions/Percents Workout 13

Name _____

1. Given 2 similar triangles, find *b*:

 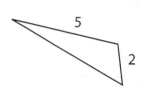

Mark's strategy:

2	1	3
5		

Mary's strategy:

2	1		5
3	6		

Molly's strategy:

Since the 3 is 1 1/2 of
2, then b must be 1 1/2
of 5. Half of 5 is 2.5,
so, 1.5 of 5 is _____.
So the answer is _____.

2. Given 2 similar triangles, find *n*:

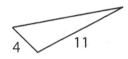 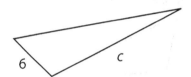

Mark's strategy:

4	2	6
11		

Mary's strategy:

4		2	1	11
6	18			

Molly's strategy:

I know that 4 is 2/3 of
6, so 11 has to be 2/3 of
something. Half of 11 is 5.5,
so 3 x 5.5 is _____.
So the answer is _____.

3. Given 2 similar triangles, find *n*:

 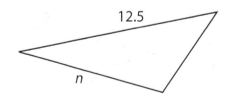

Sample Dialog from Proportion/Percents Workout 13

Teacher: What did you think about this Workout?

Angel: None of these numbers were very nice. You couldn't just look at it to solve them, you had to do some work.

Raymond: In the last two Workouts, the triangles had side lengths that were either double or half or triple or something. These were not as nicely related. But they weren't too bad.

Teacher: Talk to me about the first one. Bethany?

Bethany: It looks to me like both Mark and Mary were about getting to a 1 and then scaling back up to what they needed.

Mike: Whether you start with the ratio in the triangle of 2 to 5 or between the triangles of 2 to 3, either way, they went from the 2 to a 1. Mark had to divide 5 in half and Mary had to divide 3 in half. Then they both scaled up to what they needed. Mark needed 3 so he multiplied by 3. Mary needed 5 so she multiplied by 5.

Angel: Even though they started with different ratios in the proportion, they used the same kind of strategy to find a ratio to 1 and then scale up.

Raymond: Molly's strategy is more like using a non-unit ratio. The ratio between 3 and 2 is 1 to 1 and a half. So the ratio between the missing side and 5 also has to be 1 to 1 and a half.

Teacher: Would it work to model Molly's strategy this way?

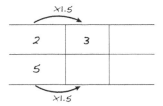

Bethany: Yes, that helps me see what Molly was thinking. It's like asking, "What is 1 and a half of 5?"

Teacher: So, which of these strategies did you like best for this problem?

Bethany: Now that I get Molly's, I think I like it. It seems the most direct.

Teacher: Is Molly's using a within triangles ratio or a between triangles ratio?

Raymond: It's between the 2 triangles. It's the ratio of 2 on the one triangle to 3 on the other.

Teacher: Did Mark and Mary do the same, get to a ratio of 1 strategy, on the second problem?

Mike: No, Mark was going from 4 to 6 so he just halved the 4 to get 2 and then added them together.

Jessica: Mary did. She was building from 4 to 11, so she tripled to get 12 to 18. So she needed 1 less to go from 12 to 11. So she halved and halved to find the ratio 1 to 1.5.

Teacher: Let's look at Molly's strategy for problem 2. Who thinks they could model her strategy in a ratio table?

Harvey: I think I can. She knows that to go from 6 to 4, it's $\frac{2}{3}$, so to go from the unknown to 11, it also has to be $\frac{2}{3}$.

Raymond: I thought about it from 4 to 6, that's 1 and a half again. So the unknown has to be 1 and a half of 11, that's 16.5.

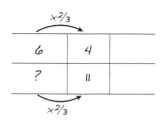 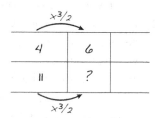

Teacher: Wonderful thinking. Now we are going to share strategies for the last problem, where there are no sample strategies given, just the 2 triangles. What relationships did you use?

Rachel: I thought about 4 to 5 as 80%. So I needed to find 80% of 12.5. So, 10% is 1.25, 20% is 2.5, 40% is 5, and 80% is 10.

Mark: I also thought about getting from 5 to 4. So I started with the ratio of 5 to 12.5 in a ratio table with the goal of multiplying to get the 5 to 4. I divided both by 5 to get the ratio of 1 to 2.5. Then I scaled up by 4 to get to the ratio of 4 to 10.

Amaia: I decided to start with the ratio of 5 to 4 and work the 5 up to 12.5. So, I doubled 5 and got the ratio of 8 to 10. Then half of 5 gives the ratio of 2 to 2.5. Add those together and you get 10.

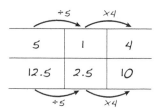

÷5	×4			×2		10 + 2.5
5	1	4		5	10	2.5	12.5
12.5	2.5	10		4	8	2	10
÷5	×4			×2		8 + 2

Teacher: Which strategy do you like the best?

Proportions/Percents Workout 14

Name _____

Solve the proportions:

1.
$$\frac{4}{6} \quad \frac{x}{21}$$
x = _____

2.
$$\frac{a}{24} \quad \frac{5}{20}$$
a = _____

3.
$$\frac{8}{36} \quad \frac{10}{b}$$
b = _____

4.
$$\frac{c}{5} \quad \frac{93}{6}$$
c = _____

Sample Dialog from Proportion/Percents Workout 14

Teacher: What relationship did you use for the first problem?

Amaia: I looked at getting from 6 to 21. Six times 3 is 18 and then half again is 21. So 4 times 3 is 12 and half again is 14. Four is to 6 as 14 is to 21.

Matthew: I know that 4 to 6 is the same as 2 to 3. There are three sevens in 21, so I'm looking for a number with two sevens, that's 14.

Abigail: I thought about getting the 6 to the 4 so I set up the ratio 6 to 21 and worked from the 6. One-third of 6 is 2, and ⅓ of 21 is 7. Now just double to get 4 to 14 and the answer's 14.

4	12	2	14
6	18	3	21

4	2	14
6	3	21

6	2	4
21	7	14

Teacher: Nice strategies. Does anyone have any questions? No? Which strategy, now that you can look at all of these relationships, do you like the best and why?

Travis: I like Matt's, thinking of the ratio 2 to 3 and seeing the three 7s in 21. That feels clever to me.

Allie: Yes, I don't know if that will always be so obvious, but here it is so you might as well use it.

Travis: To make that work though, you have to be able to think about 4 to 6 as 2 to 3 and see the three 7s in 21. Interesting.

Teacher: Excellent point. I wonder if knowing that 21 is divisible by 3 helps? Let's share strategies with the next problem. What relationships did you capitalize on?

Travis: I found that one easy. Five to 20 is just times 4. So a must be 6 because 6 times 4 is 24.

Amaia: You could also look at the 20 to 24 as the ratio of 5 to 6. Then you've answered the question, a must be 6.

Allie: How did you know that 20 to 24 is equal to 5 to 6?

Amaia: Because there are five 4s in 20 and six 4s in 24.

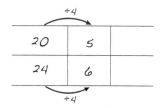

Teacher: Thank you for explaining. Let's talk about the third problem.

Abigail: Nothing jumped out at me so I decided to simplify the 8 to 36. That is 2 to 9. Now multiply 2 by 5 to get 10, so multiply 9 by 5 to get 45.

Travis: I kind of did the same thing as Abigail, but I simplified the 8 to 10 and got 4 to 5. Then you scale up by 9 and I also got 45.

Heather: I also used the 8 to 10 but scaled up by 4 to get 32 to 40. I still needed 4 to get from the 32 to 36, so that's half of the 8 to 10, which is 4 to 5. Add the 40 to the 5 and I got 45 also.

8	2	10
36	9	45

8	4	36
10	5	45

8	32	4
10	40	5

Teacher: Excellent reasoning. The last problem?

Jeremy: Nothing jumped out at me, so I decided to work from 6 to 5. To get from 6 to 5, I found 2, then 1, then ½, and then doubled 2½.

Susanne: Couldn't you just have doubled the 2 and added the 1, instead of finding the ½?

Jeremy: Oh, man! Yes, I could've. Nice catch, Susanne.

Susanne: Well, I wish I would've done it that way. I started with 6 to 5 and worked the 6 up to 93. First 6 to 60 and 50, half that to 30 and 25, add those together to 90 and 75. Then I just needed 3 more. I can get that from the 30 by dividing by 10 to get 3 and 2.5. Add those together to get 93 and 77.5.

6	2	1	½	2½	5
93	31	15.5	7.75	38.75	77.5

6	2	1	4	5
93	31	15.5	62	77.5

6	60	30	90	3	93
5	50	25	75	2.5	77.5

Teacher: Which of these do you like the best?

Trevor: I like the one that Jeremy started and Susanne finished! Nice team work!

Travis: Yeah, to go from 6 to 5 by finding 2, doubling to 4 and adding 1. I guess that works well if finding the 2 is easy.

Teacher: What do you mean?

Travis: Finding 2 from 6 means you divide by 3. Dividing 93 by 3 was easy. Other numbers might not be so easy, like 92. But it worked here.

Proportions/Percents Workout 15

Name _____

Solve the proportions:

1.

$$\frac{4}{5} \bigg| \frac{10}{x} \qquad x = \underline{\hspace{2cm}}$$

2.

$$\frac{a}{8} \bigg| \frac{6}{15} \qquad a = \underline{\hspace{2cm}}$$

3.

$$\frac{7}{b} \bigg| \frac{6}{9} \qquad b = \underline{\hspace{2cm}}$$

4.

$$\frac{c}{10.5} \bigg| \frac{5.5}{16.5} \qquad c = \underline{\hspace{2cm}}$$

Proportions/Percents Workout 16

Name _____

Fill in the blanks to find 91% of 60, _____.

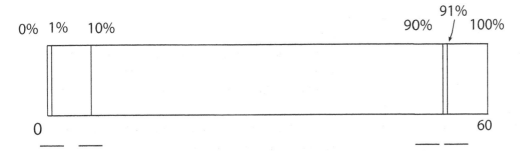

Fill in the blanks to find 12.5% of 60, _____.

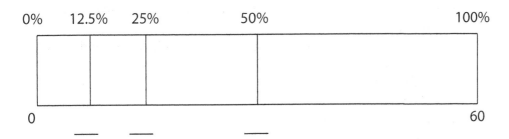

Fill in the blanks to find 125% of 60, _____.

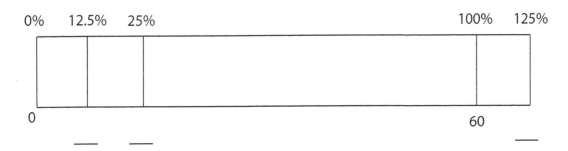

Show how you could find 40% of 60, _____.

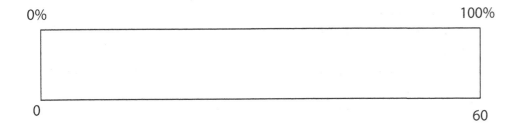

Sample Dialog from Proportion/Percents Workout 16

Teacher:	We have been doing some problem strings with percents and percent bars. What is going on in this Workout?
Martin:	I think they all have to do with 60.
Bailey:	Yeah, they are finding percents of 60.
Teacher:	The directions are to fill in the blanks to see how these students found these percents. Do you think you are going to fill in the blanks in order?
Hannah:	No, because look at the second one. I bet you don't know 12.5% of 60 right off the bat, but you do know 50%.
Teacher:	Does that make sense? If you can't figure out what goes in a blank, you might need to look at the other blanks on that percent bar. Then maybe the ones you have filled in will help you with the others.

Students work.

Teacher:	How do you think the student found 91% of 60?
Noe:	I think they found 10% first because that's easy, 6. Then 1% is 0.6. Now you can subtract 10% from 100% to get 90% and 60 minus 6 is 54. Now you add the 1% to get 91%, that's 54 plus 0.6 — 54.6!
Teacher:	People agree with Noe? Disagree? Everyone agrees? OK, how about the next one, 12.5% of 60?
Iralda:	Easy, just find 50%, which is 30, cut that in half for 25%, 15. In half again makes 12.5% and that is 7.5.
Teacher:	What do you think, everyone? These are pretty easy so far, right? What about 125% of 60?
Sebastian:	For a minute, I thought that there were just some extra things hanging around in this one. Why would you need 25% and 12.5%? Then I tried to figure out how they found 125% and I realized that they used the 12.5% and scaled up by 10.
Julio:	What do you mean?
Sebastian:	If you know 12.5% is 7.5, then you can multiply them both by 10 and get 125% is 75.
Julio:	Oh, I see how you could do that. I just used the 25% that is 15 and added it to the 100% of 60 and I also got that 125% of 60 is 75.
Teacher:	Nice thinking, both of you! Let's share some strategies for the last problem, finding 40% of 60. What were you thinking?
Joel:	I know 50%, 30, and 10%, 6. So 40% is 50% minus 10% and that means 30 minus 6. So it's 24.
Teacher:	Did everyone follow that? Yes? Other thinking?
Kyle:	I also found 10% of 60 is 6, so just times 4 to get 40%, that's 24.
Teacher:	So you both used 10%, Joel by going a bit over with 50% and subtracting 10% and Kyle by multiplying 10% by 4. What else?
Itzel:	I also used 10% but I doubled to get 20% and that's 12, then double to get 40% and double 12 is 24.
Teacher:	That 10% is pretty handy! What else might 10% be really handy in finding for other problems?
Danielle:	It's easy to find 1% from 10%, just divide by 10.

Reagan: You can also find 5% by cutting it in half.

Arlene: So then you would have 15% by adding the 10% and the 5% together.

Teacher: This Workout was pretty straightforward. Now that we have the format down, I wonder if we can use what we learned to solve more difficult problems in the next Workouts.

Fill in the blanks to find 42% of 24, _____.

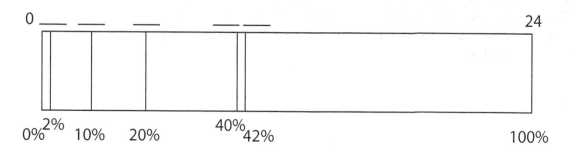

0 ___ ___ ___ ___ ___   24

0% 2% 10%   20%   40% 42%   100%

Fill in the blanks to find 49% of 24, _____.

1%
0%   10%   49% 50%   100%

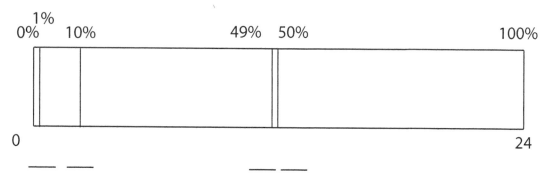

0   24

___ ___   ___ ___

Fill in the blanks to find 130% of 24, _____.

0%   10% 20%   100%   120%

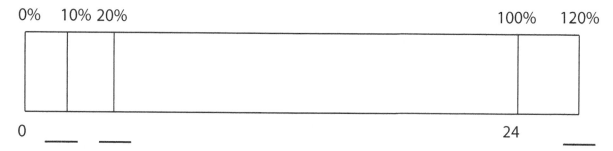

0   ___   ___   24   ___

Show your strategy for finding 90% of 24. 90% of 24 is _____.

0%

0   24

Proportions/Percents Workout 18

Name _____

Fill in the blanks to find 95% of 36, _____.

0 ___ ___   ___ 36

0% 5% 10%   95% 100%

Fill in the blanks to find 33% of 36, _____.

0% 3% 10%   20%   30% 33%   100%

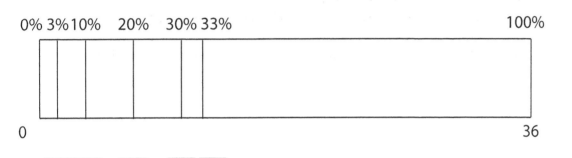

0   36

___ ___ ___   ___ ___

Fill in the blanks to find 78% of 36, _____.

0% 3%   50%   _____% 78%   100%

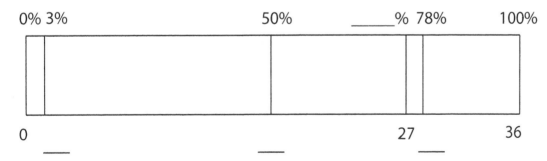

0 ___   ___   ___   27   36

___   ___   ___

Show your strategy for finding 36% of 78. 36% of 78 is _____.

0%   100%

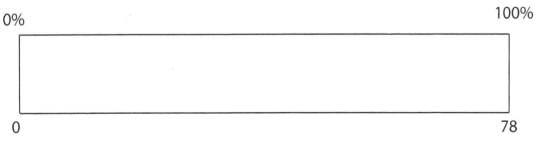

0   78

Sample Dialog from Proportion/Percents Workout 18

Teacher: On this Workout, I want to ask you about the last two problems. Some of you were wondering if the last problem was an error. No, it's the question I wanted you to answer. What answers did you get for the third problem and the last problem?

Chloe: Let's see, for number 3, I got 28.08 and for the last one I got . . . humm . . . it looks like I got the same thing, 28.08. I hadn't noticed that. Did I goof?

Teacher: Did Chloe goof? Did anyone else get those results, the same results? *The teacher intends to capitalize on the students' disequilibrium.*

Most of the students raise their hands.

Teacher: That's weird. What an interesting coincidence. What was the third problem?

Marcus: What is 78% of 36?

Teacher: And the last problem?

Marcus: What is 36% of 78? They just switch the numbers?

Teacher: What is Marcus talking about?

Jane: The numbers are just swapped. That's odd. I wonder if that happens all of the time.

Teacher: That is a great wonder. I wonder too. Let's keep our eyes out for that.

Proportions/Percents Workout 19

Name _____

Four students found 66% of 20. Fill in the blanks and figure out the relationships each student used to solve the problem. What is 66% of 20? _____

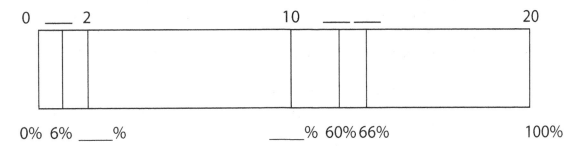

0 ___ 2   10 ___ ___   20

0% 6% ____%   ____% 60% 66%   100%

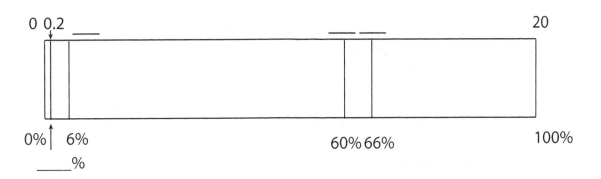

0 0.2 ___   ___ ___   20

0% 6%   60% 66%   100%

____%

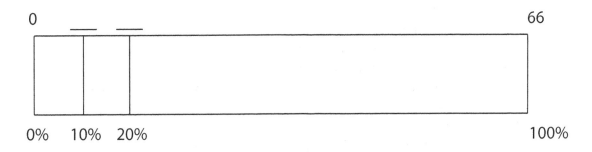

0   ___ ___   66

0%   10%   20%   100%

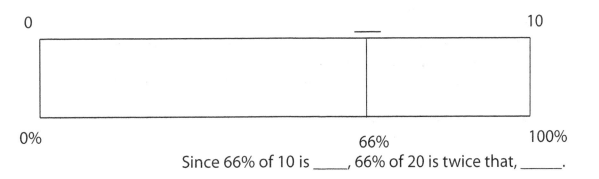

0   ___   10

0%   66%   100%

Since 66% of 10 is ____, 66% of 20 is twice that, _____.

©2014 Pamela Weber Harris from *Lessons and Activities for Building Powerful Numeracy*. Portsmouth, NH: Heinemann.

Sample Dialog from Proportion/Percents Workout 19

Teacher: Now that you've all worked on this, let's talk about these strategies for finding 66% of 20, starting with the first one. Jack?

Jack: I think this person knew that 20 is 100% and worked from there. I am guessing they found the 2 first, that's 10%. From there, you can find the 10 by multiplying by 5, so that's 50%.

Molly: I see how you multiplied by 10, but I think you could just reason that 10 is half of 20, so 50%.

Jack: Sure enough! Now that you've got 10% and 50% you can get 60%, so that's 2 plus 10 is 12. Then you can figure the 6% by dividing by 10, so 12 divided by 10 is 1.2.

Teacher: Why do you think they found 6%?

Jack: Because they are looking for 66%. And now they have 60%, 12, and 6%, 1.2, so 66% is 13.2.

Kate: You found the 6% from the 60%? I was trying to find the 6% first so I could multiply by 10 to get the 60%. I get it.

Teacher: Good work. How about the second strategy, Kate?

Kate: Yes, this one made more sense to me. Find the 1%, that's 0.2. Then multiply that by 6 to get 1.2. Now you can get 60% by multiplying by 10, 12, and then add back the 6% of 1.2 to get 13.2.

Teacher: Now that you understand both the first two strategies, do you have a favorite? *It's not really about finding a favorite strategy. This question helps prompt students to generalize about the strategies as they compare them.*

Kate: It is easy for me to find 1% if I know the 100% so I usually do that. I had to multiply 1% of 20, 0.2, by 6 to get 6% and then I could scale up to get 60%. The first strategy added the 10% and the 50% to get the 60% and then scaled down to get the 6%. I don't know . . . I think they are both pretty similar and took about the same amount of steps.

Teacher: Anyone else?

Riley: I like the other two so much more that it's hard to care about the top two.

Teacher: Let's talk about the third strategy. Riley?

Riley: This is that switcheroo thing. Instead of finding 66% of 20, they found 20% of 66.

Teacher: How?

Riley: They found 10%, 6.6, and doubled it to 20%, 13.2.

Teacher: Why does that switching thing work?

Riley: We talked about it the other day when we did those problems that had the same answer.

Kate: It's the commutative property.

Brandon: Finding the percent of a number is like multiplication and in multiplication, you can switch the factors around.

Carter: It's like either 0.66 times 20 or 0.20 times 66. Either way you get the same answer.

Natalie: I really like that strategy, but I don't always think of it. Maybe after today, I'll start looking for that.

Teacher: It's a nice relationship that can come in handy, that's for sure. Would someone start us talking about the last strategy? Is that a typo? Why is the total 10? I thought we were looking for 66% of 20, not 10?

Courtney: I wondered about that at first. I started working with it and then figured out what this person was doing. I think it's like, if I can find 66% of 10, then I can double that to get 66% of 20.

Teacher: What is 66% of 10?

Courtney: It's just 6.6. I kind of thought about 66% of 100 — that's easy, just 66. So 66% of 10 is a place-value shift, 6.6.

Teacher: And now that you have 66% of 10?

Courtney: You can double that to get 66% of 20, 6.6 times 2 is 13.2.

Teacher: So, which of these do you think is the most clever?

Taylor: I really like the swapping one.

Teacher: Where you use the commutative property to come up with an easier problem?

Taylor: Yes, it is very easy to find 20% of anything — just 10% doubled.

Scott: Yeah, but that only works if the numbers are nice when you switch them.

Taylor: True, but they are nice in this problem.

Ashley: I like the bottom one. Finding a percent of 10 is pretty easy. Then you just double to get the percent of 20.

Teacher: Does that also depend on how nice the numbers are?

Ashley: Absolutely. If the number wasn't 10 or something nicer like 100, it wouldn't work.

Teacher: Great discussion, folks! Let's see if we can apply some of these strategies in our other work.

Proportions/Percents Workout 20

Name _____

Four students found 88% of 25. Fill in the blanks and figure out the relationships each student used to solve the problem. What is 88% of 25? _____

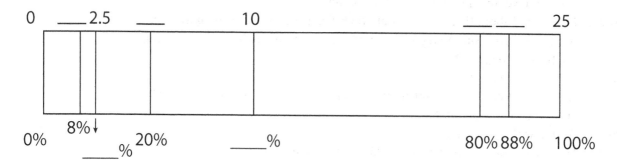

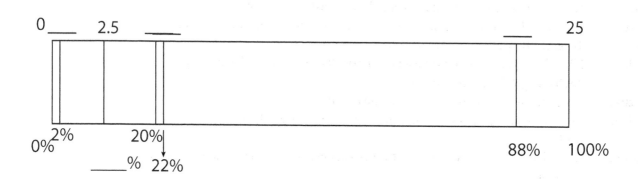

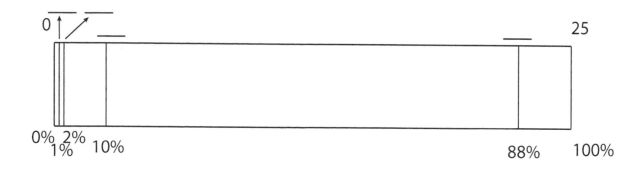

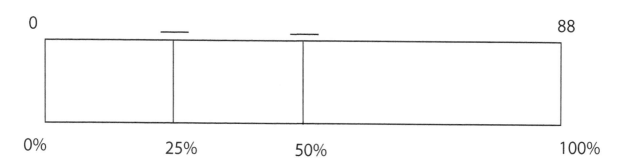

Proportions/Percents Workout 21

Name _____

Fill in the blanks to find: 22 is _____% of 40.

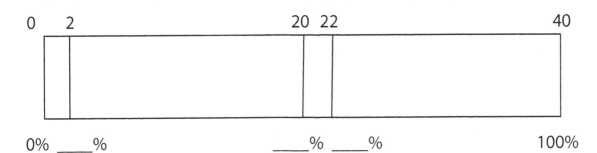

0   2   20 22   40

0% ____%   ____% ____%   100%

Fill in the blanks to find: 16 is _____% of 40.

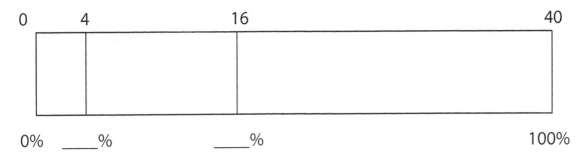

0   4   16   40

0%   ____%   ____%   100%

Fill in the blanks to find: _____% of 40 is 5.

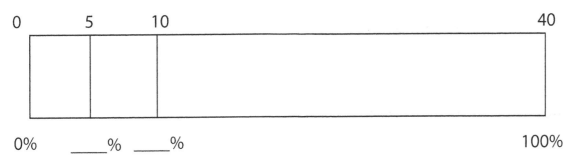

0   5   10   40

0%   ____% ____%   100%

Show your strategy for finding 34 is _____% of 40.

0   40

0%   100%

Proportions/Percents Workout 22   Name _____

1.   Three students found the percent that 16 is of 20. Fill in the blanks and figure out the relationships each student used to solve the problem. 16 is _____% of 20.

a.

| 0 | 4 | | 16 | 20 |

```
 0              4                          16        20
 ┌──────────┬──────────────────────────┬──────────┐
 │          │                          │          │
 │          │                          │          │
 └──────────┴──────────────────────────┴──────────┘
 0%         _____%                      _____%   100%
```

b.

```
 0    2                                  16        20
 ┌──┬───────────────────────────────┬──────────┐
 │  │                               │          │
 │  │                               │          │
 └──┴───────────────────────────────┴──────────┘
 0%   10%                             _____%   100%
```

c.   *I know that to find the percent, I can use*

          the ratio 16/20 = ____/10 = _____%

2.   Which strategy do prefer and why?

3.   Show your strategy for finding: 48 is _____% of 80.

```
 0                                                    80
 ┌──────────────────────────────────────────────────┐
 │                                                    │
 │                                                    │
 └──────────────────────────────────────────────────┘
 0%                                                 100%
```

Proportions/Percents Workout 23

Name _____

Three students solved a problem. Fill in the blanks. What problem were they all solving?

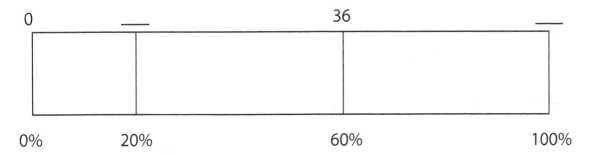

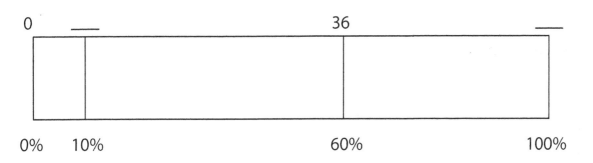

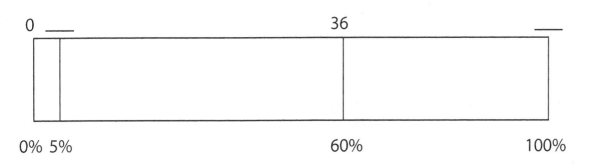

Proportions/Percents Workout 24   Name _____

Students solved different problems. Fill in the blanks. What problem did each solve?

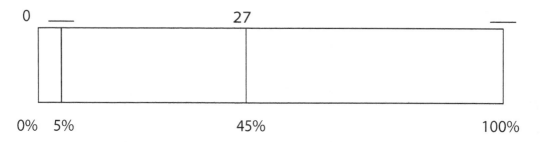

1. Write the problem and the answer:

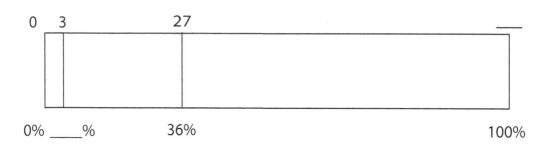

2. Write the problem and the answer:

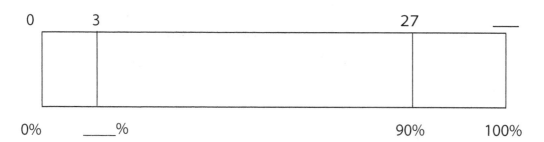

3. Write the problem and the answer:

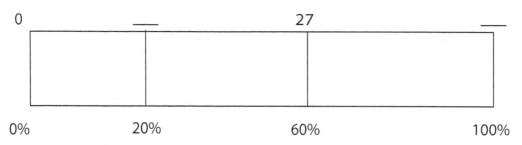

4. Write the problem and the answer:

Proportions/Percents Workout 25

Fill in the blanks. Show your thinking.

1. 51 is 60% of _____

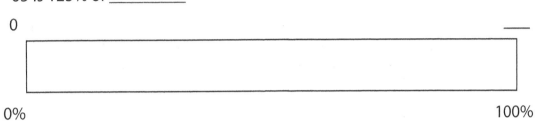

2. 65 is 125% of _____

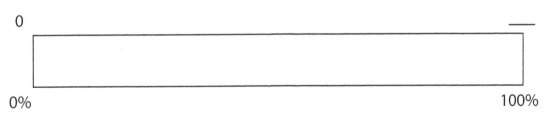

3. 15 is 30% of _____

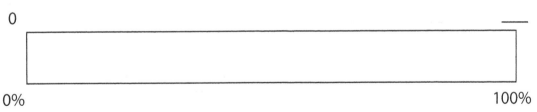

4. 81 is 45% of _____

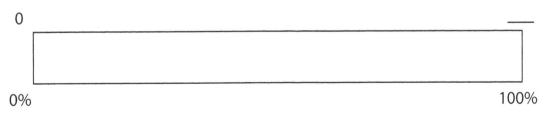

5. 18 is 40% of _____

Sample Dialog from Proportion/Percents Workout 25

Teacher: These problems were just wide open, right? Solve any way you want to. Let's hear about your strategies.

Cole: First, I always put the numbers down where I think they go. So, the 51 and the 60% are lined up with each other a little past the halfway point.

Teacher: Like this?

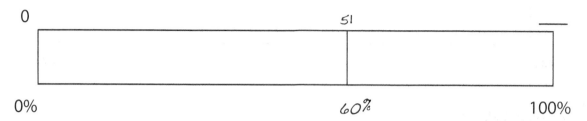

Cole: Yes. Then I need to get from the 51 to the missing total, so I think about how to get from 60 to 100. Since there is not an easy way, I look for factors of 60 that are also factors of 51. So, I divided them both by 3 to get 17 corresponding with 20%.

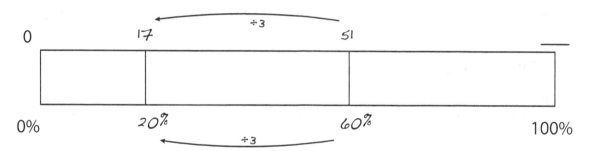

Cole: Now that I have 20%, I can get to 100% by multiplying by 5. So 17 times 5 is 85.

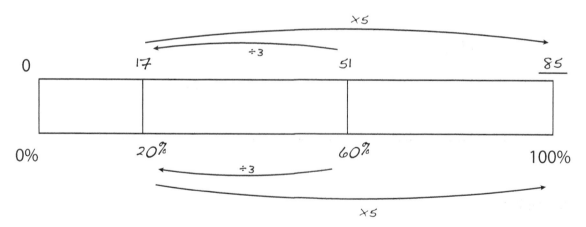

Teacher: Nice. Let's hear a strategy for the second problem, 65 is 125% of what?

Kaylene: I put the numbers on the percent bar but I had to extend the bar to be ¼ longer so I could show the 125%.

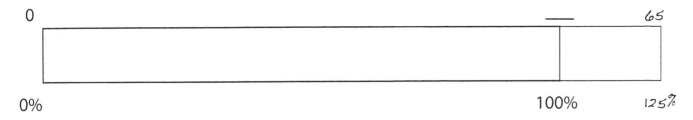

Kaylene: I didn't know how to get from 125% to 100%, so I divided both the 125% and the 65 by 5 to get 13 and 25%. Then I multiplied both by 4 because 25 times 4 is 100 and then 13 times 4 is 52.

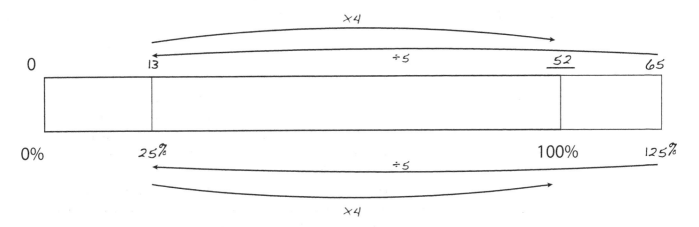

Teacher: Excellent. Let's talk about the third problem: 15 is 30% of what number?

Jackson: I put the 15 and the 30% on the percent bar. By estimating, I know that the answer is going to be a little more than 3 times 15, so more than 45. I don't know how to get 30% to 100%, so I scaled down by dividing both by 3 to get 5 and 10%. Then to get 10% to 100%, multiply by 10 and I got 50 is the 100%. And that's a bit more than 45 so I am confident that I got it.

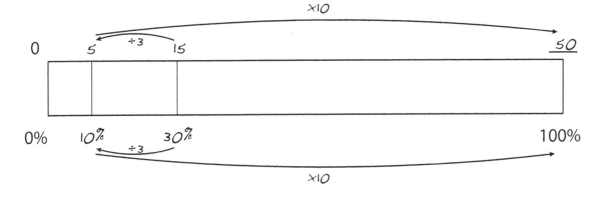

Teacher: Wonderful. Who will share their thinking for the fourth problem: 81 is 45% of what number?

Riley: After putting the 81 and the 45% on the percent bar, I looked for things I could divide the 45 by to get a number that would multiply up to 100%. I tried 9 and got 9 and 5%. Then I multiplied both of those by 20 and I got 180 and 100%. So 81 is 45% of 180.

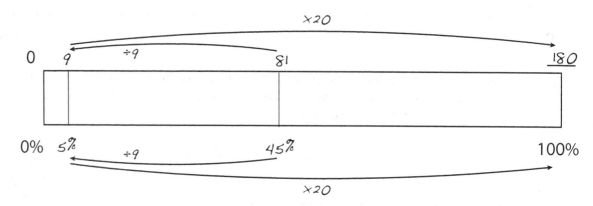

Teacher: It seems to me like you are all doing some similar things. Who can describe the thinking that is going on here? *The teacher knows that describing the reasoning is an opportunity for students to construct the relationships involved.*

Tucker: We are all trying to get to 100%. None of these problems' percents were factors of 100, so they didn't multiply to 100 nicely.

Jane: So we have to mess with them to find a factor of 100 by dividing both the number and the percent by the same thing to try to get to a factor of 100.

Tucker: Then we can multiply to 100 and as long as we do the same thing to the number and the percent, it works.

Teacher: Did someone do something similar on the last problem, finding 18 is 40% of some number?

Kate: Yes. I estimated where the numbers went on the percent bar and that helped me think that the answer would be a bit more than double the 18. I divided the 18 and 40% by 2 to get 9 and 20%. Then I multiplied them by 5 to get 45 and 100%.

Teacher: And is 45 a bit more than double 18?

Kate: Yes, double 18 is 36 so 45 is a bit more than that.

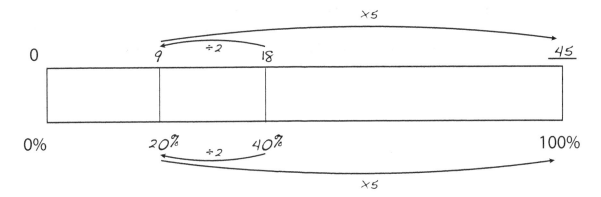

Teacher: Tell me about this pattern I am seeing in the arrows. What is going on with these arrows to the left and then arrows to the right?

Jack: The arrows to the left start with what you know and work to get a factor of 100 in the percent.

Kennedy: The arrows back to the right are the multiplication that takes you to the 100%. Then you have the total you are looking for.

Teacher: What question did all of these problems ask?

Molly: They gave you a number and a percent and you have to find the total.

Riley: They ask, this number is a certain percentage of an unknown number. Find the unknown number.

Teacher: What do you think you would do if you couldn't find a nice, friendly factor to divide by? *The teacher knows that not all problems will have nice, friendly factors. This nudges students to generalize for such cases.*

Tucker: You would have to find out how to get from the given percent to 100%. You could do that with division. Then you would multiply the given number by that factor.

Ann: Yes, divide the 100% by the number to find out the factor to get from the number to 100%. Then you have the factor. Just multiply it by the number you are given. That will give you the total.

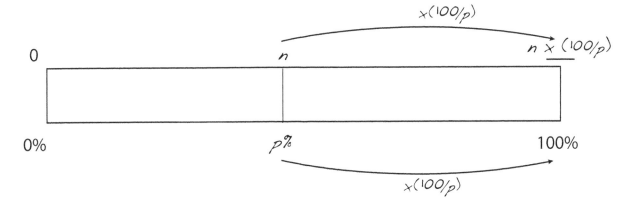

Teacher: Do you think you need to memorize that?

Jack: No, you can just think it through. Besides, most of the time, you can figure it out by scaling down and then scaling back up. The numbers have to be pretty ugly for you to need to do anything else.

Problem Strings

Addition

The strings for addition include the following strategies:

- ▶ Adding a Friendly Number (Leading to Decimals and Fractions)
- ▶ Get to a Friendly Number (Leading to Give and Take)
- ▶ Swapping
- ▶ Use Factoring to Add (Leading to Collecting Like Terms)
- ▶ Integer Addition

Adding a Friendly Number (Leading to Decimals and Fractions)

Use the adding a friendly number strings to build place-value concepts and students' ability to think about the values of the numbers, instead of performing a series of rote steps. These strings are constructed with paired problems in which the first problem sets up a friendly number for students to use with the next problem(s). Model the problems on open number lines to help students grapple with the numbers. For example, 10 is a friendly number in the problem 67 + 10. Then the next problem (67 + 14) builds from there. Since students already have 67 + 10 = 77, then they can just add 4 more, usually by adding 3 to get to 80 and then 1 for 81 (Figure 5.1). Similarly, 3.8 + 2 leads to 3.8 + 2.5 (as shown) and 8.48 + 0.2 leads to 8.48 + 0.23. For the last problem, which does not have an immediate helper problem, students may start with 8.48 + 0.3 and then tack on the 0.04.

67 + 10
67 + 14
378 + 100
378 + 130
3.8 + 2
3.8 + 2.5
8.48 + 0.2
8.48 + 0.23
8.48 + 0.34

FIGURE 5.1

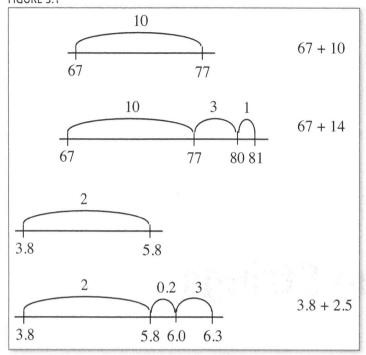

For whole numbers, the friendly numbers are often multiples of 10, 100, or 1,000. For decimals, the friendly numbers are often 1, 0.1, or 0.01. For fractions, the friendly numbers are often 1 and other whole numbers. In the first three strings, the addends in the second of the paired problems are just slightly over a friendly number. The second set of strings involves problems with addends that are just slightly under a friendly number, so students go over and adjust. (See the "Subtraction" strings section on page 223 for related subtraction strings.)

Add a Friendly Number That Is a Bit Under and Then Adjust		
$66 + 20$	$39 + 20$	$28 + 40$
$66 + 26$	$39 + 23$	$28 + 46$
$347 + 200$	$2,000 + 4,279$	$0.65 + 200$
$347 + 250$	$2,800 + 4,279$	$0.65 + 250$
$347 + 255$	$7.9 + 2$	$4\frac{2}{3} + 3$
$3\frac{4}{5} + 2$	$7.9 + 2.2$	$4\frac{2}{3} + 3\frac{2}{3}$
$3\frac{4}{5} + 2\frac{3}{5}$	$0.3 + 5.78$	$99\frac{2}{7} + 1$
$3\frac{4}{5} + 2\frac{1}{2}$	$5.78 + 0.36$	$99\frac{2}{7} + 1\frac{6}{7}$

Add a Friendly Number That Is a Bit Too Much and Then Adjust		
45 + 40	33 + 60	58 + 30
45 + 39	33 + 58	58 + 29
649 + 200	2,648 + 2,000	0.67 + 0.30
649 + 198	2,648 + 1,999	0.67 + 0.29
3.68 + 2	$4\frac{3}{5}$ + 3	42.74 + 30
3.68 + 1.99	$4\frac{3}{5}$ + $2\frac{4}{5}$	42.74 + 29.97
0.34 + 0.20	$11\frac{5}{8}$ + 4	$19\frac{3}{10}$ + 10
0.34 + 0.19	$11\frac{5}{8}$ + $3\frac{7}{8}$	$19\frac{3}{10}$ + $9\frac{9}{10}$

As before, model the problems on an open number line, as shown in Figure 5.2 for two of the fraction problems.

FIGURE 5.2

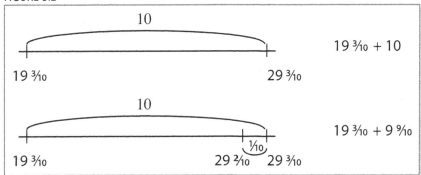

Get to a Friendly Number (Leading to Give and Take)

The get to a friendly number strings are designed to help students construct the strategy of keeping one addend whole and decomposing the other addend to get to a friendly number. Each problem stands alone with no helper problems. The problems deal with different magnitudes — tens, hundreds, thousands, tenths, hundredths, and fractions. Each time, students choose a friendly number for the particular magnitudes in the problem (such as choosing 100 as a friendly number for 99 + 67: students can take 1 from 67 to get 100 + 66, a simpler problem). This builds their sense of number space — nearness, neighborhood, between.

99 + 67
133 + 499
3,988 + 5,194
4.9 + 3.2
5.45 + 2.97
$9\frac{9}{10}$ + $4\frac{2}{5}$
$29\frac{7}{8}$ + $6\frac{1}{4}$

If students struggle to do anything more efficient than make many small jumps or use the traditional algorithm for every problem, consider starting with the get to a friendly number strings first. These strings consist of grouped problems where the first problem sets up the rest. The first problem of each group is easy and helps students construct the idea of getting to a friendly number as they get a feel for what a friendly number is.

As students begin to get to a friendly number and then make bigger and bigger jumps, they begin to give and take in concert. They give to one addend to get to a friendly number while simultaneously taking from the other addend. As more students do this, move to the give and take strings to give students experience giving and taking with many different magnitudes.

Model get to a friendly number strategies on a number line. You can model give and take strategies either on an open number line or with an equation, as shown in Figure 5.3.

FIGURE 5.3

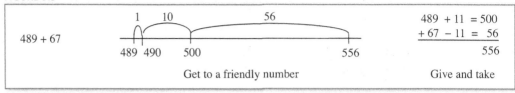

489 + 67	Get to a friendly number	Give and take

Get to a friendly number (number line): 1, 10, 56 arcs over 489 490 500 ... 556

$$489 + 11 = 500$$
$$+ 67 - 11 = \underline{56}$$
$$556$$

Get to a Friendly Number		
58 + 2	1,388 + 12	$5\frac{7}{8} + \frac{1}{8}$
58 + 6	1,388 + 25	$5\frac{7}{8} + \frac{1}{4}$
489 + 1	1,388 + 63	$3\frac{5}{6} + \frac{1}{6}$
489 + 11	8.57 + 0.03	$3\frac{5}{6} + \frac{5}{6}$
489 + 67	8.57 + 0.08	$3\pi/4 + \pi/4$
9.6 + 0.4	8.57 + 0.43	$3\pi/4 + \pi/2$
9.6 + 0.7	8.57 + 0.49	$5\pi/6 + \pi/3$
3.57 + 0.04	2.9 + 0.5	

Give and Take		
399 + 435	49 + 23	289 + 198
2,164 + 5.998	$4\frac{9}{10} + 2\frac{3}{10}$	3.9 + 15.42
4.2 + 0.9	589 + 196	7.62 + 5.98
0.99 + 0.47	$3\frac{3}{4} + 2\frac{3}{8}$	0.67 + 23.96
0.97 + 1.96	$2\frac{3}{8} + 5\frac{7}{8}$	364.3 + 2.9
22.89 + 6.14	$3\frac{5}{6} + 2\frac{1}{3}$	1,399.7 + 42.6
3.99 + 208.08	$69\frac{2}{3} + 19\frac{5}{6}$	$99\frac{21}{22} + 16\frac{1}{2}$

Swapping

Use swapping strings when students have a good handle on the give and take strategy. The problems are grouped in twos or threes. Have students solve the first in each group any way they want. The next problem(s) in the group have the same answer as the first problem. This will intrigue many students. Ask them to explain why they think this is happening. The last problem in each group lends itself nicely to the give and take strategy. These problems can lead to a nice discussion of the associative property, which is at work as students swap place-value

49 + 92
99 + 42
391 + 239
339 + 291
399 + 231
2.9 + 9.4
2.4 + 9.9

pieces. For example, 391 + 239 can be written (300 + 90 + 1) + (200 + 30 + 9). Commutating and reassociating yields (300 + 90 + 9) + (200 + 30 + 1) = 399 + 231, which, using a little give and take, is simply 400 + 230.

For the last problem of the third string, ask students to describe what numbers lead to good swapping problems. Then, have students put their answers to the test by writing their own swapping problems and defending their choices.

Swapping		
92 + 39	49.4 + 16.8	0.19 + 0.93
32 + 99	46.8 + 19.4	0.99 + 0.13
5.49 + 3.91	49.8 + 16.4	$9\frac{3}{8} + 3\frac{7}{8}$
5.91 + 3.49	19.4 + 8.9	$12\frac{3}{10} + 9\frac{9}{10}$
5.99 + 3.41	0.458 + 0.983	$91\frac{2}{5} + 9\frac{4}{5}$
$9\frac{1}{5} + 3\frac{9}{10}$	39.4 + 41.7	91.4 + 9.8
$9\frac{1}{5} + 3\frac{1}{5}$	1.39 + 19.92	Write your own

Use Factoring to Add (Leading to Collecting Like Terms)

An advanced strategy involves using common factors in addends to add. It leads to greater understanding with collecting like terms in algebra. These strings consist of paired problems in which the first problem is a whole number addition problem and the second problem is equivalent to the first, but it is written using factors to represent the addends. The numbers are such that there are common factors. For example, 28 + 14 can be solved nicely by giving 2 to 28 to get 30 + 12 = 42. However, after students see the second problem, $4 \cdot 7 + 2 \cdot 7$, many will see a connection between the problems—that you can just find that four 7s and two 7s are six 7s, or 42. The next paired problems, 49 + 21 and $7 \cdot 7 + 3 \cdot 7$, are even more pointed because $10 \cdot 7$ is so friendly.

28 + 14
$4 \cdot 7 + 2 \cdot 7$
49 + 21
$7 \cdot 7 + 3 \cdot 7$
63 + 77
36 + 18
$6 \cdot 6 + 3 \cdot 6$
$6x + 3x$

The next problem is related but given without the paired factor representation, 63 + 77. Students begin to look *into* the addends to find common factors: $9 \cdot 7 + 11 \cdot 7 = 20 \cdot 7$. The next paired problems change the common factor to 6. The punch line of the string, the last problem, $6x + 3x$, asks students to consider the sum of 6 things plus 3 of those things, 9 things or $9x$.

Model student addition strategies on an open number line. Model the sums of products problems as repeated addition on an open number line. Keep the jumps proportional as shown in Figure 5.4.

FIGURE 5.4

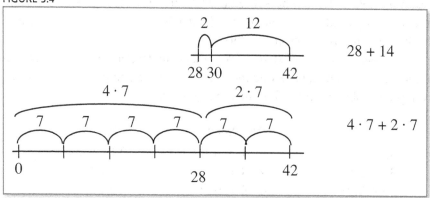

The three following strings play with different factors and continue to build toward collecting like terms. In the second and third strings, alternate problems are written in the opposite order (4 · 2 + 7 · 4, for instance) to get students to use the commutative property. These strings end with expressions like $9e + 7e$, $9a + 11a$, and $11\pi + 9\pi$. See page 223 in the "Subtraction" strings section for similar strings with subtraction.

16 + 48	24 + 56	28 + 49
2·8 + 6·8	3·8 + 7·8	4·7 + 7·7
72 + 88	88 + 72	16 + 28
9·8 + 11·8	11·8 + 9·8	4·4 + 7·4
54 + 48	54 + 36	84 + 36
9·6 + 8·6	6·9 + 4·9	12·7 + 12·3
10·6 + 7·6	81 + 99	132 + 108
$9y + 7y$	$9a + 11a$	11·12 + 9·12
$9e + 7e$		$11\pi + 9\pi$

Integer Addition

Use integer addition strings after students have experience adding and subtracting positive integers using open number lines to represent their strategies and after they have had an introduction to the meaning of integers. By juxtaposing several problems that have the same two answers, students sort out what is happening in each case; for instance, what happens when you add -34 to 25 or 34 to -25. There is no rule memorizing here. Students simply start with one of the addends and add the other. Including a subtraction problem helps students build connections between addition and subtraction.

34 + 25
$-34 + 25$
$34 + -25$
$-34 + -25$
34 − 25

Some problems in these strings have numbers that you can simply add by place value (3.7 + 5.6), while others lend themselves to a give and take strategy (49 + 36) or an over strategy (64 + −29).

Integer Addition		
49 + 36	64 + 29	3.7 + 5.6
−49 + −36	64 − 29	−3.7 + −5.6
49 + −36	64 + −29	3.7 + −5.6
−49 + 36	−64 + −29	−3.7 + 5.6
49 − 36	−64 + 29	5.6 − 3.7

Use a context (such as money, altitude, or temperature change) for the first several times you deliver these strings.

The dialog that follows shows the string beginning with 49 + 36. Notice that the teacher gives the problem in the context of money and debt. As the student describes a strategy, the teacher models the student strategy on an open number line. The teacher asks students to clarify what they mean and invites them to restate other students' ideas.

Teacher: Let's start the string today with an easy problem. I have $49 and I earned $36. How much money do I have? *Writes 49 + 36.*

Peter: $49 and $1 is $50 and $35 is $85.

$$49 + 36 = 85$$

Teacher: Great! For our next problem, I start out in debt $49. Then I get even more in debt by adding a debt of $36. *Writes −49 + −36.*

Paul: So, start at −49 because you're in debt. Then you have to go more negative, to the left 36. I did it by jumping left + to −50 and then 35 to −85.

Teacher: Why did you say you have to go more negative, to the left?

Paul: Because I am more in debt. I owe more. I owed 49 and now I owe more.

$$-49 + -36 = -85$$

Teacher: Super! For the next question, you start with $49 and then you take on a debt of $36. *Writes 49 + −36.*

Mary: I started at 49 and just subtracted 36. It's easy because you can just subtract.

Teacher: What about those numbers made it easy?

Mary: You can just take 30 from 40 and 6 from 9, that's 13. I didn't have to mess with the numbers to make it easy. They already were friendly.

Teacher: Why did you subtract? I said that you added a debt. Shouldn't you have added?

Mary: Adding a debt is getting rid of money. It is subtraction.

$49 + {-36} = 13$

Teacher: OK, this time, you start with a debt of $49 and then earn $36. Now how much money do you have? *Writes −49 + 36.*

Luke: I started at −49 because it's a debt. Then I jumped 30 to get to −19 and then 6 to get to −13. So we're still in debt 13.

$-49 + 36 = -13$

Teacher: The next problem is starting with $49 and spending $36. *Writes 49 − 36.*

Annie: Again, this is easy. Just subtract. In fact, I just looked up to where we had already done it, 13.

Paul: What do you mean? That problem was adding a negative. This one is subtracting.

Annie: They end up with the same thing because if you start on 49 and add a debt of 36, that's just like taking away 36 dollars of your money.

$49 - 36 = 13$

Mary: Check it out—the numbers are just moving around the board.

Teacher: What do you mean?

Mary: The answer is either 85 or −85 or 13 or −13. Huhhhh . . .

Teacher: What do you think that is all about?

John: If you add 49 and 36, you get 85. If they're both positive, the sum is positive. If they're both negative, the sum is negative.

Teacher: Can someone restate that with debt?

Esi: If you have money and get more, you have a positive amount of money. If you're in debt and then go more in debt, you owe more money.

Teacher: Great! But what about the 13s?

Paul: Thirteen is the difference between 49 and 36.

John: Yeah, but why did we get −13?

Peter: When you start in debt 49 and get 36 bucks, you're still in debt!

LESSONS AND ACTIVITIES FOR BUILDING POWERFUL NUMERACY

FIGURE 5.5

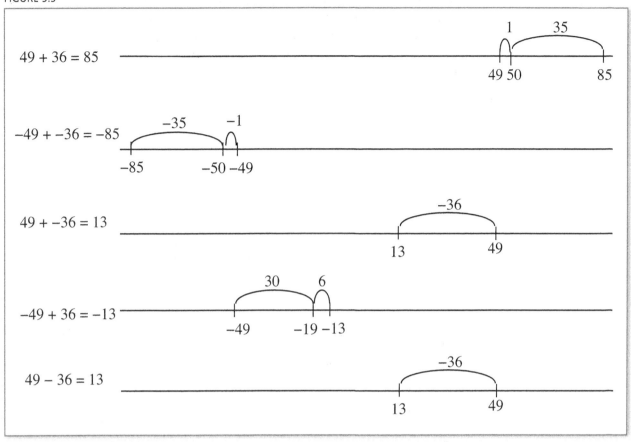

Subtraction

The strings for subtraction include the following strategies:

- ▸ Removal (Leading to Decimals and Fractions)
- ▸ Difference Versus Removal (Leading to Decimals and Fractions)
- ▸ Constant Difference(Leading to Decimals and Fractions)
- ▸ Integer Subtraction
- ▸ Integer Subtraction (Leading to Add the Opposite)

Removal (Leading to Decimals and Fractions)

Use removal strings to build place value and a sense that students can think about the values of the numbers, instead of performing a series of rote steps. These strings are constructed with paired problems where the first problem leads to a friendly number that students could use with the next problem. Students must grapple with the place value of the numbers; they are aided in this struggle with the helper problem and by the teacher modeling the problems on open number lines (Figure 5.6). For example, with $32.7 - 0.7$, the result is a friendly 32. The

$32.7 - 0.7$
$32.7 - 0.9$
$2.89 - 0.89$
$2.89 - 0.93$
$16.36 - 0.36$
$16.36 - 0.47$
$8.42 - 0.54$

next problem builds from there. Since students already have 32.7 − 0.7 = 32, then they can just subtract 0.2 more to find 32.7 − 0.9, resulting in 31.8. Similarly, 2.89 − 0.89 leads to 2.89 − 0.93 and 16.36 − 0.36 leads to 16.36 − 0.47. For the last problem, there is the potential to start with 8.42 − 0.42 and then remove the extra 0.12. Model student strategies on an open number line.

FIGURE 5.6

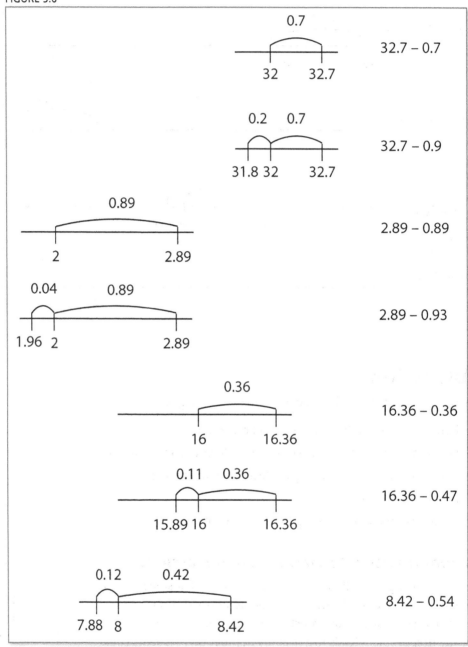

Removal		
Remove to a Friendly Number	**Remove a Friendly Number**	**Remove a Friendly Number That is Too Big and Adjust**
2.4 − 0.4	8.2 − 2	6.2 − 4
2.4 − 0.7	8.2 − 2.3	6.2 − 3.9
3.92 − 0.92	4.23 − 3	11.33 − 10
3.92 − 0.97	4.23 − 3.34	11.33 − 9.95
502.5 − 2.5	63.8 − 53	56.6 − 40
502.5 − 3.7	63.8 − 53.9	56.6 − 39.99
6⅝ − ⅝	7⅜ − 5	5⅕ − 4
6⅝ − ⅞	7⅜ − 5½	5⅕ − 3⅘
7.3 − 0.5	7.3 − 5.4	7.3 − 2.98

Below are some examples of number lines you could use to model problems from the "Remove a Friendly Number That Is Too Big and Adjust" string.

FIGURE 5.7

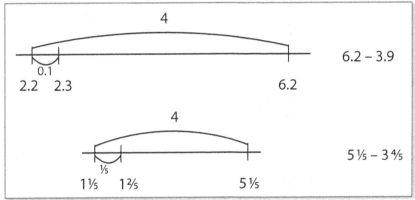

Difference Versus Removal (Leading to Decimals and Fractions)

Difference versus removal strings build a sense of when to find the difference between numbers that are relatively close together or remove a relatively small number from a relatively big number. These strings are constructed with paired problems where one problem has numbers relatively close together (easy to find the distance between them) and one problem has numbers that are relatively far apart (easy to remove). For example, with 32 − 3, it is easy to remove 3. For 41 − 39, the distance between the numbers (2) is easy to find. In the next pair, 497 is close to 502 and 24 is easy to remove from 312. The problems switch up the order so that students cannot just guess which type of problem will be next. Model these problems on an open number line, emphasizing where the answers end up on the number line (Figure 5.8). For difference/distance strategies, the answer is on the top (not on the number line itself) because the answer is the distance between the numbers, it is

32 − 3
41 − 39
502 − 497
312 − 24
4,006 − 11
3,009 − 2,989
5.2 − 4.9
3.1 − 0.4
6.03 − 5.97
4.1 − 0.15

the number you have moved on the number line. For removal strategies, the answer is the number you land on, because the answer is the result after removing one number from the other.

FIGURE 5.8

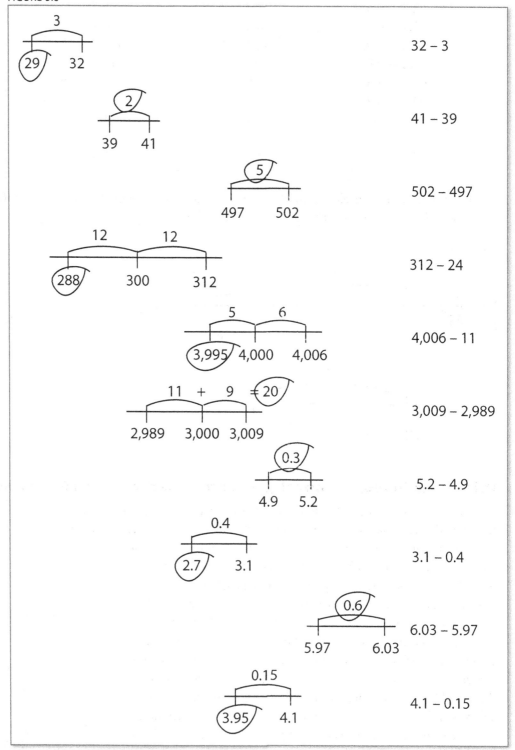

32 – 3

41 – 39

502 – 497

312 – 24

4,006 – 11

3,009 – 2,989

5.2 – 4.9

3.1 – 0.4

6.03 – 5.97

4.1 – 0.15

LESSONS AND ACTIVITIES FOR BUILDING POWERFUL NUMERACY

| Difference Versus Removal Strings with: | | |
Decimals	Same Minuend Partners	Fractions
$6.2 - 5.9$	$7.2 - 6.9$	$3\frac{1}{6} - 2\frac{5}{6}$
$8.3 - 0.7$	$7.2 - 0.5$	$9\frac{1}{8} - \frac{3}{8}$
$4.11 - 0.12$	$7\frac{3}{8} - \frac{5}{8}$	$5\frac{1}{7} - \frac{2}{7}$
$5.05 - 4.96$	$7\frac{3}{8} - 6\frac{7}{8}$	$6\frac{2}{5} - 5\frac{4}{5}$
$18.03 - 17.97$	$200.4 - 198$	$4\frac{1}{4} - 3\frac{7}{8}$
$14.16 - 0.19$	$200.4 - 0.8$	$7\frac{1}{6} - \frac{1}{3}$
$0.42 - 0.03$	$12\frac{1}{5} - \frac{5}{10}$	$8\frac{1}{5} - \frac{3}{10}$
$0.81 - 0.79$	$12\frac{1}{5} - 11\frac{9}{10}$	$11\frac{1}{10} - 10\frac{4}{5}$

Constant Difference (Leading to Decimals and Fractions)

With constant difference strings, students practice finding the difference between numbers as they build intuition for creating equivalent problems by shifting the distance between numbers up and down the number line. These strings group problems with the same answer. Begin by asking students to solve the problems using both a removal and a difference strategy. Model both strategies on an open number line for the first 1 to 3 problems, depending on how your students are doing with both strategies. For the rest of the problems, model the difference strategy, lining up the number lines appropriately so that there is the potential for the equivalence to become apparent. As students become aware, acknowledge that the answers are all the same, but continue to model difference strategies for the problems, including $80 - 33$. Write the equivalences as equations (e.g., $83 - 36 = 80 - 33$) and wonder aloud if students could use this idea to create an equivalent problem that is easier to solve. If needed, provide the two problems, $87 - 40$ and $77 - 30$ (Figure 5.9). The last problem, $143 - 96$, may appear at first glance to have a different answer and may surprise students because the same distance, 47, has been shifted farther from the starting point than the rest.

$82 - 35$
$74 - 27$
$85 - 38$
$76 - 29$
$83 - 36$
$80 - 33$
$87 - 40$
$77 - 30$
$143 - 96$

FIGURE 5.9

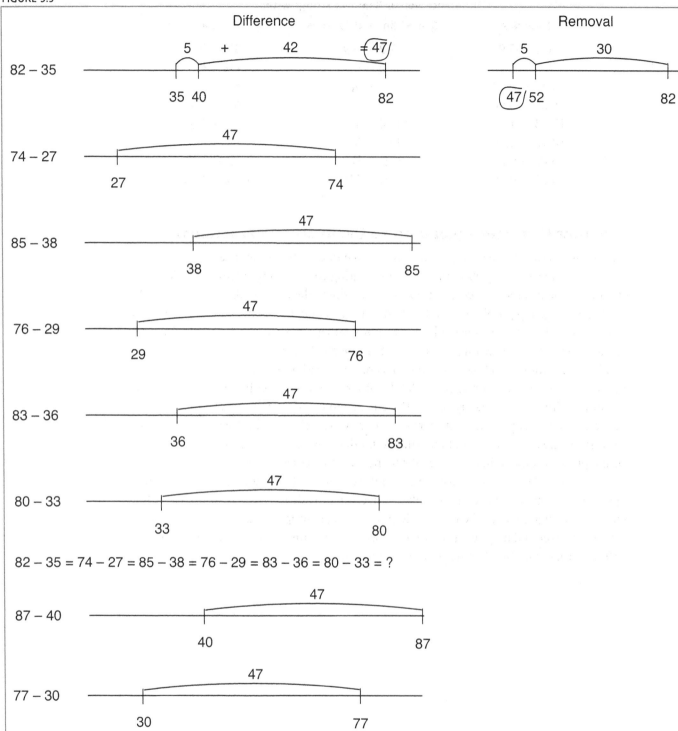

82 − 35 = 74 − 27 = 85 − 38 = 76 − 29 = 83 − 36 = 80 − 33 = ?

Constant Difference Strings with:		
Decimals	**Decimals**	**Fractions**
6.6 − 2.9	7.1 − 4.3	$8\frac{1}{5} - 6\frac{3}{5}$
7.1 − 3.4	6.6 − 3.8	$7\frac{2}{5} - 5\frac{4}{5}$
7.6 − 3.9	5.7 − 2.9	$8 - 6\frac{2}{5}$
6.4 − 2.7	6.3 − 3.5	$7\frac{3}{5} - 6$
7.4 − 3.7	6.4 − 3.6	$5\frac{3}{10} - 3\frac{2}{5}$
6.7 − 3.0	6.8 − 4.0	$4\frac{4}{5} - 2\frac{9}{10}$
7.7 − 4.0	5.8 − 3.0	$5\frac{1}{2} - 3\frac{3}{5}$
12.4 − 8.7	14.7 − 11.9	$5\frac{1}{10} - 3\frac{1}{5}$
8.3 − 3.8	19.2 − 9.8	$4\frac{9}{10} - 3$
Helpful Partners	**Little Shifts**	**Bigger Shifts**
3,352 − 1,566	7.2 − 5.9	541 − 352
3,356 − 1,570	7.3 − 6.0	589 − 400
3,386 − 1,600	81 − 49	3.32 − 1.38
3,786 − 2,000	6.5 − 4.8	3.94 − 2.00
453 − 265	131.4 − 99.7	5,063 − 2,894
488 − 300	3,870 − 199	7.34 − 5.078
5.36 − 2.79	9.6 − 0.99	1,654,236 − 3,655
5.57 − 3	4.01 − 0.88	

Integer Subtraction

Use these integer subtraction strings to sharpen students' ideas about subtracting integers by helping students parse out when to think in terms of removal, when to think in terms of finding the difference, and how to use those notions in tandem. In this string, the first four problems are two paired partners. In the first problem the first number (minuend) is greater than the second number (subtrahend). The second problem reverses the order. Students typically reason using removal to find that when subtracting a larger number from a smaller number, the answer is negative. If the students do not mention it, the teacher wonders aloud about finding the difference with these subtraction problems — it seems to work with some

8 − 5
5 − 8
12 − 10
10 − 12
3 − 7
11 − 22
6 − 9

(when the answers are positive) and not with others (when the answers are negative). If students only use distance, without considering the sign of the answer, then all subtraction problems would have a positive solution. If students use distance, they must also consider removal to determine the sign of the solution. The teacher leads a discussion about using both strategies in tandem, difference and removal, to reason about integer subtraction problems and students may apply this in the last few problems.

Brittany, a seventh-grade math teacher, starts an integer subtraction string by reminding students about the contexts they have been using for integers (such as money, football, elevation, and temperature) and uses a familiar whole number problem, 8 − 5, in order to set the stage for an integer subtraction string. She barely pauses after asking, just long enough for students to think of the answer, and she models a *distance* strategy. "If I have $8 and I spend $5, I have only $3 left. So, we can think about removing the $3. We can also think about 8 minus 5 as the difference between 8 and 5, right? I'll model that quickly."

Removal   Difference/Distance

  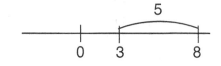 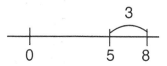

Brittany continues, "What if I have $5 and I spend $8?" as she writes 5 − 8, and students respond, "You're in debt." "You owe money." "You owe $3."

Brittany: What if this question was about football?

Jonathan: You started 5 yards in front of the line of scrimmage and lost 8 yards. You're 3 yards behind the line of scrimmage.

Brittany: *Wanting to make one more contextual connection:* What about temperature?

Sydney: It's really cold, 5 degrees and then it goes down 8 degrees, so you are at 3 degrees below 0.

Brittany: And how do I write that I owe $3, am behind the line of scrimmage 3 yards, or chilly at 3 degrees below 0?

Rayshauna: Negative 3 or the opposite of 3.

Brittany: Excellent, and we can say the opposite of 3 because . . .?

Rayshauna: It's on the opposite side of 0 than positive 3.

Now that Brittany has connected to students' past experience, she wants to pose a possible confusion for students to work through. "We said that we can think about subtraction as removal and also as difference/distance, right? What about for 5 − 8? What is the distance between 5 and 8? Is it negative 3? Help me here." She draws an open number line next to the problem 5 − 8 = −3 with the distance of 3 between 5 and 8

Removal   Difference/Distance

  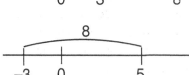 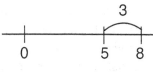

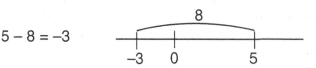 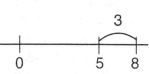

Riley: This time, you're subtracting a bigger number. Like, 8 is bigger than 5, so it's going to have to be negative.

Logan: In all the subtraction problems I can think of that I've ever done, it's always been a number minusing something smaller than it.

Lainey: Yeah, we haven't been starting with a number and subtracting more than it. I wonder if that's what is going on. Maybe when the numbers are normal, a number minus a smaller number, then the answer's always positive. But when you subtract more than you start with, it's going to be negative.

Brittany: That's interesting. I hear you using removal to justify why the answer is negative. Start with a number. If you remove something smaller, that's what you're used to, the answer is positive. You still have some yards left, the temperature is above 0, you're standing above sea level. But if you start with a number and remove something bigger that it, then the answer is negative. You're behind the line of scrimmage, the temperature has fallen below 0, you are below sea level. Is that what you are saying?

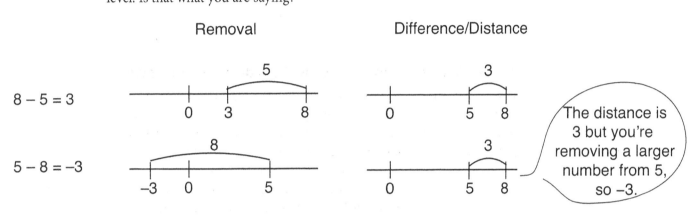

The students agree and Brittany gives them another set of partner problems to chew on, $12 - 10$ and $10 - 12$. Students agree that the answers are 2 and -2, respectively.

Brittany: How are you thinking about $10 - 12$?

Trey: The distance between 10 and 12 is 2, but since you're taking away a bigger number than 10, the answer's -2.

Riley: Or you can think that you're at 10 and you go back 12, that lands you on -2.

Brittany: Let's see if we can use both of your reasonings to figure this next problem, $3 - 7$.

Ashton: You can start at 3 and move back 7, so you land on -4.

Caitlyn: The difference between 3 and 7 is 4, but you're removing a bigger number than 3 so it's -4.

Brittany: I hear that one way to think of this is to remove — to back up on the number line. The other way seems like a combination — you can find the difference, but then use removal to decide if the answer is positive or negative. Interesting.

Brittany continues the same questioning, drawing out both ways of thinking for the rest of the problems. She will bring back the combination thinking (finding the distance between the minuend and the subtrahend and then reasoning about removal to decide on the sign of the number) in the next problem strings, where using removal alone fails —

when you try to remove negative numbers. With those problems, Brittany will help students continue to construct the combination strategy and then lead to the equivalent strategy of adding the opposite of the subtrahend.

Integer Subtraction Strings with:		
Negative Integers	**Integers**	**Constant Difference**
7 − 4	9 − 5	4 − (−4)
4 − 7	5 − 9	−5 − (−13)
−3 − (−5)	5 − (−9)	2 − (−6)
−5 − (−3)	−9 − 5	0 − (−8)
−13 − 2	−5 − 9	15 − 7
−13 − (−2)	9 − (−5)	8 − 0
−8 − (−1)	−5 − (−9)	−8 − (−16)
−8 − 1	(−9) − (−5)	

Integer Subtraction (Leading to Add the Opposite)

These integer subtraction strings help students construct the notion that subtracting a number can be thought of as adding the opposite of the number. These strings are constructed with paired problems where one problem features subtraction and the other features adding the opposite. The teacher delivers the paired problems in integer contexts, where the action verb is represented by subtraction and the addition of a loss is represented by adding a negative. Students discuss the equivalence and make sense of the relationship for subtracting positive numbers. For example, losing 7 yards puts you at the same place as incurring a loss of 7 yards or spending \$7 puts you in the same place as incurring a debt of \$7: $-8 - 7 = -8 + -7$. Students apply the generalization to the last, unpaired problems that feature subtracting a negative number, such as $4 - (-7)$.

−8 − 7
−8 + −7
9 + −12
9 − 12
3 − 7
3 + −7
4 − (−7)
−3 − (−9)
−6 − (−2)
$a + -b$

Brittany, the seventh-grade teacher we saw earlier, starts the string by asking the students to remind her of some of the contexts they have been using to reason about integers. The students respond with football, temperature, elevation, and debt.

Brittany writes the first problem on the board, *−8 − 7*, as she says, "One of the plays last night made me cringe! Do you remember when the football team lost 8 yards and then lost 7 yards? That's our first problem in the string today. How far back did they end up from the line of scrimmage?" She purposefully suggests a removal situation.

Timothy: They would be 15 yards back.
Brittany: *Models the removal on open number line and writes the −15.*

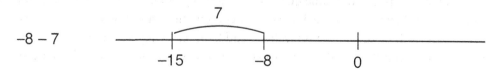

LESSONS AND ACTIVITIES FOR BUILDING POWERFUL NUMERACY

She continues by writing −8 + −7 *on the board.*

Brittany: Then later the team lost 8 yards and then after the next play I heard the announcer say, "Oh no, now they have a loss of 7 yards." Where are they now? *She times the* + *symbol with "have" and the* −7 *with "a loss of 7 yards."*

Hunter: They are back 15 yards.

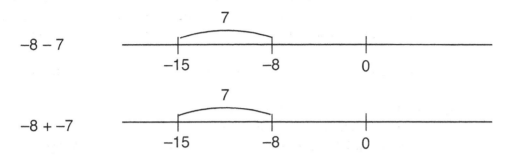

−8 − 7

−8 + −7

Brittany: *Wants to bring attention to the equivalence and start the students considering why.* Hmmm . . . They both have the same answer. . . . Interesting. The next problem in the string is about elevation. John started 9 feet above sea level and then walked 12 feet down. Where is he? *She writes* 9 + −12 *on the board.*

Lauren: He went down, right? He's 3 feet below sea level, −3, because it takes 9 to get to 0 and then 3 more to finish the 12 puts you at 3 below or −3.

9 + −12

Brittany: John started 9 feet above sea level and then *fell* 12 feet. Where is he? *She writes* 9 − 12 *on the board and times the subtraction symbol with the words "fell 12 feet."*

Juwan: It's the same again, starting at 9 and falling 12 puts you 3 below, so −3.

Brittany models this right below the partner problem.

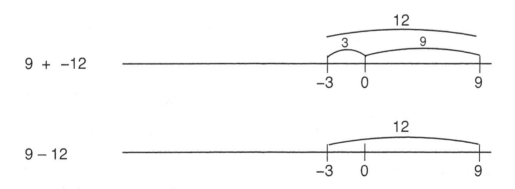

9 + −12

9 − 12

Brittany: *Draws attention to the equivalence by asking a question.* So, we've got 2 situations so far where the answers were the same, so −8 − 7 = −8 + −7 and

9 + −12 = 9 − 12. She writes the equivalencies on the board as she speaks.
What do you think about that? How would you describe what's going on?

Sidney: It makes sense that if you fall, it's like a negative.

Ashton: Plus a negative means you are going backwards, so it's the same thing as subtracting.

Brittany: Hmm . . . what do the rest of you think? Is subtracting a number the same thing as adding the opposite of that number? In other words, subtracting a 7 is like adding its opposite, plus −7? And subtracting a 12 is like adding its opposite, + −12?

Chelsea: I think so. If you think about removing when you see subtraction, it's like adding a negative.

Brittany: And we've been removing, haven't we? Losing yards, falling feet. Let's try another situation. The temperature is a chilly 3 degrees. It drops 7 degrees. How cold will it be? *As she writes 3 − 7, she follows with another question.* The temperature is a chilly 3 degrees. We predict we will have a drop of 7 degrees. How cold will it be?

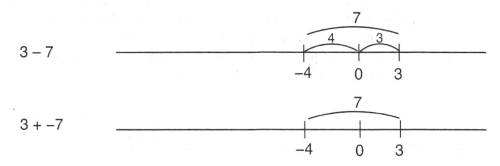

$3 - 7$

$3 + -7$

Brittany: Hmmm . . . ? I wonder if it's always true that subtracting a number is like adding its opposite. Let's do some investigating with different numbers and using the distance/difference strategy for subtraction. What about a problem like 4 − (−7)? Removing a negative number is a bit weird, so let's look at the distance between these guys. *She puts 4 and −7 on an open number line and labels the distance.*

$4 - (-7)$

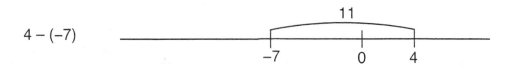

Brittany: So, the difference between −7 and 4 is 11. What question do we need to answer now?

Kennedy: From the number 4 are you removing a bigger or smaller number? Negative 7 is smaller, so the answer is positive 11.

Brittany: *She records the answer.* Is that equivalent to adding the opposite here? Work on that for a bit. What would you get if you found 4 − (−7) by adding the opposite of negative 7?

Students work.

Marissa: Yes, because 4 plus the opposite of negative 7 is 4 plus 7 and that's 11. It works!

Brittany: Let's try another one. Please find −3 − (−9). *She writes it on the board.*

The students reason similarly about the equivalences for that problem and for the next, −6 − (−2). Brittany finishes the string asking students to generalize.

Brittany: If this is true, what could we write about any subtraction problem, *a* − *b*?

Emma   Instead of thinking about subtraction, you can add the opposite of the number.

Brittany: *She records this on the board as a* − *b* = *a* + −*b*. Great work today!

FIGURE 5.10

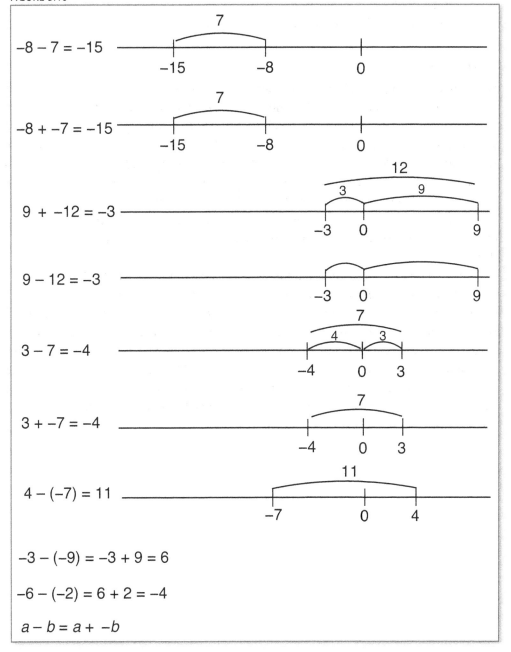

$$-3 - (-9) = -3 + 9 = 6$$

$$-6 - (-2) = 6 + 2 = -4$$

$$a - b = a + -b$$

Multiplication

The strings for multiplication include the following strategies:

- ▶ Chunking
- ▶ Doubling and Halving
- ▶ Over and Under
- ▶ Five Is Half of Ten
- ▶ Factor to Multiply
- ▶ Using Fractions to Multiply Whole Numbers and Decimals
- ▶ Using Proportional Reasoning
- ▶ Same Strategies, Smaller Numbers (Basic Facts)

Chunking

Use chunking strings to help students realize that multiplication problems can be broken into manageable chunks. Use an open array to model student strategies. The open array model can help students gain spatial sense about the commutative property because a 90×3 array has the same area as a 3×90 array, $90 \times 3 = 3 \times 90$. The open array model also can help students develop the distributive property, that $92 \times 3 = (90 \times 3) + (2 \times 3)$, because the 90×3 and the 2×3 arrays are chunks of array that combine to form the 92×3. These strings are constructed with sets of three problems where the first two problems can be used to solve the third.

90×3
2×3
92×3
17×10
17×2
17×12
62×4

The first set of three strings that follow uses whole numbers. Model these on open arrays, maintaining the orientation such that the first factor is the number of rows and the second is the number of columns, so that the arrays in the strings are sometimes wide and sometimes tall, depending on the order of the factors. This brings out the distributive property spatially as students have to decide how to combine the chunks to obtain the desired rectangle. For example, a 4×56 array is created by putting 4×50 and 4×6 next to each other. The array for 22×18 is created by stacking 20×18 and 2×18 on top of each other (Figure 5.11). Refrain from *telling* students how to combine the arrays. Let them tell you.

FIGURE 5.11

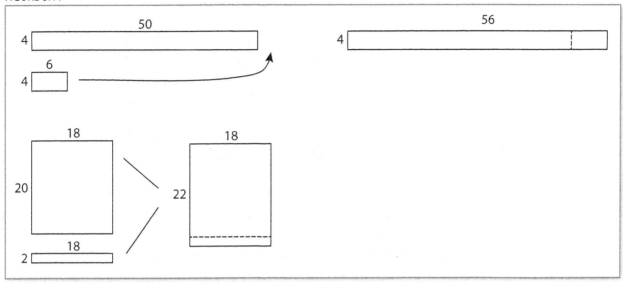

Whole Numbers		
4 × 50	70 × 6	80 × 3
4 × 6	8 × 6	7 × 3
4 × 56	78 × 6	87 × 3
20 × 18	21 × 10	33 × 10
2 × 18	21 × 4	33 × 3
22 × 18	21 × 14	33 × 13
12 × 13	11 × 18	13 × 21

The next strings, called special chunks strings, work on having students recognize that they can readily find products of a factor that is a two-digit number where the digit is repeated, like 22, 33, and 44. For example, once students have found twice a number, $2n$, they can easily find 20 times that number, $20n$, and then add those chunks to get 22 times that number, $(20 + 2)n = 22n$. The second and third strings also employ the over and under strategy, so you may want to do some over and under strings (see the "Over and Under" section that follows) before you do these strings. For example, the problem after 88 × 37 is 87 × 37. Alternatively, you could leave out the over and under problems, like 87 × 7, 43 × 43, 28 × 67, and 43 × 22 until students have more experience with over and under relationships.

Special Chunks		
26 × 2	2 × 37	36 × 3
26 × 20	4 × 37	36 × 30
26 × 22	8 × 37	36 × 33
26 × 4	88 × 37	28 × 6
26 × 44	87 × 37	28 × 66
2 × 47	43 × 2	28 × 67
4 × 47	43 × 4	44 × 22
44 × 47	43 × 44	43 × 22
114 × 42	43 × 43	

The following single-digit practice extension strings help students practice single-digit facts, because each set of problems starts with a single-digit fact. The next problems build from that fact, using manageable chunks to find larger products. As you deliver these strings, take time to have students share how they quickly find a single-digit fact if they do not already have it at their fingertips. Emphasize using multiplicative relationships to quickly solve these facts. For example, 7×6 can be found by doubling $7 \times 3 = 21$ to get 42. Deemphasize skip-counting by asking students what products they know that can help them find the desired fact.

Chunking—Single-Digit Practice Extensions		
7 × 6	5 × 9	3 × 8
70 × 6	5 × 90	30 × 8
77 × 6	5 × 99	33 × 8
8 × 4	9 × 55	6 × 9
8 × 40	4 × 8	66 × 9
8 × 44	4 × 88	7 × 9
9 × 3	8 × 44	77 × 9
9 × 33	7 × 55	9 × 44

The next group of strings use chunking with decimals. To do these strings, students should already have some understanding of the place-value shifts involved in dividing by 10. For example, they should understand how to find 0.4×23 if they know $4 \times 23 = 92$. Model these strings in a ratio table (Figure 5.12).

Chunking—Decimals		
2×23	7×3	3×4
4×23	7×6	3×6
0.4×23	7×0.3	3×0.6
2.4×23	7×6.3	3×4.6
6×5	4×4	8×9
6×4	4×8	8×0.1
6×0.4	4×0.8	8×9.1
6×5.4	4×4.8	9×3.2
3×2.3		

FIGURE 5.12

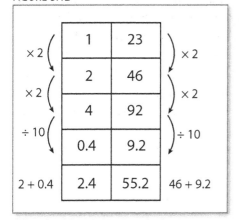

Doubling and Halving

These doubling and halving strings are designed to help students construct the strategy of multiplying one factor by a number and the other factor by the reciprocal of the number, $a \times b = a \times c \times b \times 1/c$. At its simplest, you double one factor and halve the other, resulting in an equivalent product. The spatial analogue is that you double one dimension of a rectangle, halve the other, and the resulting rectangle has the same area (Figure 5.13). The strings are designed with pairs and triples of equivalent problems. Emphasize the equivalence and wonder aloud why this might be. The last problem in each string is given without a helper problem. Model the strings with arrays and equations.

5×42
10×21
24×1.5
3×12
18×2.5
9×5
2.5×4.5

FIGURE 5.13

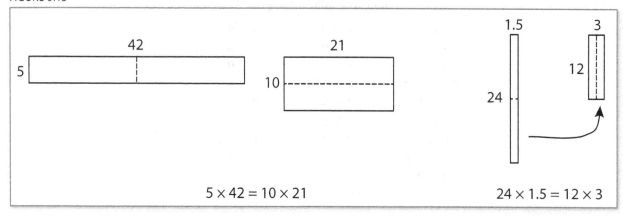

$$5 \times 42 = 10 \times 21 \qquad 24 \times 1.5 = 12 \times 3$$

When delivering the strings, emphasize the relationships between equivalent problems. Bring out the doubling and halving, tripling and multiplying by ⅓, and so on. The point is not that each individual problem in the string should be solved with this strategy. Some problems, like 24 × 1.5, can be solved just as easily by adding 24 to half of 24 as by doubling and halving. However, these problems help build the double/half relationships in the learner's mind, and then the learner can use the relationships to solve other problems that are readily solved by doubling and halving, such as 2.5 × 4.5, 12.5 × 16, 1.4 × 3.5, and 4.5 × 1.8.

Use the strings with mixed-number factors when students have had some experience multiplying mixed numbers.

24 × 9	18 × 3	2⅓ × 33
8 × 27	6 × 9	11 × 7
72 × 3	2 × 27	15 × 3⅕
36 × 8	24 × 2¼	3 × 16
9 × 32	3⅓ × 9	6 × 8
12 × 24	24 × 9	7½ × 21
12.5 × 16	1.4 × 3.5	4.5 × 1.8

Over and Under

The over and under strings are designed to help students construct the strategy of finding a friendly product that is a bit too much or too little and adjusting as needed. This first string begins with a single-digit fact, 5 × 6, and builds to 50 × 6 using the relationship of 10 times. It then asks, if fifty 6s is 300, then what is fifty-one 6s, 51 × 6, and then forty-nine 6's, 49 × 6? The next problem is 0.1 × 6, which leads to removing that tenth of 6 from 50 × 6 = 300 to get 49.9 × 6. The next problem, 0.5 × 6, leads to 49.5 × 6 by removing half of 6 from 50 × 6 = 300. The last problem could be found by adding the 49.5 × 6 = 297 and 50 × 6 = 300 but could also be found by removing half of 6 from 100 × 6 = 600. The string emphasizes going a little over or under an easy-to-find friendly number by finding tenths of 6 and half of 6.

5 × 6
50 × 6
51 × 6
49 × 6
0.1 × 6
49.9 × 6
0.5 × 6
49.5 × 6
99.5 × 6

Following are whole number and decimal strings. Model the whole number strings with arrays. Model the decimal strings with ratio tables.

Over and Under—Whole Numbers		
6×7	7×8	9×9
60×7	7×80	8×90
59×7	7×79	8×89
6×70	70×8	9×6
6×69	69×8	9×60
8×5	9×4	9×59
8×50	90×4	7×9
8×49	89×4	69×9
9×59	3×19	79×8

The following strings deal with over and under relationships using decimals as one of the factors.

Over and Under—Decimals		
6×8	7×7	6×7
6×80	7×70	6×70
6×79	7×69.9	6×69
6×0.1	7×0.5	6×0.1
6×79.9	7×69.5	6×69.9
6×0.5	8×8	6×68.9
6×79.5	8×80	6×69.5
60×8	8×79.5	9×6
0.1×8	8×79.9	89.5×6
59.9×8	9×89.9	89.9×6
9×49	9×89.5	

Use language such as "five sixes" when talking about 5×6, to help students unitize, as in the dialog that follows for the first whole number over and under string.

Brittany: What is 6 times 7? I'm looking for six 7s.

Carlos: It's 42.

Brittany: I'll model that on an array. *Brittany draws a 6 by 7 array and labels the area 42.* What is 60 times 7, sixty 7s?

Logan: That's 10 times 42, so 420. *Brittany draws a 60 by 7 array and labels the area 420.*

Brittany: So, we have sixty 7s is 420. How much is fifty-nine 7s, 59 times 7? *As she says this, she writes 59×7.*

Trey: That is 1 less 7, so 420 minus 7 is 413. *Brittany draws another 60 by 7 array and then removes a 1 by 7 array to end up with a 59 by 7 array.*

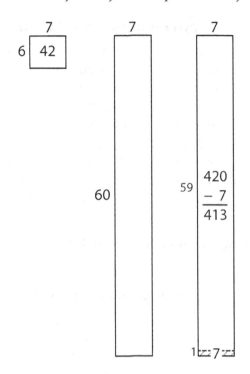

Brittany: The next problem is 6 times 70. *She writes 6 × 70.*

Riley: That is also 420. It's like the 10 is with the 70 instead of the 60.

Sydney: Starting with 6 times 7 is 42, you can find 60 times 7 and 6 times 70, both 10 times 42, 420.

Brittany: Nice reasoning. The next problem is 6 times 69. *She writes 6 × 69.*

Lainey: I found 6 times 60, 360, and added it to 6 times 9, 54. That's 414.

Lupita: I kind of did what we did before, I cut off one 6. We had seventy 6s and you asked for sixty-nine 6s, so that's 1 less 6. I also got 414. *Brittany models these strategies, lined up with proportional arrays so students can see how they relate.*

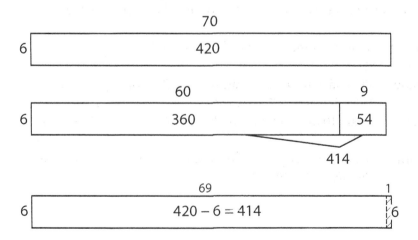

LESSONS AND ACTIVITIES FOR BUILDING POWERFUL NUMERACY

Brittany continues the string similarly with the related problems 8 × 5, 8 × 50, and 8 × 49. She then ends the string with 9 × 59, given without helper problems to see what students will do. Depending on students' responses, she may do more of these strings to help students continue to construct these relationships, or she may move on to other relationships if she sees that most students are using the over and under strategy.

Five Is Half of Ten

32 × 10
32 × 5
15 × 32
32 × 0.5
32 × 1.5
100 × 32
50 × 32
150 × 32
149 × 32

Use five is half of ten strings to help students build multiplicative relationships with the number 10, the base of our number system. The problems are grouped in twos or threes in which students can find half of a problem to solve another: 32 × 10 = 320, so 32 × 5 is half of 320, which is 160. All the groups are related; 50 × 32 is half of 100 × 32 but is also 10 times 5 × 32 and 100 times 0.5 × 32. All of these place-value relationships can be brought to the forefront for students to consider. The last problem of the string is an over and under problem, 149 × 32, which can be found by using 150 × 32 and subtracting one 32 or starting with 15 × 32 and removing 0.1 × 32 and then scaling up. Model student strategies in ratio tables.

Five Is Half of Ten with Whole Numbers		
10 × 47	10 × 37	19 × 0.5
5 × 47	5 × 37	19 × 10
47 × 15	100 × 37	19 × 5
14 × 47	50 × 37	19 × 15
100 × 47	49 × 37	19 × 100
99 × 47	99 × 47	19 × 50
50 × 47	150 × 37	19 × 150
55 × 47	15 × 37	19 × 149
47 × 155	1.5 × 37	19 × 145

The next sets of strings use the five is half of ten strategy with decimals. The first set of three mostly involves finding the products of decimals and whole numbers, such as finding 0.49 × 66. The next set of three deals with finding of the products of whole numbers and decimals, such as starting with 2.3 and finding 49 × 2.3, leading to multiplying decimals, such as finding 4.5 × 3.2.

Five Is Half of Ten with Decimals		
0.5 × 46	10 × 66	29 × 0.5
1.5 × 46	5 × 66	29 × 50
15 × 46	66 × 0.5	5 × 29
50 × 46	0.1 × 66	29 × 0.1
46 × 150	5.1 × 66	29 × 0.05
46 × 1,000	4.9 × 66	0.15 × 29
46 × 500	0.49 × 66	29 × 0.14
46 × 498.5	49 × 0.66	14 × 0.29
10 × 2.3	10 × 4.2	10 × 3.4
9 × 2.3	9 × 4.2	9 × 3.4
5 × 2.3	90 × 4.2	90 × 3.4
0.5 × 2.3	5 × 4.2	5 × 3.4
100 × 2.3	95 × 4.2	0.5 × 34
99 × 2.3	50 × 4.2	50 × 3.4
9.9 × 2.3	49 × 4.2	49 × 3.4
50 × 2.3	45 × 4.2	4.9 × 3.4
49 × 2.3	4.5 × 3.2	49.5 × 3.4

The dialog that follows shows Brittany delivering the string starting with 10 × 2.3 to her seventh-grade class.

Brittany: For today's string, we're going to talk about bottles of eye drops. Each bottle holds 2.3 ounces. *Brittany starts a ratio table with bottles:ounces and 1:2.3. What if I had 10 bottles of eye drops that each hold 2.3 ounces? What is 10 times 2.3? She writes 10 in the ratio table.*

bottles	1	10
ounces	2.3	

Timothy: That's 23. *Brittany fills in the ratio table with 10:23.*

bottles	1	10
ounces	2.3	23

Brittany: Did anyone get anything different? No? Timothy, how do you know that 10 bottles hold 23 ounces total?

Timothy: It's 2.3 times 10. I think about times 10 as a place-value shift. Instead of ten 2.3s, you can think of 2.3 tens. If you put 2.3 in the tens place, that's 23.

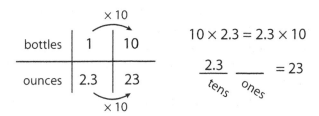

$$10 \times 2.3 = 2.3 \times 10$$

$$\underset{\textit{tens}\quad\textit{ones}}{\dfrac{2.3}{}} = 23$$

Brittany: Some of you have been telling me that when you multiply by 10, you just "add a zero." Would that work here? Is 2.3×10 equal to 2.30?

Hunter: No, the number has to shift in the place-value, so it's not 2.30, it's 23.

Brittany: Great! Next, I am wondering how many ounces we'd have if we had 9 bottles of eye drops? *She writes a 9 in the ratio table.*

Lauren: I got 20.7 ounces, 23 minus 2.3 is 20.7. *Brittany records 20.7 in the ratio table and models Lauren's strategy.*

			$10 - 1$
bottles	1	10	9
ounces	2.3	23	20.7

$23 - 2.3$

Brittany: What if we had 5 bottles? How many ounces would we have?

Marissa: Since 5 is half of 10, I just found half of 23 and that's 11.5.

$\div 2$

bottles	1	10	9	5
ounces	2.3	23	20.7	11.5

$\div 2$

Brittany: Now we have half a bottle. How many ounces? *Brittany writes 0.5 in the table.*

Alex: Half of 2.3 is, let's see, 1.15.

Brittany: How did you do that?

Alex: I found half of 2, that's 1. Then half of 30 cents is 15 cents, so 1.15.

Sidney: I used the 5 that we already had. To get from 5 to 0.5, you divide by ten, so 11.5 divided by 10 is 1.15.

$\div 2 \qquad \div 10$

bottles	1	10	9	5	0.5
ounces	2.3	23	20.7	11.5	1.15

$\div 2 \qquad \div 10$

Brittany: Nice! Now we have 100 bottles. How many ounces in 100 bottles?

Ashton: You could shift the 2.3 twice or the 23 once to get 230.

Brittany: Now we want to know how many ounces are in 99 bottles.

Emma: I took away 2.3 from 230 because 99 bottles is 1 less bottle than 100. That's 227.7.

Brittany: So you took 1 bottle from 100 bottles and you removed the corresponding 2.3 ounces from the 230 ounces? Nice work.

							100 − 1
bottles	1	10	9	5	0.5	100	99
ounces	2.3	23	20.7	11.5	1.15	230	227.7
							230 − 2.3

Juwan: I took the 9 ounces and multiplied by 10 to get 90 ounces, that's 207 ounces. Then I added the 9 ounces to get 99 ounces. And 207 plus 20.7 is 227.7.

								90 + 9
bottles	1	10	9	5	0.5	100	99	90
ounces	2.3	23	20.7	11.5	1.15	230	227.7	2170
								217 + 21.7

Brittany: Would someone please generalize the different ways that Emma and Juwan just solved 99 times 2.3?

Adrian: You could find 100 and then take away 1 bottle. Or you could find 9, times by 10 to get 90 and then add the 9.

Brittany: I'd like you all to consider — if you were to find yourself needing to solve 99 times 2.3, which of those strategies might you find more efficient?

Juwan: I can see that mine was OK because we had already found the 9 bottles. If I had to solve the problem and we didn't already have the 9 bottles, I would probably find the 100 minus 1.

Adrian: But I bet that 9 strategy would be good for finding something times 92. You wouldn't want to find 100 and subtract 8. You could find 9, 90 and then add 2.

Brittany: Nice thinking! What about 9.9? That's a bit of a stretch because we don't usually talk about 9.9 bottles, but can we use relationships to find 9.9 times 2.3?

Kennedy: I got 22.77. First I found 0.1 times 2.3 and then I subtracted 0.1 from 10 to get 9.9 and 23 minus 0.23 is 22.77.

								10 − 0.1	
bottles	1	10	9	5	0.5	100	99	9.9	0.1
ounces	2.3	23	20.7	11.5	1.15	230	227.7	22.77	0.23
								23 − 0.23	

Collin: I also got 22.77 but I divided the 99 by 10 to get 9.9. So 227.7 divided by 10 is 22.77.

							÷ 10	
bottles	1	10	9	5	0.5	100	99	9.9
ounces	2.3	23	20.7	11.5	1.15	230	227.7	22.77

÷ 10

Brittany: Great relationships!

Brittany finishes the string with 50×2.3 and 49×2.3 and students relate these problems to the 5×2.3, the 0.5×2.3, and half of the 100×2.3. Then they find 1 less bottle than 50 to get 112.7 ounces in 49 bottles.

Factor to Multiply

The factor to multiply strings are designed to help students consider the factors of the factors in a multiplication problem. These strings consist of paired problems where the first problem is a multiplication problem and the second problem is equivalent to the first, where factors of the numbers have been reassociated to create a factor of 10. The other factors can be multiplied by that 10. For example, 14×45 can be solved easily by re-associating and commuting $14 \times 45 = (7 \times 2) \times (5 \times 9) = 7 \times (2 \times 5) \times 9 = (7 \times 9) \times (10) = 63 \times 10 = 630$. When students note the equivalence with the second problem, 10×63, many are intrigued. The last two problems are given with no equivalent helper.

14×45
10×63
35×16
10×56
55×22
35×120

Model student strategies on arrays or ratio tables, as needed. Write the equivalencies as they come up: $14 \times 45 = 10 \times 63$. Wonder aloud what might make them equivalent.

42×25	44×15	120×35
10×105	10×66	100×42
18×15	16×45	45×160
27×10	72×10	72×100
18×35	35×22	180×55
125×14	24×25	48×75

Using Fractions to Multiply Whole Numbers and Decimals

Use fractions to multiply whole numbers and decimals strings after students have experience using fractions as operators, such as finding ¼ of 24 and ¾ of 36. These strings are helpful for students to construct relationships between using a fraction, like ¼, as an operator and multiplying by the equivalent decimal, 0.25. These relationships are helpful in decimal multiplication for factors like 0.24, 0.26, 0.74, 0.76, and the corresponding whole numbers, 24, 26, 74, 76. In this string, start by having students share a few whole number multiplication strategies for 25 × 24. Then have them share their thinking for ¼ of 24. For 0.25 × 24, some students may grind out a decimal strategy and others may recognize the equivalence to the ¼ of 24 problem. Either way, once students have an answer, ask them to consider the pattern in the problems and answers for the first three problems. Discuss the place values involved. As students work on each of the remaining problems, continue to discuss place value and using fractions as operators. Model student strategies with ratio tables and equations.

The following strings have some problems whose factors have whole number quarters (e.g., ¼ of 32 is 8, and so ¾ of 32 is 24). These strings also include other problems whose factors take a bit of work to find the quarters: ¼ of 18 can be found by halving 18 to 9 and halving again to 4.5. Also, ¼ of 18 can be found by finding ¼ of (16 + 2) = ¼ of 16 + ¼ of 2 = 4 + 0.5 = 4.5. The strings also use the over and under strategy to go from 0.25 × 16 to 0.24 × 16 and 0.26 × 16.

| 25 × 24 |
| ¼ of 24 |
| 0.25 × 24 |
| 0.01 × 24 |
| 0.26 × 24 |
| 0.24 × 24 |
| 0.25 × 28 |
| 0.75 × 28 |
| 0.76 × 28 |
| 76 × 28 |

Using Fractions		
25 × 32	25 × 16	¼ × 88
26 × 32	¼ × 16	0.25 × 88
¼ × 32	¾ × 16	0.26 × 88
0.25 × 32	0.75 × 16	0.26 × 89
0.26 × 32	0.76 × 16	0.24 × 88
0.24 × 32	0.25 × 18	0.24 × 89
0.75 × 32	0.26 × 18	0.75 × 88
0.74 × 32	26 × 18	0.75 × 26
0.76 × 32	26.1 × 18	75 × 0.26

Using Proportional Reasoning

Use proportional reasoning strings to help students reason proportionally as they use equivalent ratios to multiply. These strings use many of the same multiplicative relationships developed in the previous multiplication strings, but bring them all together to focus on reasoning proportionally using a ratio table as a tool. Each string finds many products using one specific factor, such as 17, as shown in this first string. In this string, students can use previous problems with strategies including chunking, over and under, and place-value shifts as they multiply and divide by multiples of 10. Help students make connections by drawing out the place-value relationships. Model student strategies on a ratio table. Deliver the strings that follow in the context of a unit rate; for example, 1 bag has 19 donut holes, 1 pack has 47 mints, and 1 package has 37 candies (as Brittany did with eye drops for the five is half of ten strategy discussed earlier in this section).

| 2 × 17 |
| 4 × 17 |
| 8 × 17 |
| 10 × 17 |
| 9 × 17 |
| 5 × 17 |
| 100 × 17 |
| 99 × 17 |

Whole Numbers		
2 × 47	2 × 37	19 × 2
4 × 47	10 × 37	19 × 0.5
8 × 47	9 × 37	19 × 10
10 × 47	5 × 37	19 × 5
9 × 47	15 × 37	19 × 15
5 × 47	20 × 37	19 × 100
15 × 47	19 × 37	19 × 50
14 × 47	100 × 37	19 × 150
100 × 47	91 × 37	19 × 149
99 × 47	99 × 37	19 × 145

Decimals		
2 × 4.1	2 × 2.4	2 × 3.3
4 × 4.1	10 × 2.4	4 × 3.3
8 × 4.1	9 × 2.4	8 × 3.3
10 × 4.1	90 × 2.4	10 × 3.3
9 × 4.1	5 × 2.4	9 × 3.3
5 × 4.1	95 × 2.4	90 × 3.3
100 × 4.1	9.5 × 2.4	5 × 3.3
92 × 4.1	45 × 2.4	85 × 3.3
9.2 × 4.1	4.5 × 2.4	8.5 × 3.3

Same Strategies, Smaller Numbers (Basic Facts)

Same strategies, smaller numbers strings help students automatize the "basic facts." These strings use many of the same multiplicative relationships developed in the previous sections, but bring them all together, focusing on smaller numbers. Each string finds many products using one specific factor, such as 7, as shown in this first string. Note that in this string, some problems are repeated. This is to subtly suggest that students could use that problem to reason about the next problem. It is not necessary that students use the suggestion, but by mentioning it, you invite students to make connections between the problems and students may begin to use the relationships. Each time a problem is repeated in the string, say something like, "And what was 2 times 7 again?" Model student strategies with arrays and ratio tables only as needed.

2 × 7
4 × 7
8 × 7
2 × 7
3 × 7
6 × 7
10 × 7
9 × 7
10 × 7
11 × 7
6 × 7
12 × 7

Pam: Abby, what is 2 times 7, 2 sevens?
Abby: 14.
Pam: And 4 times 7?
Abby: 28.
Pam: How do you know?

Abby:	If 2 times 7 is 14, then 4 times 7 is double that, 28.
Pam:	What about 8 sevens, 8 times 7?
Abby:	Double that, 56.
Pam:	What if I hadn't asked you 4 times 7 first? How could you find it?
Abby:	Double, double, double, 14, 28, 56.
Pam:	Nice. What was 2 times 7 again?
Abby:	14
Pam:	Three times 7, 3 sevens?
Abby:	21.
Pam:	If 3 sevens is 21, how much is 6 sevens, 6 times 7?
Abby:	Um, 42.
Pam:	How did you get that?
Abby:	Double 21.
Pam:	So, if you know 3 sevens, you can double 21 to get 6 sevens? Great. How about 10 times 7?

The following three problems strings provide experience with different facts and relationships.

2 × 6	2 × 8	4 × 10
4 × 6	3 × 8	4 × 9
8 × 6	4 × 8	4 × 10
9 × 6	8 × 8	4 × 5
10 × 6	10 × 8	4 × 2
5 × 6	9 × 9	4 × 3
6 × 6	10 × 8	4 × 6
2 × 6	5 × 8	4 × 7
3 × 6	2 × 8	4 × 2
6 × 6	3 × 8	4 × 4
7 × 6	6 × 8	4 × 8

Division

The strings for division include the following strategies:

- ▶ Multiply Then Divide
- ▶ Partial Quotients
- ▶ Over and Under
- ▶ Five Is Half of Ten
- ▶ Constant Ratio
- ▶ Using Proportional Reasoning

Multiply Then Divide

Use multiply then divide strings to transition students from multiplication to division. Use an open array to model student strategies for both the multiplication and division problems. The open array model can help students gain spatial sense about the distributive property, that $192 \div 6 = (180 \div 6) + (12 \div 6)$, because the $180 \div 6$ and the $12 \div 6$ can represent arrays that combine to form the $192 \div 6$ (Figure 5.14).

6×30
6×2
6×32
$180 \div 6$
$12 \div 6$
$192 \div 6$
$204 \div 6$
$186 \div 6$

FIGURE 5.14

These strings are constructed with sets of three problems where the first two problems can be used to solve the third. The second half of the string is based on the first half, using the relationship between multiplication and division. The last problems suggest using the over and under strategy.

The first set of three strings that follows uses whole numbers and the second set decimals.

Whole Numbers		
41×10	52×2	86×10
41×2	52×20	86×5
41×12	52×22	86×15
$410 \div 41$	$1{,}040 \div 52$	$860 \div 86$
$82 \div 41$	$104 \div 52$	$430 \div 86$
$492 \div 41$	$1{,}144 \div 52$	$1{,}290 \div 86$
$403 \div 31$	$966 \div 42$	$735 \div 35$

Decimals		
3.2×10	2.4×2	8.6×1
3.2×3	2.4×0.2	8.6×0.1
3.2×13	2.4×2.2	8.6×1.1
$32 \div 3.2$	$4.8 \div 2.4$	$8.6 \div 8.6$
$9.6 \div 3.2$	$0.48 \div 2.4$	$0.86 \div 8.6$
$41.6 \div 3.2$	$5.28 \div 2.4$	$9.46 \div 8.6$
$37.2 \div 3.1$	$3.36 \div 1.6$	$6.82 \div 3.1$

Partial Quotients

Use partial quotient strings to build a spatial sense of the distributive property. Students can use chunks they know to help them figure out chunks they do not know. These strings are similar to those in the "Multiply Then Divide" section, but the corresponding multiplication problems are not provided first in each string. Model student strategies on an open array.

$260 \div 26$
$52 \div 26$
$312 \div 26$
$540 \div 54$
$1{,}080 \div 54$
$162 \div 54$
$1{,}242 \div 54$
$672 \div 21$

These strings are constructed with sets of three problems where the first two problems can be used to solve the third. The last problem has no helpers.

Kim, a fifth-grade teacher, begins the string by asking, "With a division problem like $260 \div 26$, where do the numbers go on an array?" A dialog ensues.

Michaela: The 26 is a dimension. We don't know the other one.
Nick: The 260 is the area. It goes in the middle and the 26 goes on one side.

Kim draws part of an open array and labels it.

$260 \div 26$

```
            26
      ┌──────────────┐
  ?   │     260
      └──────────────┘
```

Kim: What is 260 divided by 26?
Gabi: It's 10 because 10 times 26 is 260. *Kim fills in the missing dimension and finishes the equation.*

$260 \div 26 = 10$

```
            26
      ┌──────────────┐
 10   │     260      │
      └──────────────┘
```

Kim: What is 52 divided by 26? And what would the array look like? *She writes the expression $52 \div 26$.*

Kat: The array will be shorter, 2 by 26 because 52 divided by 26 is 2. *Kim sketches the array and finishes the equation. Note that the arrays are lined up and proportional. This is important so that students have the opportunity to notice the relationships and use them for subsequent problems.*

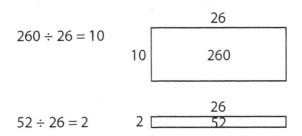

$260 \div 26 = 10$

$52 \div 26 = 2$

Kim: The next problem is 312 divided by 26. Before you solve that, tell me what the array will look like. *She writes $312 \div 26$.*

Marissa: The array will look like a something by 26 with an area of 312. It will have the same width as the rectangles you have already drawn. *Kim draws and labels a partial open array.*

$312 \div 26$

Kim: And what is 312 divided by 26? What is that missing dimension? Twenty-six by what is 312? Vincent, how did you find that missing dimension?

Vincent: I knew that 26 by 10 is 260, so I added another 26 and got 286. That wasn't enough, so I added one more 26 and got 312. So 12 by 26 is 312, or 312 divided by 26 is 12. *Kim models his strategy.*

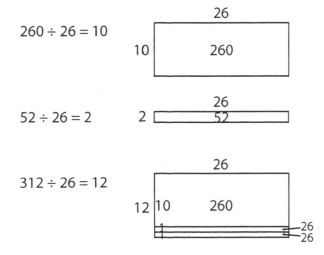

$260 \div 26 = 10$

$52 \div 26 = 2$

$312 \div 26 = 12$

Kim: And Elijah? What did you do?

Elijah: I looked at what we already had. Since 260 and 52 is 312, I knew that I could just put those two arrays together to get a 12 by 26 and that would give me 312 for the area. *Kim models that strategy next to the previous one, so that they line up. This helps nudge students to considering bigger chunks of arrays in their work because they can see the smaller chunks encompassed in the bigger chunks.*

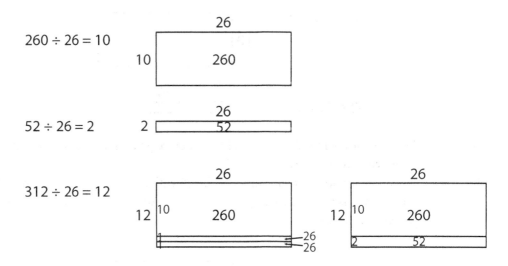

$260 \div 26 = 10$

$52 \div 26 = 2$

$312 \div 26 = 12$

Kim continues the string and then at the end, asks students to discuss what they think about the problems they solved today.

Gilbert: To solve division problems, I can think about multiplication.
Marissa: I can use chunks I know to find chunks I don't know.
Brianna: Ten times a number can be a good starting place.

Following are more partial quotient strings. The first set uses whole numbers and the second set decimals.

Whole Numbers		
$520 \div 52$	$96 \div 32$	$88 \div 22$
$104 \div 52$	$64 \div 32$	$44 \div 22$
$624 \div 52$	$160 \div 32$	$132 \div 22$
$420 \div 21$	$2{,}130 \div 71$	$360 \div 18$
$63 \div 21$	$71 \div 71$	$54 \div 18$
$483 \div 21$	$2{,}201 \div 71$	$414 \div 18$
$567 \div 27$	$205 \div 41$	$713 \div 31$

Decimals		
23 ÷ 2.3	6.6 ÷ 2.2	8.8 ÷ 4.4
6.9 ÷ 2.3	4.4 ÷ 2.2	4.4 ÷ 4.4
29.9 ÷ 2.3	11 ÷ 2.2	13.2 ÷ 4.4
84 ÷ 4.2	81 ÷ 8.1	20.4 ÷ 5.1
4.2 ÷ 4.2	8.1 ÷ 8.1	15.3 ÷ 5.1
88.2 ÷ 4.2	89.1 ÷ 8.1	35.7 ÷ 5.1
9.2 ÷ 2.3	50.4 ÷ 2.4	70.4 ÷ 3.2

Over and Under

These over and under strings continue to use the distributive property, but they narrow in on finding quotients that are a little over or under a friendly quotient. For example, $198 \div 18 = (180 \div 18) + (18 \div 18) = \frac{180}{18} + \frac{18}{18} = 10 + 1 = 11$. These strings are constructed with sets of problems that all have the same divisor. Students find friendly quotients for that divisor and then work a bit over and under. Until students have facility using ratio tables as a tool, use a context for these strings. Say, "If a bag of chips has 18 chips in it, how many bags contain 180 chips?" as you write the expression *180 ÷ 18* and fill in a ratio table with the ratio 1:18 and 180: ___.

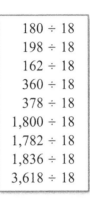

180 ÷ 18
198 ÷ 18
162 ÷ 18
360 ÷ 18
378 ÷ 18
1,800 ÷ 18
1,782 ÷ 18
1,836 ÷ 18
3,618 ÷ 18

Figure 5.15 models the first four problems in a ratio table:

FIGURE 5.15

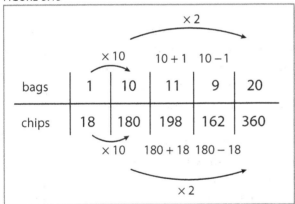

The first set of three strings that follows uses whole numbers and the second set decimals.

Whole Numbers		
58 ÷ 29	162 ÷ 81	208 ÷ 52
580 ÷ 29	1,620 ÷ 81	260 ÷ 52
609 ÷ 29	1,539 ÷ 81	520 ÷ 52
522 ÷ 29	243 ÷ 81	468 ÷ 52
2,900 ÷ 29	2,511 ÷ 81	2,548 ÷ 52
2,871 ÷ 29	2,349 ÷ 81	5,252 ÷ 52
2,958 ÷ 29	8,019 ÷ 81	1,040 ÷ 52
5,742 ÷ 29	7,938 ÷ 81	988 ÷ 52

Decimals		
45 ÷ 4.5	4.7 ÷ 4.7	20.8 ÷ 2.08
4.5 ÷ 4.5	9.4 ÷ 4.7	22.88 ÷ 2.08
49.5 ÷ 4.5	94 ÷ 4.7	18.72 ÷ 2.08
40.5 ÷ 4.5	89.3 ÷ 4.7	4.16 ÷ 2.08
36 ÷ 4.5	47 ÷ 4.7	41.6 ÷ 2.08
450 ÷ 4.5	51.7 ÷ 4.7	43.68 ÷ 2.08
445.5 ÷ 4.5	42.3 ÷ 4.7	208 ÷ 2.08
900 ÷ 4.5	474.7 ÷ 4.7	212.16 ÷ 2.08
904.5 ÷ 4.5	460.6 ÷ 4.7	205.92 ÷ 2.08

Five Is Half of Ten

Use these five is half of ten strings to work on the relationship between 5 and 10 with division. Use a ratio table to model student strategies. These strings are constructed with the same divisor, using products of the divisor and 10, 5, 100, 50. Look for place-value connections between the problems and suggest them if students do not. For example, if students have found that $70 \div 14 = 5$, they can use that to find $700 \div 14 = 50$. Model a couple of students' alternate strategies for some problems and explore why they work and the connections between them. For example, to find $210 \div 14$, students could multiply the 70 by 3 to get $210 \div 14 = 5 \times 3 = 15$ (Figure 5.16).

140 ÷ 14
126 ÷ 14
70 ÷ 14
210 ÷ 14
224 ÷ 14
700 ÷ 14
672 ÷ 14
728 ÷ 14
1,400 ÷ 14
1,372 ÷ 14

FIGURE 5.16

Or students could add the 140 and 70 to get the 210 for a corresponding dividend of
10 + 5 = 15 (Figure 5.17).

FIGURE 5.17

				10 + 5
1	10	9	5	15
14	140	126	70	210
				140 + 70

The first set of strings that follows uses whole numbers and the second set decimals.

Whole Numbers		
260 ÷ 26	4,200 ÷ 42	2,700 ÷ 27
130 ÷ 26	420 ÷ 42	2,673 ÷ 27
156 ÷ 26	210 ÷ 42	1,350 ÷ 27
390 ÷ 26	630 ÷ 42	4,050 ÷ 27
364 ÷ 26	6,300 ÷ 42	2,025 ÷ 27
1,300 ÷ 26	4,116 ÷ 42	405 ÷ 27
650 ÷ 26	2,142 ÷ 42	4,077 ÷ 27
676 ÷ 26	6,090 ÷ 42	4,455 ÷ 27
1,950 ÷ 26	6,258 ÷ 42	135 ÷ 27
1,924 ÷ 26	3,150 ÷ 42	3,915 ÷ 27

Decimals		
16 ÷ 1.6	52 ÷ 5.2	2.8 ÷ 0.28
14.4 ÷ 1.6	26 ÷ 5.2	28 ÷ 0.28
8 ÷ 1.6	78 ÷ 5.2	1.4 ÷ 0.28
12 ÷ 1.6	260 ÷ 5.2	1.68 ÷ 0.28
120 ÷ 1.6	130 ÷ 5.2	2.52 ÷ 0.28
24 ÷ 1.6	390 ÷ 5.2	27.72 ÷ 0.28
25.6 ÷ 1.6	442 ÷ 5.2	4.2 ÷ 0.28
80 ÷ 1.6	254.8 ÷ 5.2	42 ÷ 0.28
78.4 ÷ 1.6	514.8 ÷ 5.2	42.28 ÷ 0.28
40 ÷ 1.6	525.2 ÷ 5.2	46.2 ÷ 0.28

Constant Ratio (Equivalent Ratio)

Use constant ratio strings to help students construct the relationships between division
and equivalent ratios. Division can be represented by a ratio, which can be simplified to
solve division problems. Use an open array to model student strategies for problems and
emphasize the relationships between the changing areas and dimensions: when you halve
the area and halve one of the dimensions, the other dimension stays the same; when you

32 ÷ 16
64 ÷ 8
32 ÷ 8
64 ÷ 16
16 ÷ 8
16 ÷ 4
8 ÷ 2
156 ÷ 12

double the area and keep one dimension the same, the other dimension doubles. The open array model can help students gain spatial sense about finding equivalent ratios such as $32 \div 16 = 16 \div 8 = 8 \div 4 = 4 \div 2$ which can be written $^{32}/_{16} = {}^{16}/_8 = {}^8/_4 = {}^4/_2$ (Figure 5.18).

FIGURE 5.18

The string above and the first string that follows are constructed with sets of related problems so that students can discuss the relationships between the areas and dimensions of the arrays that model those problems. The last 2 strings are designed with paired problems that are equivalent and other problems that can be easily solved by finding equivalent ratios. For example, $60 \div 7.5 = 120 \div 15 = 240 \div 30 = 24 \div 3 = 8$.

The string on the left, Quotients >1, has problems that result in quotients that are greater than 1, such as $330 \div 165 = {}^{330}/_{165} = {}^{660}/_{330} = 2$. The middle string, Quotients <1, has problems that result in quotients that are less than 1, such as $36 \div 144 = {}^{36}/_{144} = {}^{18}/_{72} = {}^2/_8 = {}^1/_4 = 0.25$. The string on the right, Decimal Divisors, works with decimal divisors, such as $36 \div 4.5 = {}^{72}/_9 = 8$.

Quotients >1	Quotients <1	Decimal Divisors
$36 \div 9$	$76 \div 8$	$500 \div 25$
$72 \div 18$	$2 \div 8$	$250 \div 12.5$
$72 \div 9$	$18 \div 72$	$330 \div 16.5$
$36 \div 18$	$36 \div 144$	$60 \div 7.5$
$12 \div 6$	$6 \div 24$	$72 \div 4.5$
$288 \div 32$	$48 \div 192$	

Brittany delivers the "Quotients >1" string, beginning with $36 \div 9$, with her students.

Brittany: Today, we'll start off with an easy one, $36 \div 9$. You need to be able to figure these quickly. What is $36 \div 9$? *Brittany writes the problem on the board.*

Riley: It's 4. *Brittany fills in the answer, $36 \div 9 = 4$.*

Brittany: I will model that on an array. What parts of the array do I label with the 36 and the 9?

Riley: The 36 is the area, the 9 is one dimension and the 4 is the other one. *Brittany draws and labels the array.*

$36 \div 9 = 4$

Brittany: The next problem is 72 ÷ 18. Before you start figuring, first tell me what the array should look like, compared to the 36 ÷ 9 array that we already have.

Caitlyn: It's got twice as much area and the side is twice as long.

Brittany: So, the area is twice as big and the known dimension is twice as long. *Brittany draws and labels the array.*

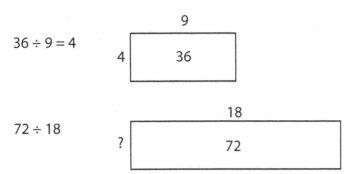

Brittany: What is the missing dimension? What is 72 divided by 18?

Timothy: I doubled 18 to get 36 and doubled that to get 72. So it's 4 eighteens. *Brittany fills in the 4 on the array and in the equation.*

Brittany: How does this 72 divided by 18 relate to the first problem, 36 divided by 9?

Tyler: It's twice as long and has twice the area.

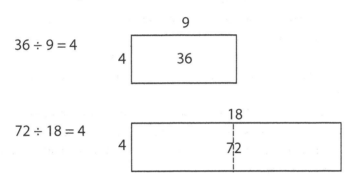

Brittany: Do you think that's always true? That if you double the area and double the dimension, that the other dimension will stay the same? Think about that while we do the next few problems. What is 72 divided by 9? What would the array look like?

Emma: I know 72 divided by 9 is 8 because 9 times 8 is like 10 times 8, 80, but minus one 8, so 72.

Collin: The array is back to where one dimension is 9.

Alex: And the area is 72. That has to be the same area as the second array. But the dimension is half of the 18. It's going to have to be taller, longer down the board.

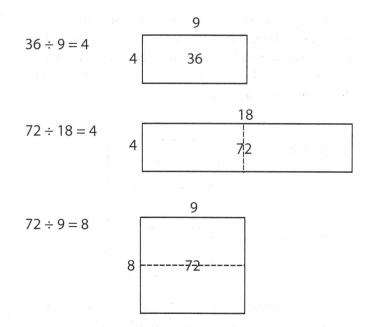

$36 \div 9 = 4$

$72 \div 18 = 4$

$72 \div 9 = 8$

The discussion continues with 36 ÷ 18 and 12 ÷ 6, where students compare the areas and dimensions (the products and factors).

Brittany: What relationships are you seeing?

Hunter: When you double the area and double the dimension, the other dimension stays the same.

Brittany: Can you say that using products and factors?

Hunter: If you double the product and one factor, the other factor stays the same.

Brittany: What else?

Lainey: If you cut both the area, product, and the dimension — the factor — in half, the other dimension, the other factor, stays the same.

Ashton: That could be helpful if we could cut the problem down to something that we already know.

Brittany: I will write what you just said in a slightly different format. *Brittany records some of the equivalencies with equations.*

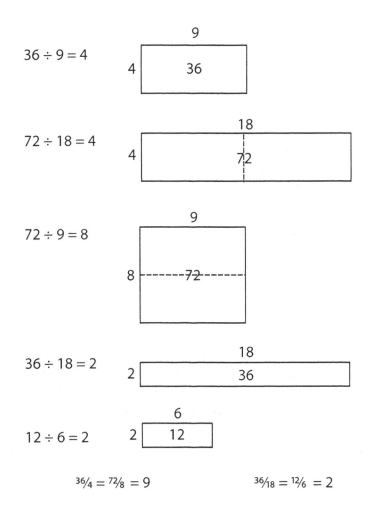

$36 \div 9 = 4$

$72 \div 18 = 4$

$72 \div 9 = 8$

$36 \div 18 = 2$

$12 \div 6 = 2$

$^{36}/_4 = {}^{72}/_8 = 9$ $^{36}/_{18} = {}^{12}/_6 = 2$

Brittany: I wonder if we could use that to think about the last problem, which is 288 divided by 32?

After students solve 288 ÷ 32, Brittany asks them to share strategies. Jonathan uses $^{320}/_{32} = 10$ to find that $^{288}/_{32} = 9$ by removing one group of 32 from 320. Chelsea doubles 32 to 64 to 128 to 256 and adds one more 32 to get $9 \times 32 = 288$, so 288 ÷ 32 = 9. Since no one mentions simplifying the ratio, Brittany brings out the relationship that $^{288}/_{32} = {}^{144}/_{16} = {}^{72}/_8 = 9$ by questioning students about the corresponding areas, dimensions, and quotients (Figure 5.19). She plans to continue to nudge these relationships in future strings.

FIGURE 5.19

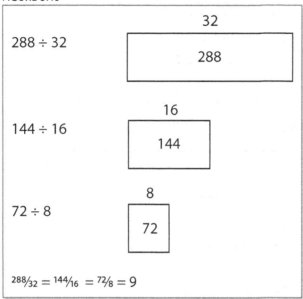

$^{288}/_{32} = {}^{144}/_{16} = {}^{72}/_8 = 9$

The following strings use the relationship of dividing by 10 or 100, so you will want to have built that relationship with students before using these strings. Because dividing by 10 and 100 results in a place-value shift, we look for problems where the divisor can be easily manipulated with multiplication to be 10 or 100. For example, $3.2 \div 5$ is equivalent to $6.4 \div 10 = 0.64$; $^{3.2}/_5 = {}^{6.4}/_{10} = 0.64$. Students can also reason that $3.2 \div 10$ is 0.32 and then double 0.32 to get $3.2 \div 5 = 0.64$. Essentially they divide by twice as much and then double the answer.

Using 10		
$165 \div 5$	$22 \div 25$	$3.2 \div 5$
$330 \div 10$	$44 \div 50$	$6.4 \div 10$
$550 \div 25$	$88 \div 100$	$490 \div 5$
$1,100 \div 50$	$75 \div 2.5$	$980 \div 10$
$2,200 \div 100$	$150 \div 5$	$49 \div 0.5$
$231 \div 5$	$130 \div 12.5$	$2.7 \div 0.5$
$1,075 \div 5$	$11 \div 12.5$	$0.88 \div 0.25$
		$1.6 \div 0.125$

Using Proportional Reasoning

Use proportional reasoning strings to help students use the ratio table as a tool to solve division problems by reasoning proportionally. Use a ratio table to model student strategies for both the multiplication and division problems. These strings are constructed based on a unit ratio; for example, 1:17. The strings start with a few multiplication problems to establish some helpful relationships, like 17×2, and then follow

17×2
17×4
17×10
$153 \div 17$
$85 \div 17$
$255 \div 17$
$238 \div 17$
$1,700 \div 17$
$1,683 \div 17$

with division problems, many that are related by a place-value shift, or are a bit over and under previous quotients. Use a context like mints in a bag. For 17 × 2, "If a bag has 17 mints, how many mints are in 2 bags?" For 153 ÷ 17, "If I have 153 mints, how many bags do I have?"

A ratio table for this string without all the marks to show strategies could look like the one shown in Figure 5.20:

FIGURE 5.20

bag	1	2	4	10	9	5	15	14	100	99
mints	17	34	68	170	153	85	255	238	1,700	1,683

The first set of three strings that follows uses whole numbers and the second set decimals.

Whole Numbers		
78 × 2	81 × 3	64 × 2
78 × 4	81 × 6	64 × 5
78 × 10	81 × 10	64 × 7
702 ÷ 78	405 ÷ 81	512 ÷ 64
390 ÷ 78	1,215 ÷ 81	640 ÷ 64
1,092 ÷ 78	2,430 ÷ 81	1,088 ÷ 64
156 ÷ 78	2,349 ÷ 81	4,480 ÷ 64
7,176 ÷ 78	4,941 ÷ 81	4,416 ÷ 64

Decimals		
4.2 × 2	3.4 × 2	5.6 × 3
4.2 × 4	3.4 × 4	5.6 × 6
4.2 × 10	3.4 × 8	28 ÷ 5.6
21 ÷ 4.2	30.6 ÷ 3.4	61.6 ÷ 5.6
37.8 ÷ 4.2	17 ÷ 3.4	50.4 ÷ 5.6
33.6 ÷ 4.2	23.8 ÷ 3.4	168 ÷ 5.6
168 ÷ 4.2	166.6 ÷ 3.4	162.4 ÷ 5.6
172.2 ÷ 4.2	132.6 ÷ 3.4	330.4 ÷ 5.6

Fractions

The strings for fraction operations include the following strategies:

▶ Using a Money Model for Addition and Subtraction
▶ Using a Clock Model for Addition and Subtraction
▶ Choosing Your Model for Addition and Subtraction
▶ Finding Equivalent Fractions for Addition and Subtraction

- ▶ Fractions as Operators
- ▶ Fractions as Decimals
- ▶ Scaling Up for Multiplication
- ▶ Trading Places
- ▶ Using Quotative Division
- ▶ Using the Constant (Equivalent) Ratio Strategy for Division

Fractions appear in many other strings in this book because those strategies also apply to specific fraction relationships. For example, when adding fractions you can give and take when one addend is close to a friendly number and it is easy to take the needed part from the other addend, like $9\frac{3}{4} + \frac{1}{2} = 10 + \frac{1}{4}$. Constant difference works well when the subtrahend is close to a friendly number, like $6\frac{1}{5} - 2\frac{4}{5} = 6\frac{2}{5} - 3 = 3\frac{2}{5}$. Doubling and halving works well for problems like $4\frac{1}{2} \times 8 = 9 \times 4 = 36$. The constant ratio strategy for division works so well for fractions that we'll devote a whole section here to it. The rest of these strategies apply specifically to fractions and are, therefore, included in this section.

The first three strings sections that follow focus on using relationships with money and time to find common denominators so that students can use the same kind of reasoning to find common denominators for uncommon fraction problems. A colleague and friend, Kathy Hale, after experiencing the money and clock model strings, related, "When we work with money and clocks, we are looking at naturally occurring common denominators, so that we can learn why we need common denominators!"

Using a Money Model for Addition and Subtraction

Use the money model for addition and subtraction strings to help students reason about adding and subtracting fractions using money equivalents. Using money relationships work well for problems where both fractions have denominators that are factors of 100. Deliver these strings in the context of money. For $\frac{1}{2} + \frac{1}{4}$, say, "What is $\frac{1}{2}$ plus $\frac{1}{4}$? I want you to think in terms of money. What do you think of when you think of $\frac{1}{2}$ in money? And $\frac{1}{4}$ in money?" Model student strategies using decimal equivalents. For example, for $\frac{3}{4} - \frac{1}{2}$, as students talk about 75 cents minus 50 cents being 25 cents, write *0.75 − 0.50 = 0.25*. Then ask students to write that money amount in terms of fractions. Since 25 cents is 1 quarter out of the 4 quarters in a dollar, $0.25 = \frac{1}{4}$. For these strings, focus less on how students do the decimal addition or subtraction (give and take or constant difference), and focus more on how students use the money context to find equivalents to fractions to solve the problems. In other words, focus the conversation around the equivalencies they used (8 dimes or 16 nickels for $\frac{4}{5}$ and 4 dimes or 8 nickels for $\frac{8}{20}$) and not how they added the resulting 0.8 and 0.4.

In all of these strings, encourage students to consider scaling up from unit fractions. For the problem $\frac{3}{10} + \frac{2}{5}$, they can find $\frac{3}{10}$ of a dollar by finding $\frac{1}{10}$ of a dollar, 0.10, and scaling up by 3, $3 \times 0.10 = 0.30$. They can find $\frac{2}{5}$ of a dollar by finding $\frac{1}{5}$ of a dollar, 0.20, and scaling up by 2, $2 \times 0.20 = 0.40$. The scaling helps them find the equivalencies to add $\frac{3}{10} + \frac{2}{5} = 0.30 + 0.40 = 0.70 = \frac{7}{10}$.

$\frac{1}{2} + \frac{1}{4}$
$\frac{3}{4} - \frac{1}{2}$
$\frac{1}{10} + \frac{1}{20}$
$\frac{1}{10} + \frac{1}{2}$
$\frac{1}{2} - \frac{3}{10}$
$\frac{7}{10} + \frac{1}{4}$
$\frac{3}{20} - \frac{1}{10}$

Answers <1	Answers >1	Mixed Numbers
$\frac{1}{5} + \frac{3}{10}$	$\frac{4}{5} + \frac{3}{4}$	$99\frac{1}{4} - \frac{3}{10}$
$\frac{7}{10} - \frac{2}{5}$	$5\frac{1}{4} - 3\frac{1}{2}$	$48\frac{1}{10} - 47\frac{3}{5}$
$\frac{1}{20} + \frac{3}{4}$	$\frac{9}{10} + \frac{7}{20}$	$3\frac{1}{20} + 4\frac{9}{10}$
$\frac{3}{4} - \frac{3}{20}$	$\frac{2}{5} + \frac{19}{20}$	$5\frac{2}{5} + 1\frac{1}{4}$
$\frac{3}{10} + \frac{2}{5}$	$2\frac{2}{5} - \frac{9}{20}$	$4\frac{2}{5} - 2\frac{7}{10}$
$\frac{4}{5} - \frac{1}{4}$	$1\frac{1}{5} - \frac{3}{4}$	$3\frac{19}{20} + 5\frac{3}{4}$

The following strings use fractions with reciprocal relationships that can be challenging for students to sort out but are very helpful multiplicative relationships to construct. For example, $\frac{1}{4}$ of a dollar is 0.25 because $4 \times 0.25 = 1.00$. Also, $\frac{1}{25}$ of a dollar is \$0.04 because $25 \times 0.04 = 1.00$. If you're finding $\frac{1}{4} - \frac{1}{25}$, you can think $0.25 - 0.04$, which gets you 0.21, which is $\frac{21}{100}$. The relationships of $4 \times 25 = 100$ can be used to find money equivalents to both quarters and twenty-fifths. Help students parse out these relationships by staying in the context of money. When they see $\frac{1}{5}$ and erroneously think nickels, ask them to consider $\frac{1}{5}$ of a dollar, \$0.20, or ask them how many nickels are in a dollar, 20.

Reciprocal Relationships		
$\frac{1}{4} - \frac{1}{25}$	$\frac{1}{50} + \frac{1}{2}$	$2\frac{1}{5} - \frac{1}{20}$
$\frac{24}{25} + \frac{3}{4}$	$\frac{1}{2} - \frac{3}{50}$	$2\frac{1}{5} - 1\frac{19}{20}$
$\frac{3}{4} - \frac{6}{25}$	$\frac{49}{50} + \frac{3}{2}$	$4\frac{1}{50} + \frac{1}{2}$
$\frac{3}{5} + \frac{3}{20}$	$\frac{27}{50} - \frac{1}{2}$	$\frac{13}{20} + 2\frac{1}{5}$
$\frac{3}{5} - \frac{3}{20}$	$\frac{11}{20} - \frac{1}{5}$	$3\frac{3}{50} - 2\frac{1}{2}$
$\frac{15}{20} + \frac{4}{5}$	$\frac{5}{20} + \frac{2}{5}$	$5\frac{1}{25} + \frac{3}{4}$

Using a Clock Model for Addition and Subtraction

Use the clock model for addition and subtraction strings to help students reason about adding and subtracting fractions by using time equivalents as found on a clock. Using relationships involving time works well for problems where both fractions have denominators that are factors of 60. Deliver these strings in the context of time. For $\frac{1}{2} + \frac{1}{4}$, say, "What is $\frac{1}{2}$ plus $\frac{1}{4}$? I want you to think in terms of a clock. What do you think of when you think of $\frac{1}{2}$ on a clock? And $\frac{1}{4}$ on a clock?" Model student strategies using fractional equivalents.

$\frac{1}{2} + \frac{1}{4}$
$\frac{3}{4} - \frac{1}{2}$
$\frac{1}{3} + \frac{1}{4}$
$\frac{1}{10} + \frac{1}{2}$
$\frac{1}{2} - \frac{1}{6}$
$\frac{7}{12} + \frac{1}{4}$
$\frac{3}{12} - \frac{1}{10}$

For a problem like $\frac{3}{4} - \frac{1}{2}$, as students talk about 45 minutes minus 30 minutes being 15 minutes, write $\frac{45}{60} - \frac{30}{60} = \frac{15}{60}$. Then ask students to write equivalencies for $\frac{15}{60}$ in terms of time. Since 15 minutes is 1 quarter out of the 4 quarters in an hour, $\frac{15}{60} = \frac{1}{4}$. Since 15 minutes is 3 5-minute chunks out of the 12 5-minute chunks on a clock, $\frac{15}{60} = \frac{1}{4} = \frac{3}{12}$. For this problem, you might even ask about 10-minute chunks. Since 15 minutes is 1.5 10-minute chunks out of the 6 10-minute chunks in an hour, $\frac{15}{60} = \frac{1}{4} = \frac{3}{12} = \frac{1.5}{6}$. This reasoning is at the heart of fraction equivalence and proportional reasoning. Because we as math teachers often want the answer expressed in the most simplified form, you could then ask students which of the equivalent fractions is in simplified form.

Many of these problems can be solved using either a time or money relationships. This is purposeful. Allow students to solve the problems however they want to, encouraging them to consider the clock model and asking students to share clock strategies.

In all of these strings, encourage students to consider scaling up from unit fractions, such as finding $\frac{5}{12}$ using a clock model by finding $\frac{1}{12}$, 5 minutes, and scaling up by 5, 5×5 minutes = 25 minutes, $\frac{25}{60}$.

$\frac{1}{3} + \frac{1}{4}$	$\frac{3}{4} + \frac{1}{6}$	$\frac{1}{4} - \frac{1}{3}$
$\frac{3}{4} - \frac{1}{3}$	$\frac{1}{4} - \frac{1}{12}$	$\frac{3}{4} - \frac{2}{3}$
$\frac{1}{10} + \frac{1}{4}$	$\frac{1}{12} + \frac{1}{15}$	$\frac{1}{3} + \frac{1}{10}$
$\frac{3}{4} - \frac{1}{20}$	$\frac{1}{6} + \frac{1}{20}$	$\frac{2}{3} + \frac{3}{10}$
$\frac{1}{4} + \frac{1}{5}$	$\frac{1}{3} - \frac{1}{30}$	$\frac{1}{3} - \frac{1}{6}$
$\frac{1}{4} - \frac{1}{5}$	$\frac{1}{2} - \frac{1}{12}$	$\frac{5}{3} - \frac{5}{6}$

Just like with the money model, the clock model can suggest challenging but helpful reciprocal relationships. For example, $\frac{1}{4}$ of a hour is 15 minutes because $4 \times 15 = 60$. Also, $\frac{1}{15}$ of an hour is 4 minutes because $15 \times 4 = 60$. Thus, $4 \times 15 = 60$ can be used to find time equivalents to both quarters and fifteenths. Help students parse out these relationships by staying in the context of time. When they see $\frac{1}{3}$ and erroneously think 3 minutes, ask them to consider $\frac{1}{3}$ of an hour, 20 minutes.

Reciprocal Relationships		
$\frac{1}{4} - \frac{1}{15}$	$\frac{1}{30} + \frac{1}{2}$	$\frac{1}{6} - \frac{1}{10}$
$\frac{2}{15} + \frac{3}{4}$	$\frac{1}{2} - \frac{1}{30}$	$\frac{5}{6} - \frac{3}{10}$
$\frac{3}{4} - \frac{6}{15}$	$\frac{29}{30} + \frac{1}{2}$	$\frac{1}{12} + \frac{1}{5}$
$\frac{2}{3} + \frac{3}{20}$	$\frac{17}{30} - \frac{1}{2}$	$\frac{2}{5} + \frac{5}{12}$
$\frac{1}{3} - \frac{3}{20}$	$\frac{11}{20} - \frac{1}{3}$	$\frac{29}{30} - \frac{1}{2}$
$\frac{5}{20} + \frac{1}{3}$	$\frac{1}{20} + \frac{2}{3}$	$\frac{2}{3} + \frac{5}{20}$

Choosing Your Model for Addition and Subtraction

Use choosing your model for addition and subtraction strings to help students reason about which model to use: money, for denominators that are factors of 100, or clock, for denominators that are factors of 60. Deliver these strings with no context, but then ask students which context they might want to use for an efficient solution. For problems where either model could be used, like $\frac{1}{10} + \frac{1}{4}$, model student strategies using decimal equivalents if they use money or using time equivalents if they use a clock. After students have shared both strategies, ask them to consider which works best for them for the particular numbers.

$\frac{1}{2} + \frac{1}{4}$
$\frac{3}{4} - \frac{1}{3}$
$\frac{1}{10} + \frac{1}{4}$
$\frac{1}{2} + \frac{1}{25}$
$\frac{1}{6} - \frac{1}{10}$
$\frac{7}{12} + \frac{1}{4}$
$\frac{3}{20} - \frac{1}{10}$
$\frac{1}{50} + \frac{1}{2}$

$\frac{1}{4} + \frac{1}{10}$	$\frac{2}{3} - \frac{5}{12}$	$\frac{1}{6} - \frac{1}{12}$
$\frac{1}{6} + \frac{3}{10}$	$\frac{9}{12} - \frac{1}{2}$	$\frac{1}{25} + \frac{4}{10}$
$\frac{3}{4} + \frac{2}{3}$	$\frac{3}{5} - \frac{9}{20}$	$\frac{3}{4} + \frac{5}{6}$
$\frac{3}{20} + \frac{3}{25}$	$\frac{13}{12} - \frac{1}{2}$	$\frac{11}{12} - \frac{1}{3}$
$\frac{11}{12} + \frac{1}{6}$	$\frac{9}{10} - \frac{3}{5}$	$\frac{9}{10} - \frac{17}{20}$
$\frac{4}{5} + \frac{7}{10}$	$\frac{4}{5} - \frac{1}{3}$	$\frac{1}{2} + \frac{7}{20}$
	$\frac{5}{4} - \frac{19}{20}$	$\frac{4}{15} + \frac{1}{12}$

Finding Equivalent Fractions for Addition and Subtraction

Finding equivalent fractions for addition and subtraction strings can open up students' repertoires for denominators that are not factors of 60 or 100. Both this problem string and the first that follows are constructed with a sequence of three problems where the first problem starts with the sum of unit fractions. The next problem has one non-unit fraction. The third problem has both addends scaled up to non-unit fractions. The last problem in the string has no helpers. Deliver these strings with the context of a race course. For example, if I walk ⅓ of the race course and then jog ¼ of the race course, the question ⅓ + ¼ means how much of the course have I traveled? Model student strategies on a double open number line.

$\frac{1}{3} + \frac{1}{4}$
$\frac{2}{3} + \frac{1}{4}$
$\frac{2}{3} + \frac{3}{4}$
$\frac{1}{5} + \frac{1}{7}$
$\frac{2}{5} + \frac{1}{7}$
$\frac{2}{5} + \frac{3}{7}$
$\frac{1}{3} + \frac{2}{5}$

The double open number line is a useful model to help students realize what they are doing as they find equivalent fractions with common denominators for the purpose of adding or subtracting fractions. It is a helpful model in part because students are "cognitively involved" in the process of choosing a course length (the common denominator) and then splitting that course into equal unit fractions. If students choose a course length of 12 to add ⅓ + ¼, when they go to mark ⅓ on the number line, they must visualize partitioning the length into 3 equal segments (Figure 5.21).

FIGURE 5.21

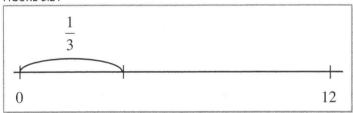

This cognitively suggests that they also need to divide the 12 into 3 equal parts, so that the ⅓ and 4 correspond. Now, the fraction part of the course is 4 out of the 12, ⁴⁄₁₂ (Figure 5.22).

FIGURE 5.22

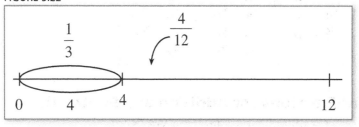

The problem ⅓ + ¼ could be modeled as shown in Figure 5.23.

FIGURE 5.23

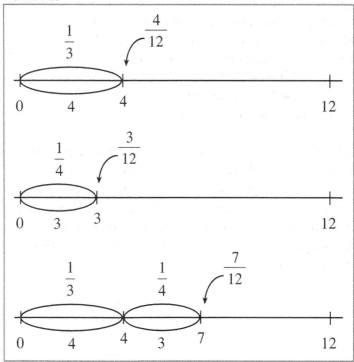

When you deliver the next problem, ⅔ + ¼, ask students, "Since we've already established that ⅓ of 12 is 4, what is ⅔ of 12? And what fraction of the course is that?" Then mark the corresponding 8 and ⅔ on the course. Generally, establish an equivalent fraction to the unit fraction, ⅓ = ⁴⁄₁₂ and then scale up, 2 × ⅓ = 2 × ⁴⁄₁₂ = ⁸⁄₁₂.

Do the same for the next problem, ⅔ + ¾, focusing on the ¼ to ¾ relationship. Since ¼ = ³⁄₁₂, then 3 × ¼ = 3 × ³⁄₁₂ = ⁹⁄₁₂. Add these on the double open number line (Figure 5.24).

FIGURE 5.24

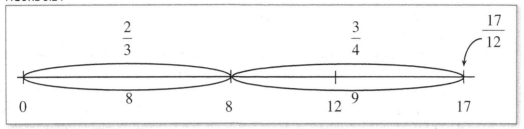

The middle string in the set that follows has denominators that are relatively prime. The last string has denominators that are not relatively prime and therefore invite a discussion about least common denominators.

¼ + ⅙	⅔ + 2/7	⅞ − ¾
¾ + ⅙	⅔ − ⅗	11/12 − ⅚
¾ + ⅚	¾ + 5/7	3/12 + ⅝
⅓ + ⅕	⅞ − ⅔	⅜ + ⅚
⅓ + ⅘		
⅔ + ⅘		
⅑ + ⅕		
4/9 + ⅖		

When students become adept at using the double open number line as a tool, and after students have ample experience multiplying using a ratio table as a tool, use the last two problem strings to model student strategies on ratio tables, with each fraction on its own ratio table. You cannot put the 2 addends on the same ratio table unless they are equivalent ratios (by definition, all ratios in a ratio table are equivalent). The problem ⅔ + ¾ could be modeled as shown in Figure 5.25:

FIGURE 5.25

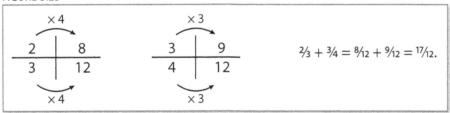

Fractions as Operators

Use fractions as operators strings to help students reason multiplicatively with fractions and to treat fractions as operators. The first couple of times you deliver these strings, you could show students an array of discrete objects and model student thinking using that array. For example, for the "36" problem string, show a 9 by 4 array of dots. Circle chunks of the array as students discuss their thinking. For example, if a student says that since half of 36 is 18, then ¼ of 36 is half of 18, 9, then circle 18 dots in

½ of 36
¼ of 36
¾ of 36
⅛ of 36
⅜ of 36
⅝ of 36
⅞ of 36
¾ of 18

one color and half of those 18 in another color. If a student says that $\frac{1}{4}$ of 36 is like 36 divided by 4, divide the dots into 4 equal groups.

An important relationship to bring out is that the fraction $(n - 1)/n$ is $1/n$ away from the unit. In other words, $\frac{7}{8}$ is just $\frac{1}{8}$ from $\frac{8}{8}$. So, when you talk about $\frac{7}{8}$ of 36, since $\frac{7}{8}$ is just $\frac{1}{8}$ of 36 away from the total, $\frac{7}{8}$ of 36 is $36 - 4.5 = 31.5$.

The first set of problem strings that follows, "Friendly Chunks," uses numbers that are pretty friendly. The next set, "Less Friendly Chunks," uses numbers that are not quite as friendly, like $\frac{1}{4}$ of 25. Encourage students to use what they know to figure out what they do not. For example, to find $\frac{1}{4}$ of 25, they could find $\frac{1}{2}$ of 25, 12.5, and cut that in half, 6.25. Alternatively, they could divide (24 + 1) by 4, so $\frac{24}{4} + \frac{1}{4} = 6 + \frac{1}{4} = 6\frac{1}{4}$.

Friendly Chunks		
$\frac{1}{2}$ of 24	$\frac{1}{3}$ of 18	$\frac{1}{8}$ of 48
$\frac{1}{4}$ of 24	$\frac{2}{3}$ of 18	$\frac{4}{8}$ of 48
$\frac{1}{8}$ of 24	$\frac{1}{6}$ of 18	$\frac{7}{8}$ of 48
$\frac{1}{3}$ of 24	$\frac{5}{6}$ of 18	$\frac{1}{6}$ of 48
$\frac{1}{6}$ of 24	$\frac{1}{2}$ of 18	$\frac{5}{6}$ of 48
$\frac{3}{4}$ of 24	$\frac{1}{4}$ of 18	$\frac{1}{2}$ of 48
$\frac{2}{3}$ of 24	$\frac{3}{4}$ of 18	$\frac{1}{4}$ of 48
$\frac{5}{6}$ of 24	$\frac{1}{9}$ of 19	$\frac{3}{4}$ of 48
$\frac{7}{8}$ of 24	$\frac{8}{9}$ of 18	$\frac{5}{4}$ of 48

Less Friendly Chunks		
$\frac{1}{3}$ of 15	$\frac{1}{5}$ of 25	$\frac{1}{3}$ of 12
$\frac{2}{3}$ of 15	$\frac{2}{5}$ of 25	$\frac{2}{3}$ of 12
$\frac{1}{5}$ of 15	$\frac{4}{5}$ of 25	$\frac{5}{6}$ of 12
$\frac{2}{5}$ of 15	$\frac{1}{2}$ of 25	$\frac{3}{4}$ of 12
$\frac{4}{5}$ of 15	$\frac{1}{4}$ of 25	$\frac{1}{8}$ of 12
$\frac{1}{2}$ of 15	$\frac{3}{4}$ of 25	$\frac{1}{16}$ of 12
$\frac{1}{4}$ of 15	$\frac{1}{8}$ of 25	$\frac{7}{16}$ of 12
$\frac{1}{8}$ of 15	$\frac{7}{8}$ of 25	$\frac{15}{16}$ of 12

Fractions as Decimals

In traditional textbooks, we often find "divide the numerator by the denominator" as the instruction for finding a decimal equivalent to a fraction. For example, to find the decimal equivalent to $\frac{2}{5}$, you would divide 2 by 5 using long division. But this does not have to be the only strategy or, in many cases, the best strategy. Most of the common fractions for which we ask students to find decimal equivalents can be reasoned about by using fractions as operators to find unit fractions and scaling up or down. These next strings use the notion of fractions as operators by thinking about $\frac{2}{5}$ of 1. Since $\frac{1}{5}$ of 1 is 0.2 (you could use money to think about $\frac{1}{5}$ of a dollar), then scale up by 2 to find $\frac{2}{5}$ of 1, 0.4.

Deliver these strings by asking, "What is the decimal equivalent to ⅕?" And then, "If - one-fifth is equivalent to 0.2, then what is *two*-fifths equivalent to?"

$\frac{1}{5}$	$\frac{1}{3}$	$\frac{1}{10}$
$\frac{2}{5}$	$\frac{2}{3}$	$\frac{12}{10}$
$\frac{4}{5}$	$\frac{1}{6}$	$\frac{1}{5}$
$\frac{1}{2}$	$\frac{5}{6}$	$2\frac{1}{5}$
$\frac{1}{4}$	$\frac{1}{9}$	$\frac{9}{5}$
$\frac{1}{8}$	$\frac{2}{9}$	$\frac{1}{4}$
$\frac{2}{8}$	$\frac{3}{9}$	$\frac{11}{4}$
$\frac{3}{8}$	$\frac{4}{9}$	$\frac{23}{4}$
$\frac{6}{8}$	$\frac{5}{9}$	$\frac{1}{8}$
$\frac{4}{8}$	$\frac{6}{9}$	$\frac{9}{8}$
$\frac{5}{8}$	$\frac{7}{9}$	$\frac{15}{8}$
$\frac{6}{8}$	$\frac{8}{9}$	$\frac{1}{3}$
$\frac{7}{8}$	$\frac{9}{9}$	$\frac{5}{3}$

Scaling Up for Multiplication

Use scaling up for multiplication strings to help students construct a scaling-up strategy for multiplying fractions. For any problem $a/b \times c/d$, first consider the product of the corresponding unit fractions: $1/b \times 1/d = 1/(b \times d)$. For example, for $⅖ \times ¼$ you first consider $⅕ \times ¼ = 1/20$. The next problem is delivered with verbal emphasis on the scale factor. For example, after students have established that $⅕$ of $¼$ is $1/20$, then ask, "What is *two-fifths* of $¼$?" as you write $⅖ \times ¼$. Model student strategies on open arrays where the factors are dimensions and the product is the area of the rectangular arrays. Note that because of the way the array supports the trading places strategy that follows, each rectangular array is drawn so that the internal units are square. The same reasoning follows for the next problem $⅖ \times ¾$, where you now emphasize that if $⅖$ of $¼$ is $2/20$, then $⅖$ of *three*-fourths must be 3 times $2/20$, $6/20$.

$⅕ \times ¼$
$⅖ \times ¼$
$⅖ \times ¾$
$⅓ \times ¼$
$⅔ \times ¼$
$¾ \times ⅔$

FIGURE 5.26

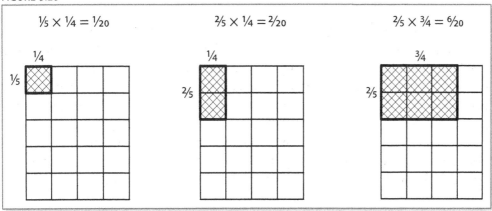

The unit fraction by unit raction string sets the stage by establishing that the product of unit fractions is a unit fraction where the denominator is the product of the factors' denominators.

Unit Fraction by Unit Fraction	Scaling Up	Scaling Up
$\frac{1}{4} \times \frac{1}{6}$	$\frac{1}{6} \times \frac{1}{4}$	$\frac{1}{3} \times \frac{1}{7}$
$\frac{1}{3} \times \frac{1}{4}$	$\frac{5}{6} \times \frac{1}{4}$	$\frac{2}{3} \times \frac{1}{7}$
$\frac{1}{5} \times \frac{1}{3}$	$\frac{3}{4} \times \frac{5}{6}$	$\frac{4}{7} \times \frac{2}{3}$
	$\frac{1}{5} \times \frac{1}{3}$	$\frac{1}{4} \times \frac{1}{5}$
	$\frac{3}{5} \times \frac{1}{3}$	$\frac{3}{4} \times \frac{1}{5}$
	$\frac{2}{3} \times \frac{3}{5}$	$\frac{2}{5} \times \frac{3}{4}$

Trading Places

Because multiplication is commutative, we can swap the numerators in fraction problems: $\frac{2}{5} \times \frac{3}{4} = \frac{6}{20}$ and $\frac{3}{5} \times \frac{2}{4} = \frac{6}{20}$, so therefore $\frac{2}{5} \times \frac{3}{4} = \frac{3}{5} \times \frac{2}{4}$. This swap can make many fraction multiplication problems easier to solve because one or both of the resulting fractions can be simplified. For example, $\frac{3}{5} \times \frac{2}{4}$ can be thought of as $\frac{3}{5} \times \frac{1}{2}$, and $\frac{1}{2}$ of $\frac{3}{5}$ is $\frac{3}{10}$. Use these strings to help students construct this strategy (Figure 5.27).

$\frac{2}{5} \times \frac{3}{4}$
$\frac{3}{3} \times \frac{2}{4}$
$\frac{4}{7} \times \frac{3}{5}$
$\frac{3}{7} \times \frac{4}{5}$
$\frac{2}{5} \times \frac{5}{6}$

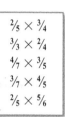

FIGURE 5.27

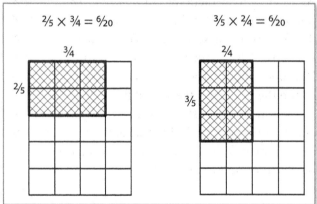

Before using these strings, you should have previously developed with students the area model for multiplying fractions and the scaling up strategy. The first problem string that follows develops the relationship that the inner array (the product of the numerators) can rotate within the outer array (the product of the denominators) and maintain an equivalent ratio of the inner area to the outer area. Therefore, if the numerators trade places, the products are equivalent. The strings consist of paired equivalent problems. The last problem is given without a partner, and it has a nice solution when the numerators trade places. The rest of the problem strings consist of problems where the trading places strategy works well. For example, $\frac{4}{3} \times \frac{9}{16} = \frac{9}{3} \times \frac{4}{16} = 3 \times \frac{1}{4} = \frac{3}{4}$.

$\frac{4}{5} \times \frac{2}{9}$	$\frac{4}{3} \times \frac{9}{16}$	$\frac{27}{4} \times \frac{2}{9}$
$\frac{2}{5} \times \frac{4}{9}$	$\frac{6}{7} \times 2\frac{1}{2}$	$\frac{7}{4} \times \frac{8}{3}$
$\frac{7}{8} \times \frac{5}{9}$	$\frac{2}{5} \times \frac{10}{3}$	$\frac{16}{21} \times \frac{7}{8}$
$\frac{5}{8} \times \frac{7}{9}$	$\frac{5}{2} \times \frac{14}{5}$	$\frac{8}{9} \times \frac{3}{4}$
$\frac{5}{6} \times \frac{3}{5}$	$\frac{3}{4} \times \frac{5}{6}$	$\frac{2}{3} \times \frac{9}{12}$

Luis, a seventh-grade math teacher, has been working with his students on the area model for multiplication of fractions and the scaling-up strategy. He starts off today's problem string.

Luis: Let's practice a few fraction multiplication problems today. How do you think about $\frac{4}{5} \times \frac{2}{9}$?

Students work for a few minutes.

Luis: Zach, tell me about your work.

Zach: First I thought about $\frac{1}{5}$ of $\frac{1}{9}$. That's $\frac{1}{45}$.

Luis: What would that array look like?

Zach: I didn't use an array.

Luis: That's OK. I'm going to model your thinking on an array. What would a $\frac{1}{5}$ by $\frac{1}{9}$ look like?

Zach: You'd have 5 rows and 9 columns and you want just the $\frac{1}{5}$ by the $\frac{1}{9}$, that little square on the upper left corner. *Luis draws the array and shades the $\frac{1}{45}$.*

$$\frac{1}{5} \times \frac{1}{9} = \frac{1}{45}$$

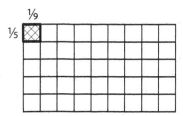

Zach: Then I scaled up by 4 because I thought about $\frac{4}{5}$ times $\frac{1}{9}$. That is 4 of those $\frac{1}{45}$s, $\frac{4}{45}$. *Luis draws the scale up by 4, $\frac{4}{45}$.*

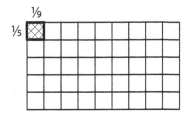

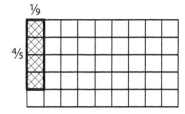

Zach: Then I scaled up by 2 because it's $\frac{2}{9}$, so that's $\frac{4}{45}$ times 2, $\frac{8}{45}$. *Luis draws the scale up by 2, $\frac{8}{45}$.*

$\frac{1}{5} \times \frac{1}{9} = \frac{1}{45}$ $\frac{4}{5} \times \frac{1}{9} = \frac{4}{45}$ $\frac{4}{5} \times \frac{2}{9} = \frac{8}{45}$

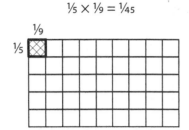 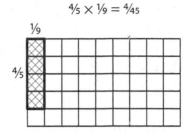 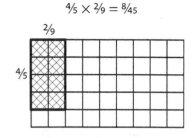

Luis: Great, so ⅘ times ²⁄₉ is ⁸⁄₄₅. Nice work. The next problem in today's string is ²⁄₅ times ⁴⁄₉.

Students work.

Luis: Alyssa, tell us about your thinking.

Alyssa: I did the same kind of thing as Zach. First it's ¹⁄₄₅, then scale up by 2 to ²⁄₄₅, then scale up by 4 to ⁸⁄₄₅. *Luis draws the progression.*

$\frac{1}{5} \times \frac{1}{9} = \frac{1}{45}$ $\frac{2}{5} \times \frac{1}{9} = \frac{2}{45}$ $\frac{2}{5} \times \frac{4}{9} = \frac{8}{45}$

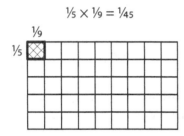 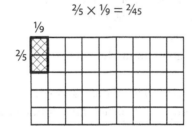 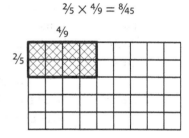

Luis: I heard some comments while you were working that the answers are the same for ⅘ times ²⁄₉ and ²⁄₅ times ⁴⁄₉. What do you think is going on here?

Richard: The numbers traded places.

Cassidy: Yeah, the numerators switched.

Santiago: It's like you did the scaling up in different orders. The first problem scaled up by 4 and then 2 and that's 8. The second problem scaled up by 2 and then 4 so it's still 8. They both have the answer ⁸⁄₄₅.

Abby: The inside arrays rotated. When you trade the numerators, the inside arrays just rotate so the area of the inside array is the same. Since the outside arrays are the same, because of the fifths and ninths, and the inside arrays have the same area, the answers are the same.

Luis: Interesting. I wonder if that always works. Let's keep practicing.

The students solve the next two problems similarly with Luis modeling the scaling up. They discuss the equivalent answers again. Luis asks students to generalize what they think is happening.

Denise: The numerators are trading places but the areas are staying the same.

Lillie: When the numerators swap, the inner arrays rotate.

Isaac: The ratio of the inner array to the outer array is the same so the answers are the same.

Luis: I wonder if that could be helpful in solving problems? The last problem in the problem string today is ⁵⁄₆ times ³⁄₅.

Johnny:	Whoa! That's cool.
Luis:	Let's let everyone solve the problem and then you can share what you just saw, Johnny. *Students work.*
Luis:	Johnny, what were you seeing?
Johnny:	I decided to trade the numerators and see what happened. You get $\frac{3}{6}$ times $\frac{5}{5}$. I didn't even really think about the arrays at all. I just saw that you could simplify those to $\frac{1}{2}$ times 1. That's just $\frac{1}{2}$!
Luis:	Can someone explain what Johnny is saying?
Laura:	He did the trading places thing so the problem became $\frac{3}{6}$ times $\frac{5}{5}$. They simplify, $\frac{3}{6}$ to $\frac{1}{2}$ and $\frac{5}{5}$ to 1. So that's $\frac{1}{2}$ times 1. That is cool.
Luis:	We'll do some more problems in the next few days and we'll start to wonder when the trading places strategy makes the problem nicer and when it doesn't really help. Good work today!

Using Quotative Division

Use quotative division strings to help students use their quotative sense of division with whole numbers to make sense of division with fractions. One way to think of quotative division is how many of the divisor divide into the dividend. For example, $24 \div 6$ can be thought of as how many 6s are in 24? For $\frac{5}{6} \div \frac{1}{6}$, how many $\frac{1}{6}$s are in $\frac{5}{6}$? This works well for division of fractions when the fractions have common denominators or denominators for which you can visualize the division. For example, to solve $1\frac{1}{2} \div \frac{1}{4}$, you could find common denominators, $\frac{3}{2} \div \frac{1}{4} = \frac{6}{4} \div \frac{1}{4}$ and then think about how many $\frac{1}{4}$s divide into $\frac{6}{4}$. But many students will be able to think about the problem by realizing that two $\frac{1}{4}$s fit into $\frac{1}{2}$, so since there are three $\frac{1}{2}$s in $1\frac{1}{2}$, there must be six $\frac{1}{4}$s in $1\frac{1}{2}$, and so $1\frac{1}{2} \div \frac{1}{4} = 6$. Students need to understand the multiplicative nature of fractions, such as $\frac{5}{6}$ as five $\frac{1}{6}$s and $\frac{3}{5}$ as three $\frac{1}{5}$s; this division strategy is a natural extension of that understanding together with quotative division. Deliver these strings by saying each problem two ways: As you write $\frac{5}{6} \div \frac{1}{6}$, *say,* "*Five-sixths divided by $\frac{1}{6}$ or, in other words, how many one-sixths are in $\frac{5}{6}$?*"

$\frac{5}{6} \div \frac{1}{6}$
$\frac{2}{6} \div \frac{1}{6}$
$\frac{1}{2} \div \frac{1}{6}$
$\frac{3}{5} \div \frac{1}{5}$
$\frac{4}{10} \div \frac{1}{5}$
$\frac{4}{5} \div \frac{1}{10}$
$1\frac{1}{2} \div \frac{1}{4}$

This opening set of problem strings works with whole numbers divided by fractions. The first string starts with three problems, all with the divisor of $\frac{1}{6}$. Draw out that the second problem is equivalent to $\frac{1}{3} \div \frac{1}{6}$ but that it may be easier to think about it as $\frac{2}{6} \div \frac{1}{6}$. This may prompt students to think about the third problem, $\frac{1}{2} \div \frac{1}{6}$, as $\frac{3}{6} \div \frac{1}{6}$. The next three problems are related, using fifths and tenths. Keep students reasoning using $\frac{1}{5} = \frac{2}{10}$. The last problem, $1\frac{1}{2} \div \frac{1}{4}$, as discussed earlier, can be solved using equivalent fractions, $\frac{6}{4} \div \frac{1}{4}$, or by reasoning about fourths and halves.

Keep students reasoning about unit fractions throughout the discussions. For example, if there are five $\frac{1}{5}$s in 1, then there must be twice that many $\frac{1}{5}$s in 2. If there are ten $\frac{1}{5}$s in 2, then there must be half as many $\frac{2}{5}$s in 2, so $2 \div \frac{2}{5}$ is 5 (Figure 5.28).

FIGURE 5.28

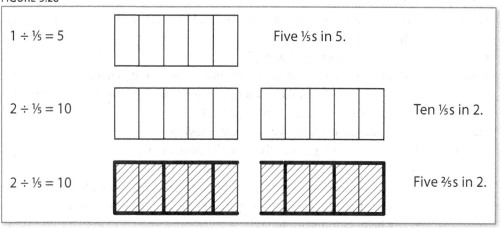

$1 \div \frac{1}{5} = 5$ Five $\frac{1}{5}$s in 5.

$2 \div \frac{1}{5} = 10$ Ten $\frac{1}{5}$s in 2.

$2 \div \frac{1}{5} = 10$ Five $\frac{2}{5}$s in 2.

Whole Numbers Divided by Fractions

$1 \div \frac{1}{6}$	$1 \div \frac{1}{5}$	$1 \div \frac{1}{4}$
$2 \div \frac{1}{6}$	$2 \div \frac{1}{5}$	$5 \div \frac{1}{4}$
$4 \div \frac{1}{6}$	$2 \div \frac{2}{5}$	$5 \div \frac{5}{4}$
$4\frac{1}{6} \div \frac{1}{6}$	$1 \div \frac{1}{12}$	$1 \div \frac{1}{8}$
$1 \div \frac{1}{3}$	$2 \div \frac{1}{12}$	$3 \div \frac{1}{8}$
$3 \div \frac{1}{3}$	$2 \div \frac{2}{6}$	$3 \div \frac{3}{8}$
$3\frac{2}{3} \div \frac{1}{3}$	$2 \div \frac{4}{12}$	$3 \div \frac{3}{4}$

The remaining three strings involve fractions divided by fractions. The first string works with sets of problems that help with mixed numbers divided by unit fractions, like $2\frac{3}{4} \div \frac{1}{4} = 2 \div \frac{1}{4} + \frac{3}{4} \div \frac{1}{4}$. The middle string works with fractions that do not have common denominators. The last problem string works with numerators that do not divide evenly, like $5 \div 2 = \frac{5}{2}$ or 2.5, therefore $\frac{5}{3} \div \frac{2}{3} = 5 \div 2 = \frac{5}{2}$ or 2.5.

Fractions Divided by Fractions

$\frac{3}{4} \div \frac{1}{4}$	$\frac{1}{3} \div \frac{1}{6}$	$\frac{3}{6} \div \frac{1}{6}$
$2 \div \frac{1}{4}$	$\frac{4}{5} \div \frac{1}{10}$	$\frac{3}{6} \div \frac{2}{6}$
$2\frac{3}{4} \div \frac{1}{4}$	$\frac{3}{4} \div \frac{1}{8}$	$5 \div 2$
$6 \div \frac{1}{6}$	$\frac{3}{4} \div \frac{2}{8}$	$\frac{5}{3} \div \frac{2}{3}$
$\frac{5}{6} \div \frac{1}{6}$	$\frac{3}{4} \div \frac{1}{3}$	$1 \div 2$
$6\frac{5}{6} \div \frac{1}{6}$	$\frac{1}{4} \div \frac{1}{8}$	$\frac{1}{5} \div \frac{2}{5}$
$3\frac{1}{3} \div \frac{1}{3}$	$\frac{2}{3} \div \frac{1}{15}$	$\frac{4}{7} \div \frac{3}{7}$

$3 \div \frac{1}{2}$
$2 \div \frac{1}{2}$
$2 \div \frac{1}{3}$
$3 \div \frac{1}{3}$
$2 \div \frac{2}{3}$
$1 \div \frac{1}{3}$
$4 \div \frac{2}{3}$
$4 \div \frac{1}{3}$

Using the Constant (Equivalent) Ratio Strategy for Division

Use the constant (equivalent) ratio for division strings to help students reason using ratio tables as a tool to divide fractions. Deliver these strings with a context. For example, for the problem $3 \div \frac{1}{2}$, you might say, "If it takes 3 cups of cheese to make $\frac{1}{2}$ of a pizza, how many cups of cheese does it take to make 1 whole pizza?" Because you are working with the ratio of 3:½, you can write that as 3 ÷ ½ or 3/½. The beauty of putting this information in a ratio table is that students can bring all of their ratio table operating experience to bear. To find the amount of cheese for 1 pizza, they multiply both 3 and ½ by 2, to get the resulting ratio of 6 cups of cheese to make 1 whole pizza (Figure 5.29).

FIGURE 5.29

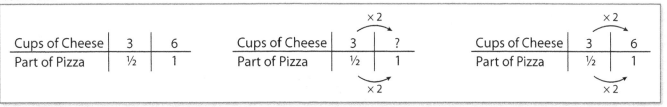

2 ÷ ¼	⅓ ÷ ⅕	3 ÷ ⅔
4 ÷ ½	⅔ ÷ ⅖	⅖ ÷ ¼
2 ÷ ½	¼ ÷ ⅕	⅔ ÷ ¾
1 ÷ ⅛	¾ ÷ ⅗	⅘ ÷ ¾
2 ÷ ⅛	⅕ ÷ ¹⁄₁₀	⅕ ÷ ⅛
4 ÷ ⅓	⅘ ÷ ⁴⁄₁₀	⅚ ÷ ²⁄₁₂
8 ÷ ⅔	⅚ ÷ ⅝	⅗ ÷ ⁴⁄₃

The middle string uses relationships of doubling, tripling, and halving ratios, which results in equivalent ratios. If it takes ⅓ of a cup of cheese to make ⅕ of a pizza, it takes ⅗ of a cup to make 1 pizza. If you double the cheese, then you can make twice the amount of pizza (and if you need twice as much pizza, you will need to double the cheese). So ⅔ ÷ ⅖ also results in ⅗ of a cup of cheese per pizza. The string is designed with paired problems, starting with dividing a unit fraction by a unit fraction. As students solve these, they realize that to find the amount of cheese for 1 pizza, they multiply both the dividend and the divisor by the denominator of the divisor. By doing so, the denominator becomes 1. If you know that ⅓ of a cup of cheese makes ⅕ of a pizza, multiplying the ⅕ pizza times 5 gives you a whole pizza. To maintain the ratio, you also multiply the ⅓ by 5 to find that you need ⅗ of a cup of cheese for that whole pizza.

Brittany gives her students the problem ⅓ ÷ ⅕ by saying, "If it takes ⅓ of a cup of cheese to make ⅕ of a pizza, how much cheese do you need to make a whole pizza?" As she states the problem, she fills in a ratio table. Brittany is aware that students might not know that the problem ⅓ ÷ ⅕ can be interpreted this way. By writing this division expression, ⅓ ÷ ⅕, as she states the problem and represents it in a familiar ratio table, Brittany is using the expression as a model of their thinking, one that she superimposes. With work, students can begin to use the model to represent their thinking. In other words, they have learned they can use a division expression to model a partitive fraction division problem (Figure 5.30).

FIGURE 5.30

Cups of Cheese	$\frac{1}{3}$	?
Part of Pizza	$\frac{1}{5}$	1

Lauren: To get to 1 pizza, I multiplied both by 5. That gets $\frac{5}{3}$ cups of cheese for 1 whole pizza. Brittany fills in the ratio table.

× 5

Cups of Cheese	$\frac{1}{3}$	$\frac{5}{3}$
Part of Pizza	$\frac{1}{5}$	1

× 5

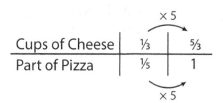

Brittany: So, I hear you saying that to find $\frac{1}{3} \div \frac{1}{5}$, you multiply both by 5. I will write that also like this: $\frac{1}{3}(5) \div \frac{1}{5}(5) = \frac{5}{3} \div 1 = \frac{5}{3}$. Why did you multiply by 5?

Lauren: To get to 1 pizza.

Brittany: And that makes the divisor 1, so once you get the divisor to be 1, the division is pretty simple. And how about this one, if it takes $\frac{2}{3}$ cups of cheese to make $\frac{2}{5}$ of a pizza, how much cheese to make 1 pizza? *Brittany writes a new ratio table.*

Cups of Cheese	$\frac{2}{3}$	?
Part of Pizza	$\frac{2}{5}$	1

Logan: First, I doubled them both to get $\frac{4}{3}$ cups of cheese to $\frac{4}{5}$ of a pizza. And I thought how I just needed one more fifth to get to a whole pizza so I thought and then I realized that if I halved instead of doubled, I'd be back at the problem before, so the answers are the same. *Brittany fills in the halving relationship.*

÷ 2

Cups of Cheese	$\frac{2}{3}$	$\frac{1}{3}$
Part of Pizza	$\frac{2}{5}$	$\frac{1}{5}$

÷ 2

Brittany: Tell me more about this. Why would Logan want to get back to the first problem, just because we already know the answer?

Abby: Because if you know what 1 is, then you can find out what the whole pizza is.

Brittany: What do you mean, "what 1 is?" One what?

Abby: The fraction on the bottom—you want it to be a unit fraction. Because if the numerator is just 1, then you can just times the fraction by the denominator to get a whole.

Brittany delivers the next two problems and students reason similarly. Brittany sums up the discussion.

Brittany: So, I am hearing that an idea is to multiply to get the divisor to be 1 and then division by 1 is simple! Let's see how you handle the last problem, $\frac{5}{6} \div \frac{5}{8}$.

Students work while Brittany fills in a new ratio table.

Brittany: Skylar, what were you thinking?

Skylar: I divided both by 5 to get $\frac{1}{6}$ and $\frac{1}{8}$. Then I needed to get rid of the 8 so that I would just have 1 pizza, so I multiplied them both by 8 and that gave me 1 and $\frac{1}{3}$ divided by 1.

Brittany: One-sixth times 8 is 1 and a third?

Skylar: It's $\frac{8}{6}$ and that's 1 and $\frac{2}{6}$, so $1\frac{1}{3}$.

Brittany: Great work.

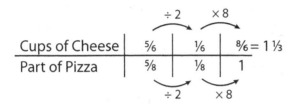

The last string begins with $3 \div \frac{2}{3}$. This gives students an easier problem to start with because they can divide a whole number, 3, by 2 and then multiply the result, 1.5, times 3. Throughout the rest of the problems in this string, Brittany pushes students toward the generalization of asking, "What can I do with multiplication to get the divisor to 1?" Students realize they can multiply both the dividend and the divisor by the reciprocal of the divisor and they end up with an equivalent ratio in which the divisor is 1. This is the standard algorithm, a fine strategy when students understand what they are doing. Notice that the string includes the problem $\frac{5}{6} \div \frac{2}{12}$, where students can multiply by the reciprocal of $\frac{2}{12}$ to get $\frac{5}{6} \times \frac{12}{2} = \frac{5}{6} \times 6 = 5$. But they could also simplify first to get $\frac{5}{6} \div \frac{1}{6}$ and then reason to figure out how many one-sixths are in $\frac{5}{6}$, 5. It's about reasoning and using relationships! Now students can reason powerfully about division of fractions, using the algorithm when appropriate.

Percents

The strings for percents include the following strategies:

- ▶ Using Friendly Percents
- ▶ Finding Unknown Percents
- ▶ Finding Unknown Referents
- ▶ Using the Commutative Property

Using Friendly Percents

Use friendly percent strings to help students learn to use friendly percents, like 50%, 10%, and 1%, to find other percentages of a given number. Use a percent bar to model student strategies. The percent bar is a helpful model because as students decide how to find 50% on the bar, they are dividing the bar into 2 equal chunks between 0% and 100%. This suggests to the mind to divide the original number, in this string 54, also by 2. To mark the 10%, students think about dividing 100% by 10 and this can help them realize they need to divide the corresponding 54 by 10. Bring out the place value patterns as they happen. For example, if students find 5% by dividing 10%, 5.4, by 2 to get 2.7, then compare that with the 50%, 27, and then similarly with the 0.5%, 0.27.

> 50% of 54
> 25% of 54
> 12.5% of 54
> 10% of 54
> 20% of 54
> 1% of 54
> 5% of 54
> 15% of 54
> 16% of 54
> 0.5% of 54
> 16.5% of 54

When delivering these strings, consider using the entire board to draw a really long percent bar. This will enable you to more correctly draw percents that are close together, so that 0%, 0.5%, 1%, and 5% are not all squished so closely together that it is difficult to see them. A really long percent bar will help students be deliberate about where to mark each percent, which can help them realize how they are dividing 100% to find the percent and therefore how to divide the original number to find the corresponding result.

Here is another sample string, with the discussion that might ensue around it.

> 100% of 15
> 50% of 15
> 25% of 15
> 10% of 15
> 5% of 15
> 1% of 15
> 11% of 15
> 0.5% of 15
> 16.5% of 15

The teacher starts leading the problem string by asking students, "What is 100% of 15?" *The first problem is often easy and sets the stage for the rest of the string.* The class responds, "15."

Teacher: That was easy, I know. But I am going to model it on a percent bar. *The choice of model is deliberate. She knows that the percent bar can become a powerful tool to help students solve percent problems.*

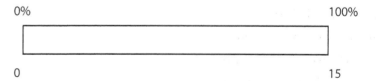

Teacher: What is 50% of 15?
Emmett: That's half, so 7.5.

The teacher adds that to the percent bar.

Teacher: Since 50% is half of 100, then you found half of 15? Great.

She helps students realize that by figuring out where the 50% relates to the 100%, that it's half, that tells students to find half of 15.

The teacher asks the next question in the string, "What is 25% of 15?" After pausing for students to think, the teacher calls on a student.

Daphne: Since 50% is 7.5, then 25% is half of that. Half of 7 is 3.5 and half of 50 cents is 25 cents. So, that's 3.75. *The teacher writes ½ of 7.5 = (½ × 7) + (½ × 0.5) = 3.5 + 0.25 = 3.75. Then she marks the percent bar. To help more students think about ½ of 7.5, she continues.*

Teacher: Anyone else?

Bay: I know that ¼ is like dividing by 4, and I know 16 ÷ 4 = 4 and 1 ÷ 4 = 0.25, so 15 ÷ 4 = 3.75.

The teacher continues with the next problem in the string, "What is 10% of 15?" waits for students to think, and then calls on a student.

Toby: 10% is like ¹⁄₁₀. So ¹⁄₁₀ of 15 is 1.5.

Teacher: How do you know ¹⁄₁₀ of 15?

Toby: Just like 10 times a number makes the number bigger, ¹⁄₁₀ of a number is one place smaller. So the 15 is 1.5.

Kathryn: 10% is 100% divided by 10, so I knew I needed 15 ÷ 10. 10 ÷ 10 is 1 and 5 ÷ 10 is 0.5 so 1.5.

Teacher: What is 5% of 15?

John: Since 10% is 1.5, 5% is half of that, 0.75.

Teacher: So, what if you didn't already know 10%, what could you do? *The string is planned for the students to use the answers they have already found. The teacher also wants them to consider what they would do if they hit the problem cold.*

John: Just find 10% because it's easy. Then 5% is just half.

Emmett: Or you could divide by 20, since 100 ÷ 5 is 20. 15 ÷ 2 is 7.5 so 15 ÷ 20 is 0.75.

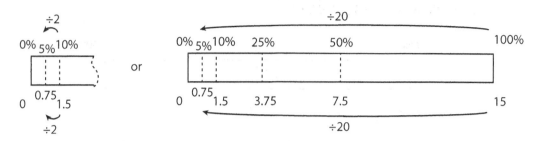

The string continues with similar reasoning for 5% and 1% of 15. Then the students use the previous problems to find 11% by adding 10% + 1% to get 1.5 + 0.15 = 1.65. And students find 0.5% of 15 by halving 1% (0.15 ÷ 2) or by dividing 5% by 10 (0.75 ÷ 10) to get 0.075.

The string ends with finding 16.5% of 15. The teacher zooms in on the percent bar to be able to see the strategies.

Daphne: I added 10 + 5 + 1 + 0.5%, 1.5 + 0.75 + 0.15 + 0.075 = 1.5 + 0.975 = 2.475.

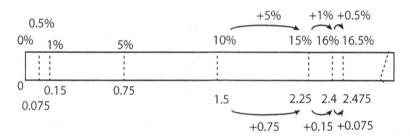

John: I used the 11 + 5 + 0.5%, that's 1.65 + 0.75 + 0.075. With a little give and take, I got 2 + 0.4 + 0.075 = 2.475.

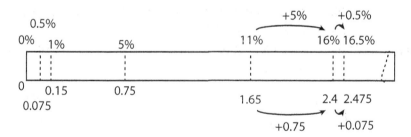

Teacher: Great thinking, everyone. You used easy percents to find others that are not so easy. Keep that in mind as we solve more percent problems.

10% of 5	50% of 27	10% of 84
20% of 5	25% of 27	5% of 84
40% of 5	10% of 27	0.5% of 84
80% of 5	20% of 27	15.5% of 84
5% of 5	1% of 27	1% of 84
25% of 5	2% of 27	25% of 84
45% of 5	48% of 27	2.5% of 84
1% of 5	98% of 27	7.5% of 84
46% of 5	27% of 27	75% of 84

Finding Unknown Percents

Use finding unknown percent strings to help students reason
when the percentage is missing. Write the problems in the same
format, but you can vary the way you say each problem: "8 is what
percent of 16?" or "What percent is 8 of 16?" or "8 is some percentage of 16. What percent?" Model student strategies on a percent bar and with fraction notation as applicable. For example, if a
student says that 8 is half of 16, you could write $^8\!/_{16} = ^1\!/_2$ and mark
the 8, 16, and 50% on a percent bar. When a student says that 4 is
half of 8 and 25% is half of 50%, mark that on the percent bar and
then ask, "Is $^4\!/_{16}$ equivalent to 25%?" (Yes, because 25% is equivalent to $^1\!/_4$.) You can write $^4\!/_{16} = 25\% = ^1\!/_4$. One possible percent
bar is shown here (Figure 5.31):

8 is ___% of 16
4 is ___% of 16
2 is ___% of 16
1 is ___% of 16
9 is ___% of 16
15 is ___% of 16
12 is ___% of 16
17 is ___% of 16

FIGURE 5.31

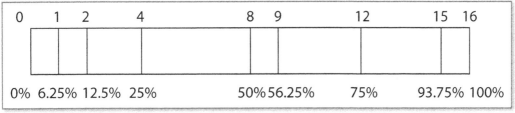

As students share strategies, encourage connections between previous problems. For
example, when finding the percent 12 is of 16, students could combine the 8 (50% of 16)
and 4 (25%) to determine that 12 is 75% of 16. The equivalent equation with fractions
would be $^1\!/_2 + ^1\!/_4 = ^3\!/_4$. You could also reason that 12 is 4, or 25%, less than 16, the 100%
(using fractions, $1 - ^1\!/_4 = ^3\!/_4 = 75\%$). You could also reason that $^{12}\!/_{16} = ^3\!/_4 = 75\%$.

5 is __% of 25	45 is __% of 90	12 is __% of 24
10 is __% of 25	22.5 is __% of 90	18 is __% of 24
20 is __% of 25	9 is __% of 90	20 is __% of 24
1 is __% of 25	18 is __% of 90	2 is __% of 24
24 is __% of 25	3 is __% of 90	6 is __% of 24
15 is __% of 25	21 is __% of 90	3 is __% of 24
19 is __% of 25	66 is __% of 90	23 is __% of 24

Finding Unknown Referents

Use finding unknown referents strings to help students construct relationships when the number corresponding to 100% on the percent bar is missing. Model each of the problems in the strings on its own percent bar. This is necessary because each 100% corresponds to a different number. For example, for the problem "12 is 50% of ___?" since 12 is 50% of 24, the 24 corresponds with the 100% on that bar. For the next problem, "12 is 25% of ___?" the answer is a *different* number, and that number, 48, is now the 100% on its own percent bar (Figure 5.32).

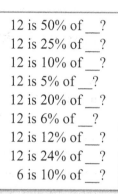

12 is 50% of __?
12 is 25% of __?
12 is 10% of __?
12 is 5% of __?
12 is 20% of __?
12 is 6% of __?
12 is 12% of __?
12 is 24% of __?
6 is 10% of __?

FIGURE 5.32

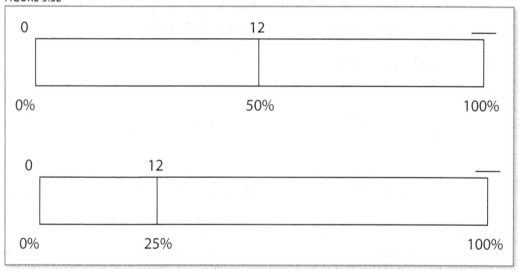

LESSONS AND ACTIVITIES FOR BUILDING POWERFUL NUMERACY

25 is 10% of __	30 is 50% of __	90 is 10% of __
25 is 25% of __	30 is 10% of __	90 is 25% of __
25 is 50% of __	30 is 60% of __	90 is 50% of __
25 is 20% of __	30 is 75% of __	90 is 60% of __
25 is 5% of __	45 is 15% of __	90 is 75% of __
50 is 50% of __	45 is 90% of __	5 is 125% of __
50 is 10% of __	45 is 30% of __	6 is 120% of __
50 is 60% of __	45 is 60% of __	9 is 112.5% of __

Using the Commutative Property

Use the commutative property strings to help students realize that there are problems for which using the commutative property to find percentages of numbers can be convenient and efficient. The strings are constructed with paired problems that have equivalent results. For example, 35% of 60 = 60% of 35. This can be extremely helpful in problems like 57% of 10 because it is much easier to find 10% of 57. Likewise, it is easier when given the problem: find 12% of 50, to find 50% of 12.

35% of 60
60% of 35
57% of 10
10% of 57
37% of 50

You can explore using the associative property with students to see why this works: 37% of 50 = 0.37 × 50 = (37 × 0.01) × 50 = 37 × (0.01 × 50) = 37 × 0.5 = 50% of 37. In the first sets of paired problems in the first string that follows, neither problem in the pair is much easier to solve than the other. Model student strategies on a percent bar. By the end of the string, one of the problems in the pair is much easier to solve than the other. This can be intriguing for students. In the next two strings that follow, the paired problems are a bit more obvious because one problem is much easier to solve than the other. Each of the three strings ends with singular problems, given without a helper. The last string consists of problems where each problem is easier to solve if you solve it by using the commutative property first. For example, it is easier to find 75% of 88 than 88% of 75.

15% of 40	40% of 22	88% of 75
40% of 15	22% of 40	53% of 10
23% of 20	80% of 99	4% of 25
20% of 23	99% of 80	64% of 20
52% of 12.5	30% of 25	12% of 50
44% of 75	13.5% of 20	

Solving Proportions

The strings for solving proportions include the following strategies:

- ▸ Using Proportional Reasoning to Multiply (Unit Rates)
- ▸ Using Proportional Reasoning to Divide (Unit Rates)
- ▸ Solving Proportions (Non-unit Rates)

Although this portion of the chapter is about solving proportions, use the first two sections that follow to develop proportional reasoning while working on multiplication and division strategies.

Using Proportional Reasoning to Multiply (Unit Rates)

Use proportional reasoning to multiply (unit rates) strings to help students reason proportionally as they use equivalent ratios to multiply. These strings use many of the same multiplicative relationships developed in the previous multiplication strings, but bring them all together focusing on reasoning proportionally using a ratio table as a tool. Each string finds many products using one specific factor, such as 17, as shown in this first string. In this string, students can use previous problems with strategies including chunking, over and under, and place-value shifts as they multiply and divide by multiples of 10. Help students make connections by drawing out the place-value relationships. Model student strategies on a ratio table. Deliver these strings in the context of a unit rate; for example, 1 bag has 19 donut holes, 1 pack has 47 mints, and 1 package has 37 candies (as Brittany did with eye drops for the five is half of ten strategy earlier in this chapter).

2×17	
4×17	
8×17	
10×17	
9×17	
5×17	
100×17	
99×17	

Whole Numbers		
2×47	2×37	19×2
4×47	10×37	19×0.5
8×47	9×37	19×10
10×47	5×37	19×5
9×47	15×37	19×15
5×47	20×37	19×100
15×47	19×37	19×50
14×47	100×37	19×150
100×47	91×37	19×149
99×47	99×37	19×145

Decimals		
2×4.1	2×2.4	2×3.3
4×4.1	10×2.4	4×3.3
8×4.1	9×2.4	8×3.3
10×4.1	90×2.4	10×3.3
9×4.1	5×2.4	9×3.3
5×4.1	95×2.4	90×3.3
100×4.1	9.5×2.4	5×3.3
92×4.1	45×2.4	85×3.3
9.2×4.1	4.5×2.4	8.5×3.3

Using Proportional Reasoning to Divide (Unit Rates)

Use proportional reasoning to divide (unit rates) strings to help students use the ratio table as a tool to solve division problems by reasoning proportionally. Use a ratio table to model student strategies for both the multiplication and division problems. These strings are constructed based on a unit ratio; for example, 1:17. The strings start with a few multiplication problems to establish some helpful relationships, like 17×2, and then follow with division problems, many that are related by a place-value shift, or are a bit over and under previous quotients. Use a context like mints in a bag: for 17×2, "If a bag has 17 mints, how many mints are in 2 bags?" or, for $153 \div 17$, "If I have 153 mints, how many bags do I have?"

17×2
17×4
17×10
$153 \div 17$
$85 \div 17$
$255 \div 17$
$238 \div 17$
$1,700 \div 17$
$1,683 \div 17$

A ratio table for this string without all the marks to show strategies could look like the one shown in Figure 5.33

FIGURE 5.33

bag	1	2	4	10	9	5	15	14	100	99
mints	17	34	68	170	153	85	255	238	1,700	1,683

The first set of three strings that follows uses whole numbers and the second set, decimals.

Whole Numbers		
78×2	81×3	64×2
78×4	81×6	64×5
78×10	81×10	64×7
$702 \div 78$	$405 \div 81$	$512 \div 64$
$390 \div 78$	$1,215 \div 81$	$640 \div 64$
$1,092 \div 78$	$2,430 \div 81$	$1,088 \div 64$
$156 \div 78$	$2,349 \div 81$	$4,480 \div 64$
$7,644 \div 78$	$4,941 \div 81$	$4,416 \div 64$

Decimals		
4.2×2	3.4×2	5.6×3
4.2×4	3.4×4	5.6×6
4.2×10	3.4×8	$28 \div 5.6$
$21 \div 4.2$	$30.6 \div 3.4$	$61.6 \div 5.6$
$37.8 \div 4.2$	$17 \div 3.4$	$50.4 \div 5.6$
$33.6 \div 4.2$	$23.8 \div 3.4$	$168 \div 5.6$
$168 \div 4.2$	$166.6 \div 3.4$	$162.4 \div 5.6$
$172.2 \div 4.2$	$132.6 \div 3.4$	$330.4 \div 5.6$

Solving Proportions (Non-unit Rates)

Use these solving proportions (non-unit rates) strings to help students reason proportionally to solve proportions. These strings use many of the same multiplicative relationships developed in the multiplication and division unit rate strings, continuing to use the ratio table as a tool, now solving non-unit rate proportions. Each string uses one ratio, like "4 pizza slices cost $5.00," and for that one ratio, solves several different proportions. The first problem in this pizza slice string could be, "If 4 pizza slices cost $5.00, how much do 2 slices cost?" This proportion can be written several equivalent ways, including: $\frac{4}{5} = 2/c$ and $\frac{4}{2} = 5/c$. As you deliver the string, help students make connections by drawing out the place-value relationships. Notice that in each problem string, students eventually find each unit rate. For example, in the pizza string, they find the cost for 1 slice ($1.25) and the number of slices for $1.00 (0.8 slices). For $1.00, you cannot even get a whole slice!

Pizza Slices	Cost
4	$5
2	
3	
1	
10	
	$10
	$1
	$2

At the end of the problem string, draw students' attention to some of the proportions they solved during the string by representing the entries in the table using standard proportion notation. For example, after the pizza string, circle the row with 3 slices and $3.75 and write the proportion $\frac{4}{5} = 3/c$ and $\frac{4}{3} = 5/c$. Ask students to consider how they would solve these proportions if they were not given in context or in a ratio table. Have students review the reasoning they used during the string. Ask students if they can think of a different way to solve the same question, now that they see the proportion written differently. For example, to solve $\frac{4}{5} = 3/c$ during the string, many students might use the fact that 2 slices cost $2.50 to find the cost of 1 slice, $1.25, and added those results to get the cost of 3 slices, $3.75. Contrast that with solving $\frac{4}{3} = 5/c$ which students might solve as shown in Figure 5.34

FIGURE 5.34

4	2	1	3
5	2.5	1.25	(3.75)

4	2	1	5
3	1.5	0.75	(3.75)

Whole Numbers

Bread Sticks	Cost
5	$2
10	
6	
3	
	$1
	$10
	$5
	$15

Cups of Chocolate Chips	Cups of Peanut Butter
2	3
4	
5	
10	
1	
1.5	
	1
	2

Cups of Pasta	Cups of Sauce
8	5
	10
	1
	9
4	
2	
1	
	4

In the following decimal strings, you could use a context of buying bulk food. The beginning non-unit rate is the price paid for a certain amount. For example, introduce the taffy string by telling students that the ticket on the bulk food tag reads $2.50 for 1.2 pounds of taffy. Then ask, "For the same price per pound, how many pounds of taffy could you buy for $5.00?" When you get to the problem in which the number of pounds (24) is given, ask, "How much would 24 pounds of taffy cost?"

Decimals

Cost	Pounds of Taffy
$2.50	1.2
$5.00	
$10.00	
$1.00	
	24
	23.52
	6
	3
	1

Pounds of Candy Drops	Cost
0.4	$1.5
	$3.00
	$6.00
	$7.50
	$3.75
4	
5	
10	
1	

Pounds of Mints	Cost
0.2	$2.40
0.4	
0.8	
0.1	
1	
	$14.40
	$48.00
	$4.00
	$1.00

As Close As It Gets

These problems are different than typical multiple-choice problems, because the exact answer is not one of the choices. The goal is for students to choose an answer that is as close to the exact answer as possible. Because the precise answer is not listed, performing a memorized series of steps is not particularly productive. It is much easier and efficient to reason to get a reasonable approximate answer. The power of using these problems comes in the discussion of students' reasoning as they justify their choices. They are particularly powerful for helping students estimate and justify the reasonableness of a number and identify friendly numbers they can use in their estimations.

Give the problems in this section one at a time to the whole group. After students have decided on their answers, call on individual students to justify those answers, as in the sample discussion below.

FIGURE 6.1

79 + 0.79
a. 7.9   b. 8
c. 79   d. 80

The teacher displays the item in Figure 6.1 and asks students to choose an answer that is the closest to the solution, reminding them that the correct answer is not listed. After students think, the teacher asks a student or two to share their thinking.

Juan: I know that 0.79 is just about 1, so 79 and almost 1 is about 80.
Sarah: I thought about money and 79 dollars and some cents is pretty close to
          80 dollars.

For the problem in Figure 6.2, students can reason that $6\frac{1}{100}$ is pretty close to 6 and there are twenty-four $\frac{1}{4}$s in 6, so $6\frac{1}{100} \div \frac{1}{4}$ is about 24.

FIGURE 6.2

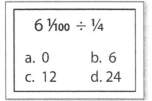

$6\frac{1}{100} \div \frac{1}{4}$	
a. 0	b. 6
c. 12	d. 24

The goal with these problems is to have students think and reason — not automatically begin to search for a memorized rule or rote algorithm. Encourage students to discuss their reasoning so that when they actually need to find exact answers, they have already thought about the reasonableness of the answer.

Since these problems are so short, you can use them when you have brief periods of time (one or two problems before the bell rings or the announcements start) or do three or four items at a time.

As close as it gets activities can be used both to introduce numeracy and in concert with strings and Workouts as students learn strategies they can apply. For example, before beginning work with multiplication of fractions, you could do several as close as it gets items to get students using estimates of fractions to multiply. Students would be thinking about the magnitudes involved and the meaning of multiplication. They would be reasoning about what it means to multiply a number times a fraction between 0 and 1 and contrast that with multiplying a number times a fraction greater than 1. You could also use the as close as it gets items in the days after you do a string or a Workout to see how students are applying the strategies from the string or Workout. Then you can adjust the next string or Workout you do and then follow up with more as close as it gets exercises. By the time students have good numerical fluency with multiplication of fractions, these items will probably be too easy and then it is time to do relational thinking exercises (see Chapter 7).

Addition and Subtraction

1. 993 + 0.3		2. 1,504 + 6.2		3. 3.219 + 5.2	
a. 993	b. 996	a. 1,560	b. 1,100	a. 3,700	b. 3.7
c. 1,000	d. 1,200	c. 1,510	d. 1,504.62	c. 8.5	d. 8

4. 4.51 + 4.49		5. 79 + 0.79		6. 5 + 5.989	
a. 8	b. 9	a. 8	b. 79	a. 6,000	b. 10,000
c. 90	d. 900	c. 80	d. 790	c. 11	d. 10

7. $-7.2 + 6.9$	8. $11.98 + 6.02$	9. $0.08 + 8$
a. -14 b. 0	a. 7 b. 18	a. 8 b. 80
c. 1 d. 14	c. 1,800 d. 1,000	c. 88 d. 800

10. $73 + 7.3$	11. $7.07 + 8$	12. $9003 + 0.9$
a. 140 b. 150	a. -1 b. 1	a. 9,000 b. 9,010
c. 80 d. 70	c. 16 d. 15	c. 10,000 d. 9,900

13. $22.01 - 11$	14. $7.6 - 0.16$	15. $0.52 - 0.02$
a. 10 b. 21	a. 6 b. 7	a. 0 b. 0.5
c. 11 d. 210	c. 7.5 d. 7.6	c. 0.4 d. 0.6

16. $9.9 - 0.8$	17. $782 - 83$	18. $3,012 - 2,998$
a. 1 b. 0.5	a. 700 b. 600	a. 0 b. 100
c. 9 d. 10	c. 800 d. 750	c. 1,000 d. 1,999

19. $5003 - 0.5$	20. $201 - 98$	21. $0.25 - 0.12$
a. 5,000 b. 4,000	a. 300 b. 100	a. 0.05 b. 0.12
c. 1,000 d. 4,500	c. 150 d. 200	c. 0.5 d. 0

22. $7.07 - 5$	23. $0.21 - 0.2$	24. $609 - 0.69$
a. 2 b. 6.95	a. 0 b. 0.1	a. 550 b. 500
c. 7.02 d. 12	c. 0.19 d. 1.9	c. 600 d. 609

Multiplication and Division

1. 0.9 × 5 a. 0 b. 2 c. 5 d. 45	2. 0.49 × 3 a. 0 b. 0.5 c. 1 d. 1.5	3. 0.1 × 15 a. 0 b. 5 c. 10 d. 15

4. 58 × 5 a. 10 b. 58 c. 300 d. 600	5. 15 × 9 a. 150 b. 200 c. 900 d. 1,500	6. 49 × 62 a. 31 b. 310 c. 3,100 d. 6,200

7. 99 × 24 a. 24 b. 240 c. 125 d. 2,400	8. 26 × 16 a. 50 b. 400 c. 800 d. 4,000	9. 74 × 36 a. 2,100 b. 2,700 c. 7,000 d. 7,500

10. 0.3 × 9 a. 0.1 b. 0.5 c. 2 d. 3	11. 1.1 × 5.9 a. 3 b. 6 c. 9 d. 15	12. 9.9 × 37 a. 37 b. 63 c. 370 d. 3,700

13. 63 ÷ 10 a. 0.5 b. 1 c. 6 d. 12	14. 8.2 ÷ 10 a. 1 b. 4 c. 8 d. 82	15. 61 ÷ 9.9 a. 0.5 b. 0.6 c. 6 d. 60

16. 802 ÷ 8 a. 0 b. 1 c. 10 d. 100	17. 703 ÷ 10 a. 0.7 b. 7 c. 28 d. 70	18. 61 ÷ 5.9 a. 1 b. 10 c. 15 d. 20

19. $32 \div 10.1$		20. $321 \div 32$		21. $1,602 \div 99$	
a. 0.3	b. 3	a. 100	b. 50	a. 0	b. 1
c. 5	d. 30	c. 30	d. 10	c. 10	d. 16

22. $1,803 \div 18$		23. $22 \div 0.99$		24. $4,942 \div 49$	
a. 100	b. 18	a. 2	b. 12	a. 0.5	b. 10
c. 10	d. 9	c. 22	d. 220	c. 100	d. 1,000

Fraction Addition and Subtraction

1. $\frac{4}{5} + \frac{9}{8}$		2. $\frac{8}{9} + \frac{9}{8}$		3. $\frac{3}{4} + \frac{1}{6}$	
a. 2	b. 1	a. $\frac{1}{2}$	b. $\frac{3}{4}$	a. 1	b. $\frac{1}{2}$
c. 3	d. 4	c. 1	d. 2	c. 1.5	d. 2

4. $\frac{5}{8} + \frac{4}{9}$		5. $\frac{10}{9} + \frac{7}{4}$		6. $6\frac{1}{4} + \frac{5}{8}$	
a. 0	b. $\frac{1}{2}$	a. $\frac{1}{2}$	b. 1	a. 6	b. 11
c. 1	d. 2	c. 2	d. 3	c. 7	d. 12

7. $2\frac{1}{3} + \frac{1}{4}$		8. $\frac{1}{8} + \frac{1}{30}$		9. $\frac{1}{100} + \frac{11}{15}$	
a. 2.5	b. 2	a. 0	b. 1	a. 0	b. $\frac{1}{2}$
c. 1	d. 3	c. 1.5	d. 2	c. $\frac{3}{4}$	d. 1

10. $\frac{8}{6} + \frac{6}{8}$		11. $\frac{10}{8} + \frac{10}{8}$		12. $\frac{3}{7} + \frac{3}{7}$	
a. $\frac{3}{4}$	b. $1\frac{1}{2}$	a. 1	b. 2	a. 1	b. 3
c. 1	d. 2	c. 8	d. 10	c. $\frac{1}{2}$	d. 7

13. $\frac{8}{6} - \frac{6}{8}$	14. $\frac{9}{10} - \frac{1}{100}$	15. $\frac{8}{10} - \frac{1}{100}$
a. 0 b. 0.5	a. 0 b. 0.5	a. 0 b. 0.5
c. $\frac{8}{4}$ d. $\frac{9}{4}$	c. 1 d. 1.5	c. 0.7 d. 0.8

16. $\frac{97}{100} - \frac{1}{30}$	17. $2\frac{4}{9} - \frac{13}{25}$	18. $\frac{66}{100} - \frac{11}{32}$
a. 1 b. 1.5	a. 0 b. 1	a. 0 b. 0.5
c. 2 d. 95	c. 0.5 d. 2	c. 0.9 d. 1

19. $\frac{74}{100} - \frac{49}{100}$	20. $\frac{10}{9} - \frac{9}{10}$	21. $5\frac{1}{5} - 2\frac{1}{2}$
a. 0 b. $\frac{1}{4}$	a. 0 b. $\frac{1}{10}$	a. $\frac{1}{2}$ b. $1\frac{1}{2}$
c. $\frac{1}{5}$ d. $\frac{3}{4}$	c. 0.75 d. 0.9	c. $2\frac{1}{2}$ d. $3\frac{1}{2}$

22. $3\frac{11}{12} - 1\frac{29}{30}$	23. $6\frac{1}{10} - 1\frac{21}{22}$	24. $2\frac{1}{3} - \frac{1}{4}$
a. 1 b. 2	a. 0 b. 1	a. 1 b. 1.5
c. 3 d. $3\frac{1}{2}$	c. 2 d. 4	c. 2 d. 2.5

Fraction Multiplication and Division

1. $3\frac{1}{5} \times 1\frac{9}{10}$	2. $\frac{1}{2} \times \frac{15}{16}$	3. $\frac{1}{4} \times \frac{49}{50}$
a. 3 b. 4	a. 0 b. $\frac{1}{10}$	a. 0 b. $\frac{1}{4}$
c. 6 d. 8	c. $\frac{1}{2}$ d. 1	c. $\frac{1}{2}$ d. 1

4. $\frac{3}{4} \times \frac{99}{100}$	5. $\frac{7}{8} \times \frac{8}{4}$	6. $\frac{9}{10} \times \frac{44}{89}$
a. 0 b. $\frac{1}{4}$	a. 0 b. 1	a. 0 b. $\frac{1}{2}$
c. $\frac{1}{2}$ d. $\frac{3}{4}$	c. 2 d. $2\frac{1}{2}$	c. 1 d. $1\frac{1}{2}$

7. $\frac{31}{60} \times 3$		8. $\frac{24}{100} \times 8$		9. $5\frac{1}{10} \times 2\frac{9}{10}$	
a. 0	b. 1	a. 0	b. 1	a. 1	b. 3
c. $1\frac{1}{2}$	d. 2	c. 2	d. 4	c. 5	d. 15

10. $3\frac{1}{3} \times 1\frac{11}{12}$		11. $\frac{16}{30} \times 4$		12. $12 \times \frac{26}{100}$	
a. 1	b. 2	a. 0	b. 1	a. 0	b. 1
c. 3	d. 6	c. $1\frac{1}{2}$	d. 2	c. 3	d. 6

13. $2 \div \frac{49}{100}$		14. $\frac{21}{40} \div 4$		15. $\frac{11}{12} \div 3$	
a. 0	b. $\frac{1}{2}$	a. 0	b. $\frac{1}{8}$	a. 0	b. $\frac{1}{3}$
c. $\frac{3}{4}$	d. 4	c. $\frac{1}{4}$	d. $\frac{1}{2}$	c. 1	d. 3

16. $3 \div \frac{24}{100}$		17. $\frac{45}{46} \div 2$		18. $\frac{1}{10} \div 100$	
a. 0	b. 1	a. 0	b. $\frac{1}{4}$	a. 0	b. $\frac{1}{2}$
c. 6	d. 12	c. $\frac{1}{2}$	d. $\frac{3}{4}$	c. 1	d. 10

19. $1 \div \frac{31}{60}$		20. $\frac{1}{8} \div 10$		21. $3\frac{99}{100} \div \frac{1}{2}$	
a. 0	b. 1	a. 0	b. 2	a. 0	b. $\frac{1}{2}$
c. $1\frac{1}{2}$	d. 2	c. 4	d. 10	c. 4	d. 8

22. $6\frac{1}{100} \div \frac{1}{4}$		23. $2\frac{1}{40} \div \frac{1}{5}$		24. $1\frac{4}{7} \div \frac{1}{2}$	
a. 0	b. 12	a. 0	b. 1	a. 0	b. 2
c. 24	d. 30	c. 2	d. 10	c. 3	d. 4

Relational Thinking

These exercises help students generalize which strategies work for each operation as they use the properties of operations and numerical relationships to work with equations. In these problems, the goal is for students to reason and decide whether a statement is true or false or to fill in the blanks of a problem such as $39 + 28 = 40 +$ ____. Encourage students not to compute each side. For example, when deciding the veracity of $27 + 64 = 30 + 61$, encourage them not to add both sides and see if they are the same, but to reason that if they move 3 from the 64 to the 27, they have 30 and 61, so the statement is true. For $2.8 + 3.9 = 3.0 + 4.0$, students can reason that you cannot increase both addends to make them friendly numbers — you cannot give-give in addition. You have changed the problem without adjusting, so the equation is false.

The problems in this chapter are given one at a time to the whole group. After students have decided on an answer, call on individuals to justify their answers. Facilitate a conversation with students about their reasoning. Help students clarify what they mean by asking other students if they agree, by inviting other students to restate the claim, and by providing nonexamples for the class to consider. These are not exercises that you give to students and walk away from; the discussion and reasoning are critical.

You can use one or two of these exercises when you have short bits of time, like before the bell rings or the announcements start. Alternatively, use a few problems to help students distinguish when to use specific strategies. For example, if students have learned to give and take with addition problems, ask them whether multiplication equations such as $49 \times 51 = 50 \times 50$ are true or false. Use arrays and the distributive property to model students' thinking about why the statement is false (Figure 7.1).

FIGURE 7.1

$45 \times 55 = (45 \times 50) + (45 \times 5) = 2250 + 225 = 2{,}475$

$50 \times 50 = 2{,}500$

So $45 \times 55 \neq 50 \times 50$

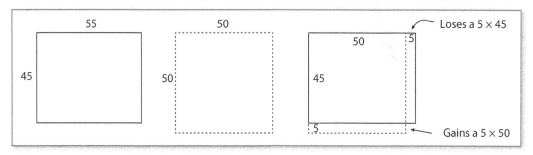

You can also use a simpler problem to wonder if giving and taking works for multiplication. Is $2 \times 5 = 1 \times 6$ true? Considering these examples can help students realize that while giving and taking works for addition, it is not a generalized strategy for multiplication.

Because relational thinking exercises help students solidify relationships and strategies, they are best done after students have experience building relationships and strategies with strings and Workouts. These exercises are great ways to assess how students are using strategies—are students using numerical relationships to compute or are they mixing up memorized steps? Are students using the magnitudes of the numbers and the meanings of the operations? Are they confusing the strategies for addition with the strategies for subtraction? If you can give and take with whole number addition, can you give and take with fraction addition? As students discuss their reasoning for these relational thinking exercises, you get a look at their current understanding.

Addition

True or False:

1. $27 + 64 = 30 + 61$

2. $2.8 + 3.9 = 3.0 + 4.0$

3. $419 + 387 = 406 + 400$

4. $0.9 + 0.3 = 1.0 + 0.2$

5. $3{,}000 + 2{,}326 = 2{,}998 + 2{,}328$

6. $8.97 + 1.54 = 9 + 1.24$

7. $2.6 + 6.9 = 1.6 + 7$

8. $5{,}364 + 2{,}750 = 5{,}114 + 3{,}000$

9. $876 + 89 = 865 + 100$

10. $3.5 + 4.96 = 3.46 + 5$

11. $3{,}699 + 178 = 3{,}700 + 177$

12. $1.9 + 36.2 = 2 + 35.2$

13. $\frac{4}{5} + \frac{1}{5} = \frac{5}{10}$

14. $5\frac{8}{9} + \frac{1}{3} = 6 + \frac{2}{9}$

15. $3\frac{9}{10} + 2\frac{1}{5} = 4 + 2\frac{1}{10}$

16. $6\frac{3}{4} + 2\frac{5}{6} = 7 + 3$

17. $4\frac{6}{7} + 3\frac{1}{7} = 5 + 3$

18. $6\frac{1}{4} + 2\frac{7}{8} = 6\frac{1}{8} + 3$

19. $\frac{4}{5} + \frac{3}{2} = \frac{7}{7}$

20. $99\frac{1}{4} + 3\frac{7}{8} = 100 + 3\frac{1}{8}$

Fill in the Blank:

1. $39 + 28 = 40 + \underline{\quad}$

2. $2.7 + 3.4 = \underline{\quad} + 3.1$

3. $115 + 798 = 113 + \underline{\quad}$

4. $4{,}436 + 2{,}897 = \underline{\quad} + 3{,}000$

5. $7{,}433 + \underline{\quad} = 7{,}439 + 6{,}994$

6. $9.6 + \underline{\quad} = 10 + 3.3$

7. $\underline{\quad} + 43 = 50 + 41$

8. $0.47 + 0.19 = \underline{\quad} + 0.20$

9. ____ + 779 = 654 + 800

10. 1,994 + 967 = 2,000 + _____

11. 15.3 + _____ = 15.6 + 12.7

12. ____ + 3.68 = 3.1 + 4

13. $\frac{5}{6}$ + $\frac{1}{3}$ = 1 + ____

14. $97\frac{4}{5}$ + $2\frac{3}{10}$ = ____ + $2\frac{1}{10}$

15. 10 + ____ = $9\frac{3}{4}$ + $4\frac{1}{2}$

16. $4\frac{2}{3}$ + $3\frac{1}{3}$ = 5 + _____

17. $5\frac{5}{8}$ + $2\frac{1}{2}$ = ____ + $2\frac{1}{8}$

18. 2 + $\frac{1}{8}$ = $1\frac{7}{8}$ + ____

19. 6 + ____ = $5\frac{11}{12}$ + $2\frac{1}{6}$

20. $4\frac{3}{5}$ + $3\frac{1}{2}$ = ____ + $3\frac{1}{10}$

Subtraction

True or False:

1. 36 − 17 = 39 − 20

2. 299 − 48 = 300 − 50

3. 2.3 − 1.8 = 4.3 − 2

4. 54 − 27 = 57 − 30

5. 3,913 − 2,999 = 3,914 − 3,000

6. 69 − 38 = 71 − 40

7. 5.26 − 2.87 = 6.39 − 3

8. 8.324 − 1.789 = 8.113 − 2

9. $4.252 - 2.654 = 4.5 - 598$

10. $0.24 - 0.19 = 0.14 - 0.19$

11. $1.46 - 0.95 = 1.51 - 1$

12. $0.371 - 0.192 = 0.379 - 0.2$

13. $7\frac{1}{5} - 3\frac{4}{5} = 8\frac{2}{5} - 4$

14. $3\frac{1}{4} - 2\frac{3}{4} = 3\frac{1}{2} - 3$

15. $23\frac{4}{7} - 20 = 22\frac{3}{7} - 19\frac{6}{7}$

16. $5\frac{1}{3} - 3\frac{2}{3} = 5 - 3$

17. $4 - 3 = 4\frac{1}{6} - 2\frac{5}{6}$

18. $6\frac{3}{5} - 3\frac{4}{5} = 6\frac{4}{5} - 4$

19. $15\frac{2}{9} - 8\frac{2}{3} = 15\frac{5}{9} - 9$

20. $12\frac{1}{5} - 7\frac{3}{10} = 12 - 7\frac{1}{5}$

Fill in the Blank:

1. $4.2 - 3.9 = \underline{\quad} - 4$

2. $1.96 - \underline{\quad} = 2 - 0.98$

3. $3{,}901 - 2{,}012 = 3{,}889 - \underline{\quad}$

4. $\underline{\quad} - 27 = 85 - 30$

5. $5.67 - 4 = 5.62 - \underline{\quad}$

6. $4.653 - 3.9 = \underline{\quad} - 4$

7. $8.2 - 3.65 = 8.55 - \underline{\quad}$

8. $5{,}678 - \underline{\quad} = 5{,}677 - 3{,}999$

9. $7.8 - 6 = \underline{\quad} - 5.96$

10. ____ − 1.99 = 3.56 − 2

11. 3.42 − 2.68 = 3.74 − ____

12. 623 − 446 = 600 − ____

13. $12\frac{3}{5} - 6\frac{4}{5} = 12\frac{4}{5} -$ ____

14. $8\frac{1}{4} - 5\frac{3}{4} = 8\frac{1}{2} -$ ____

15. $2\frac{1}{9} -$ ____ $= 2 - \frac{8}{9}$

16. $45 - 22\frac{5}{7} =$ ____ $- 23$

17. $4\frac{1}{4} - 2\frac{1}{2} =$ ____ $- 3$

18. $6\frac{7}{10} -$ ____ $= 6\frac{1}{2} - 4\frac{4}{5}$

19. ____ $- 20 = 23\frac{1}{5} - 19\frac{4}{5}$

20. $5\frac{4}{9} -$ ____ $= 5\frac{2}{9} - 3\frac{7}{9}$

Multiplication

True or False

1. $9 \times 7 = 8 \times 8$

2. $26 \times 5 = 13 \times 10$

3. $84 \times 26 = 42 \times 13$

4. $126 \times 2.5 = 31.5 \times 10$

5. $76 \times 12 = (70 \times 10) + (6 \times 2)$

6. $(20 \times 3) + (2 \times 3) = 22 \times 3$

7. $5\frac{1}{2} \times 16 = 11 \times 8$

8. $10 \times 3 = 3\frac{1}{3} \times 9$

9. $49 \times 101 = 50 \times 100$

10. $49 \times 101 = (50 \times 101) - (1 \times 101)$

11. $2.5 \times 1.6 = 5 \times 0.8$

12. $77 \times 15 = (77 \times 10) + (77 \times 5)$

13. $3\frac{1}{2} \times 14 = 7 \times 7$

14. $1\frac{1}{4} \times 2\frac{1}{3} = (1 \times 2) + (\frac{1}{4} \times \frac{1}{3})$

15. $3\frac{1}{4} \times 4\frac{3}{4} = 3 \times 5$

16. $3\frac{4}{5} \times 1\frac{4}{5} = 4 \times 2$

17. $3\frac{4}{5} \times 1\frac{4}{5} = \frac{19}{5} \times \frac{9}{5}$

18. $\frac{4}{5} \times \frac{1}{3} = 4(\frac{1}{5} \times \frac{1}{3})$

19. $\frac{2}{3} \times \frac{3}{5} = 3(\frac{2}{3} \times \frac{1}{5})$

20. $\frac{3}{5} \times \frac{2}{7} = \frac{5}{12}$

Fill in the Blank:

1. $67 \times 99 = (67 \times 100) - (\underline{} \times 1)$

2. $9 \times 5 = \underline{} \times 10$

3. $\underline{} \times 79 = (6 \times 80) - (6 \times \underline{})$

4. $84 \times 2 = \underline{} \times 4$

5. $43 \times 22 = (43 \times \underline{}) + (43 \times 2)$

6. $45 \times 140 = \underline{} \times 70$

7. $74 \times 9 = 740 - \underline{}$

8. $1.5 \times 13 = \underline{} \times 6.5$

9. $64 \times \underline{} = 32 \times 100$

10. $\underline{} \times 5.5 = 8 \times 11$

11. $36 \times 15 = 18 \times$ _____

12. ____ $\times 8 = 3.5 \times 16$

13. $18 \times 3\frac{1}{2} = 9 \times$ ____

14. $4\frac{1}{2} \times 8 = (4 \times 8) + ($___$\times 8)$

15. $\frac{3}{4} \times \frac{1}{5} =$ ____ $\times (\frac{1}{4} \times \frac{1}{5})$

16. ____ $\times 3 = 2\frac{1}{3} \times 9$

17. ____ $\times (\frac{2}{3} \times \frac{1}{4}) = \frac{2}{3} \times \frac{3}{4}$

18. $2\frac{1}{4} \times 24 =$ _____ $\times 6$

19. $3\frac{1}{2} \times 5 = ($___$\times 5) + ($___$\times 5)$

20. $7 \times$ ____ $= 14 \times 5\frac{1}{2}$

Division

True or False

1. $\frac{12}{6} = \frac{12}{3} + \frac{12}{3}$

2. $366 \div 6 = (300 \div 6) + (60 \div 6) + (6 \div 6)$

3. $244 \div 4 = 122 \div 2$

4. $\frac{16}{8} = \frac{16}{4} + \frac{16}{4}$

5. $(1{,}300 \div 13) - (13 \div 13) = 1{,}287 \div 13$

6. $\frac{32}{4} = \frac{16}{4} + \frac{16}{4}$

7. $444 \div 4 = 222 \div 8$

8. $750 \div 75 = 100$

9. $52 \div 13 = 104 \div 26$

10. $270 \div 10 = 2{,}700$

11. $505 \div 0.5 = 1{,}010 \div 1$

12. $424 \div 24 = 400 \div 20 + 4 \div 4$

13. $\frac{5}{6} \div \frac{1}{6} = \frac{5}{6}$

14. $\frac{4}{5} \div \frac{1}{5} = 4$

15. $\frac{3}{7} \div \frac{2}{7} = 3 \div 2$

16. $\frac{32}{16} = \frac{64}{32}$

17. $\frac{5}{6} \div \frac{2}{3} = (\frac{5}{6} \times \frac{3}{2}) \div (\frac{2}{3} \times \frac{3}{2})$

18. $\frac{3}{4} \div \frac{3}{5} = \frac{3}{4} \div \frac{3}{5} \times \frac{5}{3}$

19. $\frac{5}{6} \div \frac{1}{6} = 2 (\frac{5}{6} \div \frac{2}{6})$

20. $\frac{5}{6} \div \frac{1}{6} = \frac{1}{2} (\frac{5}{6} \div \frac{2}{6})$

Fill in the Blank:

1. $85 \div 5 = 170 \div \underline{\quad}$

2. $(\underline{\quad} \div 15) + (45 \div 15) = 345 \div 15$

3. $\frac{125}{25} = \frac{100}{\underline{\quad}} + \frac{25}{\underline{\quad}}$

4. $750 \div 150 = (300 \div 150) + (300 \div 150) + (\underline{\quad} \div 150)$

5. $542 \div 10 = \underline{\qquad} \div 5$

6. $15 \div 0.75 = 30 \div \underline{\quad} = \underline{\quad} \div 3$

7. $\frac{72}{8} = \frac{80}{8} - \frac{\underline{\quad}}{8}$

8. $622 \div 0.25 = 1{,}244 \div \underline{\quad} = 2{,}488 \div \underline{\quad}$

9. $264 \div 24 = (240 \div 24) + (\underline{\quad} \div 24)$

10. $0.75 \div 0.5 = 1.5 \div \underline{\quad}$

11. $\frac{54}{6} = \frac{\underline{\quad}}{6} - \frac{6}{6}$

12. (____ ÷ 82) + (82 ÷ 82) = 902 ÷ 82

13. $\frac{5}{6} ÷ \frac{1}{6}$ = _____ $(\frac{5}{6} ÷ \frac{2}{6})$

14. $\frac{2}{3} ÷ \frac{1}{4}$ = $(\frac{2}{3} ×$ ____$)$ ÷ $(\frac{1}{4} ×$ ____$)$

15. $\frac{9}{8} ÷$ ____ = 9 ÷ 4

16. $\frac{3}{7} ÷ \frac{2}{7}$ = ____ ÷ 2

17. $\frac{3}{15} ÷$ ____ = $\frac{1}{15}$

18. 3 ÷ ___ = (3 × 4) ÷ $(\frac{1}{4} × 4)$

19. (5 × 3) ÷ $(\frac{1}{3} × 3)$ = ____ ÷ $\frac{1}{3}$

20. $\frac{3}{4} ÷ \frac{9}{5}$ = $(\frac{3}{4} ×$ ___$)$ ÷ $(\frac{9}{5} ×$ ___$)$